Get the eBook FREE!

(PDF, ePub, Kindle, and liveBook all included)

We believe that once you buy a book from us, you should be able to read it in any format we have available. To get electronic versions of this book at no additional cost to you, purchase and then register this book at the Manning website.

Go to https://www.manning.com/freebook and follow the instructions to complete your pBook registration.

That's it!
Thanks from Manning!

The Mikado Method

OLA ELLNESTAM
DANIEL BROLUND

MANNING
Shelter Island

For online information and ordering of this and other Manning books, please visit
www.manning.com. The publisher offers discounts on this book when ordered in quantity.
For more information, please contact

> Special Sales Department
> Manning Publications Co.
> 20 Baldwin Road
> PO Box 261
> Shelter Island, NY 11964
> Email: orders@manning.com

Manning Publications Co.
20 Baldwin Road
Shelter Island, NY 11964

Development editors: Cynthia Kane, Frank Pohlman
Copyeditor: Andy Carroll
Proofreader: Katie Tennant
Typesetter: Gordan Salinovic
Illustrator: Martin Murtonen
Cover designer: Marija Tudor

ISBN 9781617291210
Printed in the United States of America

contents

foreword

Most software discussions, books, and articles seem to assume that development work starts with an empty codebase. The Agile literature usually presumes that the detailed learning about what is needed to solve a problem for a stakeholder community can be discovered iteratively and incrementally. This might be a valid assumption if one is starting fresh, but I seldom encounter teams with the opportunity of starting from scratch; there are always constraints. Most investment in software today involves modifications or extensions to existing applications and environments. Thus, in addition to discovering and implementing solutions to our organizational problems/opportunities, we have the constraint of fitting into the environment created by earlier development teams. We need to discover and codify not just the applicable domain knowledge, policies, and organizational goals that drive our current development work, but also to understand how the changes we make affect the existing application environment.

Everyone who has done this kind of work knows that the information we need is only weakly represented in the documentation left behind by preceding teams. One has to look at the source code to get reliable information about the constraints it imposes on additions and changes. If the source code includes an effective set of automated tests, we're in luck because tests illustrate the behavior required of the code by previous implementers to solve previous problems. If these tests pass when executed, we know that the code behaves as they expected. More often, automated tests were never created, and we're left with only the source code itself. The question then becomes how to learn what we need to know to avoid breaking previous work.

The barrier is sheer complexity. Analysis of the preexisting code has proven to be a weak tool for tackling this complexity. Much of the code we have to confront no longer communicates effectively to us the nuances we need to understand to avoid breaking it as we implement our changes, and it usually ends up taking far more time than we can afford. Therefore, after we exhaust our patience with analysis, we're forced to go ahead and take a chance at breaking the fragile existing code. What we do next is critical.

"Traditional" approaches have ended with a long, tedious, unpredictable, test-and-fix period that often consumes the second and sometimes third 90% of our project schedule. Agile and lean thinking have taught us to test immediately, integrate continuously, and fix every problem as soon as we discover it. This works well with well-structured code that's weakly dependent on its environment—provided we have an effective automated test suite. The teams who preceded us, however, have seldom had the perspective, skills, or inclination to leave us with such a foundation, because they were driven mostly by the need to get-it-done (project scope focus) even at the expense of keep-it-clean (longer-term product lifecycle focus). So we find ourselves in a hole!

The first rule of holes is this: "When you find yourself in a hole, stop digging!" Agile thinking suggests that for all the code you add to an application, you should use your refactoring, clean coding, and TDD practices to ensure that you don't make the situation worse. You'll probably have to add some higher-level automated functional tests to be able to do even this safely. Even then, complexity easily becomes overwhelming, and quality, speed, and cost all suffer. Managing this unavoidable complexity is what this book is about. Rather than permitting complexity to cascade, *The Mikado Method* enables you to discover what you need to know and address it in manageable pieces by maintaining your focus on always having a known good code base. Ultimately, this is the deepest core of Agile—always ensure that the work you have done so far is correct.

While the form of the Mikado Method is simple, it's tied closely to and greatly helps with the application of principles and practices we've learned over the last decade. It addresses individual, pair, and team-wide practices to reliably tackle changes in small steps. Ubiquitous language and the SOLID and DRY principles characteristic of clean coding practices guide our Mikado Goals and the trees of prerequisites that structure our work. Mikado Graphs help keep our packaging, dependency, TDD, and refactoring work properly focused.

The initial focus of the Mikado Method is effectively dealing with a messy reality. The long-term goal, however, is to understand the forces that drive organizations to create bad code in the first place so we can avoid creating more code that our successors will have to struggle with unhappily. When we're confronted with the normal levels of complexity in today's software, we can't keep everything we need in our heads at once. People have discovered many ways of effectively working together in complex tasks, starting with the scientific method and extending to the Theory of Constraints, empirical control systems, and pull/flow systems. The Mikado Method's approach works with all these strategies to help us stay in control.

Tom Poppendieck

preface

We once worked on an application that was used to configure the behavior of a specialized electronics module in an expensive hardware product. Our application was a part of the delivery of that product. One day, news reached our software development team that Sales had unexpectedly landed a contract with a new client. At first we didn't know what to make of it, but in time we learned that the new client needed a version of our application that was almost identical to the one we had. This was fortunate. But after further investigation, we realized that there were certain parts of the application code that under no circumstances could be shared between the new client and our old ones. We had to come up with a solution to this problem, or we couldn't deliver to the new client at all.

It finally boiled down to two possible solutions. We could duplicate the whole application, or we could restructure first and break out the parts that couldn't be shared. Our team argued for well over a week before we reached consensus. We decided that the best solution was the restructuring approach: restructure first, and then add the new functionality. This shouldn't take more than a month, or maybe two, we thought to ourselves.

We started working, and guess what? The work was more complex than we could imagine! The approach we chose was supposed to be simple, and we thought we could get away with moving some classes to new packages, fixing the compilation errors, and then adding the new functionality. But as we tried to split the application and separate sensitive information from the more general parts, we ran into trouble.

We had anticipated some trouble, but not that much. After every change we made, we got about 20 compiler errors, and as we tried to fix them, a myriad of new errors came up. When we were just about done with the new errors, the compiler moved ahead a bit, only to reveal another round of errors. Fixing those errors led to more restructurings and of course more errors.

More than two weeks went by, and we had well over a thousand files checked out and more than two hundred compiler errors. By that time, the high-level system tests, our indicator of a healthy application, had long since been put out of play because we couldn't even compile the application.

To make matters worse, the rest of the team was moving along at their regular pace, and our efforts at keeping the code in sync became more and more difficult. It became obvious that we couldn't keep up with the rest of the team, and that the complexity of the change was more than overwhelming. We were trying to behead a Software Hydra—for every head we cut off, two more grew out.

We still remember the day when we swallowed our pride and made the tough decision to revert everything we had done so far. Only later did it dawn on us that reverting the code was a defining moment in our software careers. Apart from realizing that it's never too late to turn back, we had also discovered how to approach our particular problem, and other problems like it.

Our insight was that in order to get the system in shape, we had to do almost all of the things we had already done, but we needed to do them in the opposite order. You might think this sounds crazy, but the key was to take the errors and turn them into prerequisites.

BROWNFIELD DEVELOPMENT

You've likely worked with systems like the one we described—software hydras that aren't easy to behead. For us, this is more or less the norm. We've had to clean up lots of messy code, refactor smaller and larger parts of systems, and restructure complex

The Software Hydra—for every head we cut off, two more grew out.

architecture. We've even tried rewriting code from scratch, also known as greenfield development. But we've noticed that the field doesn't stay green very long. We've long since faced it; we're stuck with brownfield development, whether we like it or not.

We, the developers, hold the fate of the code in our hands, and we're the only ones who have the power to improve it. It's our responsibility to keep the code clean and fit for its purpose. This means we have to be able to add code and improve our own code and the code of others. If computer programs don't improve, they're doomed to a slow death.

How do we approach large improvement efforts? How do we deliver while the pressure is high, because we must deploy functionality once a month, or even more frequently than that? How do we deal with huge systems that are hard to comprehend, and whose complexity makes it hard to keep all the necessary details in our heads at once? We morph systems into a new shape!

THE GOAL: MORPHING A SYSTEM

Most organizations that deliver software don't enjoy halting the development of new functionality. The stakeholders want to see value coming out as money is put in. As a result, software developers have to be able to cope with the current situation as future problems are encountered, solved, and sometimes avoided entirely.

If we want to be successful software developers, we need to learn how to morph an existing system into a desired new shape. When we say morph, we mean perform the necessary actions and steps that take us from a system of one shape to another without breaking things in between. The transitions between the different states need to be smooth and possibly add value themselves.

What complicates the process of morphing software even more is the fact that it's more or less the norm to develop software as a team. Software is very seldom developed by a single individual, and working in groups makes distributing the work possible. But teamwork also adds another dimension of complexity, and it doesn't take long to realize that the need to communicate necessary improvements within a team is essential for any real progress.

THE MIKADO METHOD

The Mikado Method is our guide to morphing. It helps us visualize, plan, and perform business-value-focused improvements over several iterations and increments of work, without ever having a broken codebase. It enhances communication, collaboration, and learning in software development teams. It also helps individuals and programming pairs stay on track while doing their day-to-day work. The framework that the method provides can help the whole team morph any system into the desired new shape.

The method itself is straightforward and simple: after you've decided on a goal, you start to build a model of required changes and dependencies by doing quick experiments.

We try to accomplish the goal in a straightforward fashion. When we can't, we create a graph of prerequisite nodes. We use the information from our quick experiments to determine whether a change can or can't be implemented right away. If a problem occurs, we roll back to the original state. By solving the prerequisites first, we work our way backwards, and the graph we build guides us toward our goal.

THE NAME OF THE METHOD

The Mikado Method gets its name from the Mikado game.

> *Mikado is a pick-up sticks game originating in Europe. In 1936 it was brought from Hungary to the USA and was mostly called pick-up sticks. This term is not very specific in respect to existing stick game variations. Probably the "Mikado" name was not used because it was a brand name of a game producer. The game got its name from the highest scoring (blue) stick "Mikado" (Emperor of Japan). The Buddhistic Chien Tung also contains a stick called "emperor." (Wikipedia, February 2011, http://en.wikipedia.org/wiki/Mikado_(game))*

To start the game, you drop the bunch of straw-sized sticks onto a surface, creating a pile. The goal is to pick up as many sticks as possible to score points, and preferably the Mikado stick, because it's the highest-scoring stick. If you're unable to pick up a stick without moving another one, the stick is put back and the turn goes to the next player. As long as you can pick up sticks without moving other sticks, your turn continues.

The trick is to pick up the easy sticks first—the sticks that have no other sticks on top of them. Eventually, by using that strategy, a player can pick up the Mikado stick and likely win the game.

The similarities between the Mikado game and restructuring software are striking. There are loads of dependencies and structural complexities in code that have to be taken into account. These dependencies have to be navigated and changed with care until you have an opportunity to do something without breaking stuff.

CHARACTERISTICS

These are some characteristics of the Mikado Method:

- It fits nicely in an incremental process.
- It's very lightweight (pen and paper, or whiteboard).
- It increases the visibility of the work.
- It provides stability to the codebase while you're changing it.
- It supports continuous deployments by finding a nondestructive change path.
- It improves communication between people.
- It enhances learning.
- It aids reflection on the work done.
- It leverages different competencies, abilities, and knowledge.
- It helps collaboration within a team.
- It scales by enabling distribution of the workload over the team.
- It's easy to use.

A THINKING TOOL

When we introduce the Mikado Method to people who develop software, we often see how they change the way they look at, approach, and talk about large structural improvements. Their perspective shifts from a very analytical view of problems to a more practical approach, where the focus is on removing the minimum number of obstacles at a time in order to achieve real results.

The effect is shorter, focused conversations that are about finding the changes that can be made without breaking the code, instead of rigorous analyzing and guessing. They get more insight on how to deal with the unnecessary complexity of a software system, and the method serves as a thinking tool when they solve difficult problems.

Even though we're becoming increasingly seasoned developers ourselves, we still find it challenging to decide where to start digging and where to take the code. The Mikado Method not only helps us find a starting point, it also shows us where to go and tells us when we're done.

We hope you'll find the Mikado Method useful, just as we have.

acknowledgments

A lot of people have contributed to this book, directly or indirectly.

Technically, it builds on the work of Michael C. Feathers, Martin Fowler, Robert C. Martin, Kent Beck, Ward Cunningham, and Joshua Kerievsky, to mention a few. The phrase "standing on the shoulders of giants" feels very appropriate when we think about how our ideas about development came to us.

We'd like to give a big thanks to our colleagues, friends, and families who supported us, and with whom we discussed the method and this book, acquiring many insights for improvements.

We'd also like to thank Laurent Bossavit for noticing the similarities between code restructuring and the pick-up-sticks game, thus eliciting the name for the method.

This book has taken many shapes. Special thanks go to the people who reviewed the book along the way and gave us great feedback on how to improve it. For the initial edition: Tobias Anderberg, Alan Baljeu, Olle Dahlström, George Dinwiddie, John Eckhardt, Steve Eckhardt, Manne Fagerlind, Thomas Gustavsson, Jakub Holý, Anders Ivarsson, Colin Jack, Torbjörn Kalin, Jan Mattsson, Luca Minudel, Staffan Nöteberg, Joakim Ohlrogge, Tom Poppendieck, Robert Postill, Måns Sandström, David Sills, Jelena Vencl-Ohlrogge, Ted M. Young, and Stefan Östergaard.

At Manning, thanks to the following reviewers: Alex Garrett, Christopher Weiss, David Madouros, David Paccoud, Ecil Teodoro, Ernesto Cárdenas Cangahuala, Jonathan Choate, Jonathan Suever, Josh Winslow, Kaleb Pederson, Mark Elston, Mark Sponsler, Paul Grebenc, Stephen Wakely, Timo Bredenoort, and Ursin Stauss.

Very special thanks to Tom Poppendieck for writing the foreword, for promoting the book, and for his excellent review work. The same thanks go to Heidi Helfand for her fantastic and relentless editing of the book in the first edition.

For the Manning edition, we've had great support and patience from the staff there: development editors Cynthia Kane and Frank Pohlmann, technical proofreader Deepak Vohra, production coordinator Kevin Sullivan, copyeditor Andy Carroll, proofreader Katie Tennant, and illustrator Martin Murtonen.

about this book

As a codebase grows large and more complicated, and they often do, there usually comes a time when you want to improve portions of it to meet new functional requirements, new legal requirements, or a new business model. You may also just want to change it to make it more comprehensible. For small changes, you can keep things straight in your head, but for larger ones the chances of getting lost on a sea of broken code increases dramatically.

As you desperately try to navigate that sea, it's easy to start labeling the code. You can come up with all sorts of names for the code, especially bad code that isn't fit for its purpose. Legacy code is one of the more popular terms, which literally means code someone (else) wrote and that you are now responsible for. Michael Feathers, in Working Effectively with Legacy Code (Prentice Hall, 2004), suggested it can be defined as code without tests, which has since become the de facto definition.

Another term for bad code is big ball of mud, popularized by Brian Foote and Joseph Yoder in their paper Big Ball of Mud (http://laputan.org/mud/). This paper describes a big ball of mud as "a haphazardly structured, sprawling, sloppy, duct-tape-and-baling-wire, spaghetti-code jungle." Some synonyms for this type of code are crap or a mess, and we can think of quite a few more in our native language (Swedish).

When code like that needs to change and trouble appears, it's easy to label the code legacy, a big ball of mud, a mess, crap, or just impossible to work with. If it's really bad, developers often distance ourselves from the code and start lobbying for a rewrite, because changing the code is perceived as too hard.

In addition to the big-ball-of-mud systems, there are at least two more types of systems that need attention. First, there are systems that look well organized, maybe even having high test coverage, but under the surface they're hard to work with or to extend. Second are the systems that look good and have served well, but don't anymore.

This book is about changing and improving all these types of systems. It offers a way to regain control over your codebase. We call it the Mikado Method.

Roadmap

Chapter 1 is an introduction to the Mikado Method. After reading this chapter, you'll understand how the method works at a high level. For some people, this will be enough to start experimenting on their own problems.

Chapter 2 shows the mechanics of the method with the use of two small examples. This chapter explains how to use the method when working with code.

Chapter 3 goes into the theory of the method in depth. After reading this chapter, you'll know the nuts and bolts of the method, and understand why and how it works.

Chapter 4 is a guide that shows how you can use the method in different working constellations, and when to start using the method on a problem. After reading this chapter, you'll understand how to get the most out of the method in a team, a pair, or on your own.

Chapter 5 presents a longer example that mimics a somewhat real scenario. This chapter will show you how to include tests and how to deal with monolithic code, a common problem for many software developers.

Chapter 6 is about emergent design and the design principles we use when we want to change a system for the better. After reading this chapter, you'll know which direction to take your code in when you change it.

Chapter 7 presents some recurring patterns we've come across when we use the method—patterns related to both drawing graphs and implementing changes. This chapter will give you ideas about how to simplify your graphs and how to go about tricky, but common, changes to code.

Appendix A is a deep dive into the concept of technical debt. This appendix will help you recognize the different types and sources of technical debt, and mitigate those at an early stage.

Appendix B is about setting the stage for an improvement effort. This appendix outlines the most common preparations needed before heading out on an improvement effort. You'll also get some tips on what to do afterward, to sustain the improvements you've made.

Appendix C contains an example in JavaScript that shows how you can use the Mikado Method to approach changes in an environment that uses a dynamically typed language.

THE CODE IN THE BOOK

The code from the longer examples in the book is available at GitHub at the links shown in this section. It is also available as a download from the publisher's website at www.manning.com/TheMikadoMethod.

You will find the code from chapter 2 at https://github.com/mikadomethod/book-example-1. In the branches of that repository, you can find the detailed steps of the two examples in that chapter.

The example in chapter 5 is available at https://github.com/mikadomethod/book-example-2. For this example, there's one branch for each graph in the chapter, with the names of the branches mapping to the goals of the graphs, respectively. The prerequisites are mostly mapped to a commit, and in some cases a couple of prerequisites are bundled in a commit.

The example in appendix C is available at https://github.com/mikadomethod/book-example-3. This example also contains detailed branches for the steps in the book.

THE GRAPHICS IN THE BOOK

We prefer and recommend using hand-drawn graphs and diagrams for work, but for clarity (and to save you from our handwriting), we've used a couple of tools to make the graphics in this book.

Most of the UML diagrams in the book are drawn using Inkscape (http://inkscape.org). The Mikado Graphs were mostly generated using Graphviz (http://graphviz.org), and sometimes drawn using Inkscape. The resulting graphics have been touched up by the Manning production team. The cartoons were drawn by Martin Murtonen of the Manning team, based on originals by Ola Ellnestam.

The font used in the graphics is Architects Daughter, a beautiful font created by Kimberly Geswein (http://www.kimberlygeswein.com). The font is free if you download it from http://www.fontsquirrel.com/fonts/architects-daughter.

Author Online

The purchase of *The Mikado Method* includes free access to a private web forum run by Manning Publications where you can make comments about the book, ask technical questions, and receive help from the authors and other users. To access the forum and subscribe to it, visit http://www.manning.com/TheMikadoMethod. This page provides information on how to get on the forum once you're registered, what kind of help is available, and the rules of conduct on the forum.

Manning's commitment to readers is to provide a venue for meaningful dialogue between individual readers and between readers and the authors. It is not a commitment to any specific amount of participation on the part of the authors, whose contribution to the forum remains voluntary (and unpaid). Let your voice be heard and keep the authors on their toes!

The Author Online forum and the archives of previous discussions will be accessible from the publisher's website as long as the book is in print.

about the cover illustration

Mikado is not only the name of the game of pick-up-sticks, or the title of the popular musical by Gilbert and Sullivan—it was the word used in the past for the emperor of Japan. The illustration on the cover of *The Mikado Method* is from an early eighteenth-century silk screen of Emperor Seiwa (844-897), the fourth son of Emperor Montoku. Before his ascension to the Chrysanthemum Throne, Emperor Seiwa's personal name was Korehito; the first member of the Imperial House to be personally named "hito." One meaning of this suffix is the Confucian concept of "ren," a virtue denoting the good feeling a human experiences when being altruistic. It later became tradition to name all male members of the Imperial Family this way.

Manning celebrates the inventiveness, initiative, and fun of the computer business with book covers based on figures from centuries ago, when life was more colorful and diverse, and when dress customs clearly differentiated a person's class, stature, profession, as well as country, region, or even town of origin. Today, it is hard to tell the inhabitants of one continent from another and many traditional costumes are only worn on ceremonial occasions. Perhaps we have traded cultural diversity for a more varied personal life—certainly for a more varied and fast-paced technological life.

about the authors

Daniel Brolund is a professional software developer who loves the creative nature of programming and teamwork. In his more than 15 years in the profession, he has successfully worked with global websites deployed on hundreds of servers, with desktop applications for just a few users, and with online gaming applications, just to mention a few. He has presented on various topics at some of the largest software conferences in the USA, around Europe, and in India.

Ola Ellnestam is a coach and mentor for both business and technical teams. He loves to combine technology, people, and business, which is why he finds software development so interesting. He has developed complex computer systems within health care, defense, and online banking fields, and he knows that software must be easy to use, extend, and deploy in order to be worth developing. More than anything else, he likes to share his findings and knowledge with others because he believes that this is how new knowledge and insight are created.

Part 1

The basics of the Mikado Method

The Mikado Method is a structured way to make significant changes to complex code. In this first part of the book, you'll be introduced to the Mikado Method and get acquainted with its core workings. You'll see an example of how to use it and learn how it's used when changing code. You'll also learn how to use it when working in different constellations. When you've finished this part, you'll be able to apply the Mikado Method to your own codebase, working alone or as part of a team.

Meet the Mikado Method

This chapter covers

- A description of the Mikado Method
- The benefits of the method
- Common situations where it works

How many times have you tried to fix something in your codebase, breaking a sweat as the changes spiral out of control? How many times has your development work started not with an empty codebase, but with an inherited system that includes the strange constraints of the previous team? You might hope to look over the documentation left behind, and to run the automatic tests and see if they pass, but what happens if there aren't any tests left behind, and all that's left is the source code? How can you understand what's going on, and how can you make big changes to code without ending up with the entire engine in pieces on the floor?

This is the perfect moment for the Mikado Method to enter the scene. It's a structured way to make significant changes to complex systems. Rather than getting caught up in the complexity of moving parts, analyzing the entire system in one large chunk, the Mikado Method lets you handle complex code a bit like you'd move furniture around in your home, one piece at a time. In the same way that you might need to move your table to fit in your sofa, and move the easy chair before

3

you can move the table, you need to change and move methods and classes around before you can fit new functionality into your complex codebase. You need to do it one step at a time.

The key to the Mikado Method is removing the fewest obstacles at a time in order to achieve real results, without breaking the code. In this chapter, we'll introduce you to the method, show you some of the benefits, and walk you through how it works.

Explaining the Mikado Method to non-techies

We've all been there, trying to explain programming to people who don't have a strong technical background. We use all kinds of metaphors like *construction*, *arts*, *crafts*, and more, and they all break down after a while. A metaphor is a model, and, quoting George E.P. Box, "essentially, all models are wrong, but some are useful."[1]

The inability to explain simple concepts in an area where you're an expert is sometimes referred to as *the curse of knowledge*.

This can happen to you too. After you've read this book, you'll know more about the method than most other people, and you'll be tempted to tell them everything, all at once, when they ask you what the Mikado Method is. We've found the simple "moving furniture" metaphor to be useful for introducing the method.

1.1   What is the Mikado Method?

When a system gets large and complicated, as they often do, there usually comes a time when you want to improve portions of it to meet new functional requirements, new legal requirements, or a new business model. You may also just want to change it to make it more comprehensible.

When you perform small changes, you can keep them in your head, but for larger ones, the chances of getting lost in a jungle of dependencies, or on a sea of broken code, increases dramatically. The Mikado Method can help you visualize, plan, and perform business value–focused improvements over several iterations and increments of work, without ever having a broken codebase during the process.

The framework that the method provides can help individuals and whole teams to morph a system into a new desired shape. The method itself is straightforward and simple, and can be used by anyone at any time. In the following section, we'll look at the core concepts, the main benefits, and when you can use them.

1.1.1   Basic concepts

There are four basic and well-known concepts that summarize the process of the Mikado Method:

- Set a goal
- Experiment

---

[1] George E.P. Box and Norman R. Draper, *Empirical Model-Building and Response Surfaces* (Wiley, 1987), p. 424.

- Visualize
- Undo

When used together in the Mikado context, these concepts are the core of the method. Without these key pieces, the method can't help you make changes without breaking the codebase. By no means are these concepts new, but put together in the context of the method, they become very powerful.

SET A GOAL

To set a goal, think about what you want for the future and about some code that needs to change. Suppose you have a package or module with several web services that's already responsible for too much. Maybe you'd want the goal to be, "The admin services are in a separate package that can be deployed without the customer web services." After you've clearly stated the goal, write it down. The goal serves two purposes:

- A starting point for change
- The endpoint, or success criteria, of the change

The goal is also the basis of your next *experiment*.

EXPERIMENT

An *experiment* is a procedure for making a discovery or establishing the validity of a hypothesis. In the Mikado Method, you use experiments to change the code in order to achieve the goal, so that you can see what parts of the system break. Whatever breaks gives you feedback on the prerequisites needed before you can achieve the goal. A typical experiment would be to move a method from one class to another, extract a class, or reduce the scope of a variable. The goal and the prerequisites are what you visualize.

VISUALIZE

Visualization happens when you write down the goal and the prerequisites necessary to achieve it.

Figure 1.1 shows a small graph. The contents of a Mikado Graph normally come from the experiments. Besides the changes to your system, the graph is the only artifact of the Mikado Method. The Mikado Graph illustrates the goal and all the prerequisites for achieving that goal, and it tells you what your next step is.

UNDO

When an experiment for implementing a goal or a prerequisite has broken your system, and you've visualized what you need to change in the system to avoid that outcome, you want to *undo* your changes to restore a previously working state. In

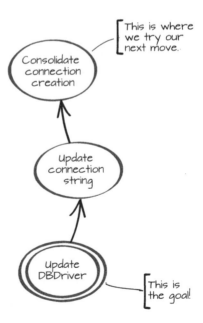

Figure 1.1   A Mikado Graph with a goal and two prerequisites

the Mikado Method, you'll always visualize your prerequisites, and then undo your breaking changes. This process—experiment, visualize, undo—is iterated for each of the prerequisites, for the next layer of prerequisites, and so on. At some point, a prerequisite won't break the system, and you can unwind the graph of prerequisites.

In order for the experiments and the undoing to be meaningful, the code needs to be in a known working state when the experiments start. When we get to section 1.2, we'll take you step by step through the method, and then this will make a bit more sense.

Of these four concepts, the undo part is what people struggle with most. At first, undoing feels very unintuitive and wasteful. But it's not waste; it's an important part of the learning process, and we'll continue to stress the undo part as you learn the method.

1.1.2 *When to use the Mikado Method*

If you want to be a successful software developer, you need to learn how to morph an existing system into a desired new shape. Maybe you've tried to implement a new feature, but the system is constantly working against you. Maybe you've thought once or twice that it's time to stop developing new features for a while and clean up a bit. Maybe you've worked on a refactoring project, or you've tried to do a bigger improvement to your system, but you weren't able to pull it off, so you just threw it all away. Maybe you constantly feel like the puzzled man in figure 1.2.

Figure 1.2 Being able to change the shape of things is a highly desirable skill

> **DIFFERENT DEVELOPMENT APPROACHES** The Mikado Method is agnostic to the development approach used, as long as there's room for executing the system and getting feedback from your actions. We've found it works very well together with the iterative and feedback-intense approaches of Extreme Programming, Scrum, and Kanban.

It's likely that you've been in at least one of the situations just described, and we know that the Mikado Method and this book could have helped. It doesn't really matter if the code was yours or someone else's; it doesn't matter if the code was old or new. Sooner or later that shiny new greenfield project, where everything can fit in your head and changes are easy to perform, will become more and more complex. As time passes, the code fades just like grass does when it's heavily used and visited. The greenfield turns brown, and sooner or later you, or your successors, become afraid of changing code. You end up stuck with *brownfield development,* and you need to be able to morph code you're afraid of touching, in midflight. Let's look at a few common scenarios where the Mikado Method can help.

IMPROVE A SYSTEMS ARCHITECTURE IN FLIGHT

When you've hit a wall and a design doesn't lend itself easily to change, you can become frustrated. It could be an API that's hard to understand and your customers are complaining, or maybe your nightly batch jobs barely complete because the data that needs to be processed has increased by a factor of ten. At times like that, the code can seem so complex, and the only way to solve your problems may seem to be stopping development and focusing solely on improving the codebase for a while, or maybe running an improvement effort as a side project.

Improvement projects make stakeholders nervous, and rightfully so, because they see nothing of value coming out. What you want to do is use the Mikado Method to change an architecture in small steps, allowing improvements and continuous delivery of new features to coexist in the same branch.

BROWNFIELD DEVELOPMENT

Brownfield development is probably the most common situation for developers to be in, and in order for business to continue, an existing application infrastructure is necessary. Whether you're adding a new feature or improving existing functionality, the Mikado Method helps because it enables you to work with what you've got and to improve on it. Brownfields need to change just like any other system, but often you don't know the whole codebase inside out, so changes become inefficient or downright scary. The Mikado Method provides a way for you to take on a reasonable number of improvements for each feature.

REFACTORING PROJECTS

Imagine that you want to extract a reusable module from a heavily entangled system, or to replace an external API that's used all over and deep into your codebase. Improvements like that are really big, and they usually take several weeks, or even months, to complete. They also require a nondestructive way forward, or you won't be able to ship your product.

The common way to temporarily achieve nondestructiveness is to start a "refactoring project" on a "refactoring branch" to keep it away from the rest of development, but at the price of a nasty and destructive merge at the end. The Mikado Method helps you uncover a nondestructive path in your regular development flow and keeps you on track as you perform each task, even if the effort takes months. If you use the Mikado Method for these kinds of improvements, separate refactoring projects on diverging branches can be avoided entirely, and the changes can be checked in on a day-to-day basis.

The lifespan of a Mikado Graph

It doesn't matter if you're using the Mikado Method for in-flight improvements, brownfield development, or instead of refactoring projects. The Mikado Graph will look pretty much the same, and it works equally well.

The lifespan of the graph will differ, however, depending on the change you want to perform. Our experience tells us that big improvements take longer, and they generally benefit from the graph being visible and easy for many to access during that time. Try putting the graph on a whiteboard in a common area. For smaller changes that takes less time to perform, pen and paper is probably more appropriate.

1.1.3   Benefits of the method

You now know that the Mikado Method is a way to improve code without breaking it, and you know what situations would be good candidates for using it. Now let's look at its benefits.

STABILITY FOR THE SYSTEM

Stakeholders will love the Mikado Method because it provides stability to the system while changing it. No more, "We can't release now; we're in the middle of a monster merge." The Mikado Method path to change is a series of small, nondestructive changes instead of the big, nasty integration at the end of a refactoring project.

INCREASED COMMUNICATION AND COLLABORATION

From a team's perspective, the Mikado Method works really well. Due to its visual nature, interested parties can watch the Mikado Graph evolve, and then follow along as the changes are performed and checked off on the graph. By also communicating through the graph, collaboration becomes easier and a change effort can be spread across the team. This way the whole team's competencies, abilities, and existing knowledge can be contributed, and the workload can also be distributed throughout the team.

LIGHTWEIGHT AND GOAL FOCUSED

Last, but not least, developers find the Mikado Method quick to learn and easy to use. The method has very little ceremony and consists of a lightweight process that requires almost no additional tools—just pen and paper or a whiteboard. Its simplicity helps you keep your eye on the prize. As a bonus, you can use the Mikado Graph you develop from the process to assist you when you reflect on the work done, and this improves learning.

Hopefully we've now piqued your interest in the method, and you can see where it could be beneficial in your work. Now you must be wondering how it works.

1.2   The Mikado Method recipe

We believe that code isn't a piece of art; it's supposed to do a job. We also believe that if a part of the code doesn't stop the rest of the system from evolving, we don't need to understand that part; we leave it as it is. On the other hand, if that code needs to be changed or understood, we want an effective way to do that. At that point, we turn to the Mikado Method, and it helps us deal with difficult situations when the code change gets too complex to fit in our heads.

In this section, we'll look at how the method actually works. We'll go through it step by step, so that by the end you'll be ready to jump into chapter 2, where you'll see your first example and how to apply the method.

1.2.1   How to work with the Mikado Method

Figure 1.3 shows what the Mikado Method looks like in a compound format. It shows our recommendation for performing changes to a system that's too large for analyze-then-edit, which means basically any production system in the world. Let's go through the steps of the process one by one.

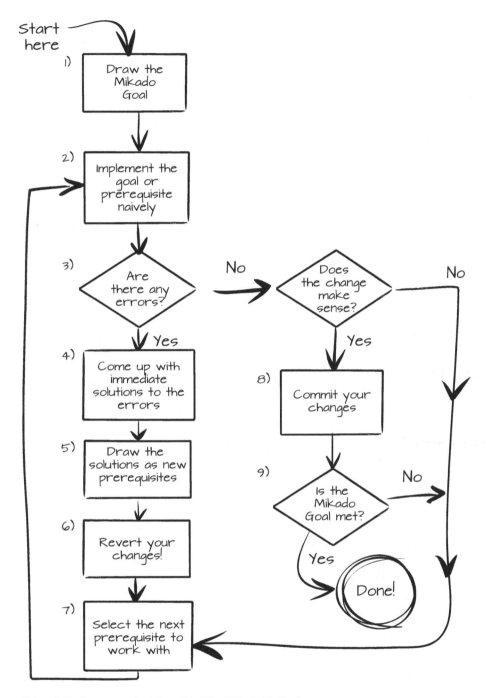

Figure 1.3 A process chart describing the Mikado Method

STEP 1: DRAW THE ORIGINAL MIKADO GOAL

The best place to start is with a concrete task, or maybe a user story. Choose a task that needs to be accomplished. The task will be your original goal: the *Mikado Goal.*

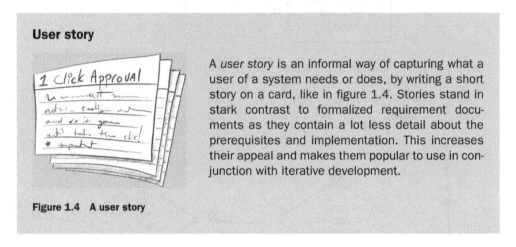

User story

A *user story* is an informal way of capturing what a user of a system needs or does, by writing a short story on a card, like in figure 1.4. Stories stand in stark contrast to formalized requirement documents as they contain a lot less detail about the prerequisites and implementation. This increases their appeal and makes them popular to use in conjunction with iterative development.

Figure 1.4   A user story

Write the Mikado Goal on a piece of paper, with a double circle around it to mark it as the original goal, as shown in figure 1.5. Replace "Mikado Goal" with a short description of an explicit goal for your application or system, like "Store report as .csv file," or "Use HTTPS for all API calls."

Figure 1.5   Start with the goal, replacing "Mikado Goal" with your task or story.

The double circle is there to indicate where it all starts. This goal will be your focus for the moment, and anything you do from now on is to help you reach this goal.

STEP 2: IMPLEMENT THE GOAL NAIVELY

Try to implement the goal right away, as this is probably the easiest way to determine what obstacles are in the way. We call this the *Naive Approach.* The idea is to make an experiment without analyzing the consequences too much. The restrictions or dependencies of your system will usually be surfaced by the compiler or your tests. An example of an actionable goal is "Move user-related classes to project X."

Sometimes a goal isn't actionable, and it can't be naively implemented. For example, "Make algorithm Y twice as fast" isn't something that's directly actionable, but you can add prerequisites such as "Write performance test" and "Replace linear array iteration search with hash table." In those cases, you need to do a minimal bit of analysis of the goal to find some prerequisites that can be tried. Analyzing isn't wrong, but it's a bit risky. If you *only* analyze the situation, you can easily spend several hours on something that you could determine by making a change, recompiling the code, and making a test run.

STEP 3: FIND ANY ERRORS

Is there anything that's stopping you? Are there compiler errors? Are there tests that don't run, or other obvious problems? All these errors have their origin in the dependencies that restrict you, and they're the reason you're having problems reaching your goal. If you don't have any errors, skip to step 8.

An example of an error could be a compiler message indicating that there are too few arguments to the createUser(..) method, probably due to the newly made change. Other common sources of problems are runtime exceptions and errors, such as null-pointer exceptions. These problems are hard to find by just reading the code, so an automated test suite is helpful. The test suite minimizes your effort and delay when identifying these problems.

STEP 4: COME UP WITH IMMEDIATE SOLUTIONS TO THE ERRORS

All errors you find need to be taken care of before you can reach your goal. Come up with immediate solutions to the errors that will make the goal implementation possible. These errors and solutions aren't limited to the program code, but could be anything you need to fix in your system, like changing a build script, opening a firewall, or adding a new server.

Again, we'd like to point out that you shouldn't over-analyze the situation and try to predict where the solution will lead you, but try to find solutions that drive the system in a good direction. Quite often, those solutions will have more underlying restrictions or dependencies that need to be taken care of before they can be implemented. This is OK; those dependencies will be discovered and handled in future iterations of the process.

If we continue with the createUser(..) example, an immediate solution could be "Add parameters at all places where createUser(..) is called," or for a null-pointer exception, "Initialize the null field in method X."

STEP 5: DRAW THE IMMEDIATE SOLUTIONS AS NEW PREREQUISITES

Before you continue, note the solution with an arrow pointing to it from the goal, as in figure 1.6.

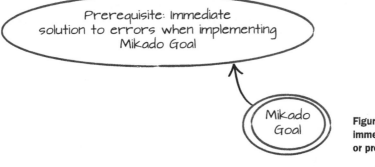

Figure 1.6 Note the immediate solution, or prerequisite.

Solutions become prerequisites to your original goal. A single solution can sometimes take care of hundreds of errors with the same root cause. In that case, draw only one prerequisite in the graph for all of those problems.

As you start to build knowledge about the system and the dependencies that stand in the way of making your changes, you'll also find ways to resolve the dependency problems, one by one.

When you can't come up with a solution to a problem, write something like "Solve the errors with the missing arguments to `createUser(..)`." This will work as a placeholder until the time has come to implement that prerequisite.

STEP 6: REVERT THE CODE TO THE INITIAL STATE IF THERE WERE ERRORS

When there are errors, you should always roll back all changes. This is extremely important! Editing code in an unknown state is very error-prone. Before you start on the next prerequisite, revert to the last known working state. Repeatability and predictability trump activity, so roll back!

Sometimes reverting is perceived as losing all your work, but it's not. In the Mikado Graph, you've accumulated loads of information and have identified all the things you need in order to get back to this state if you want to.

> ### Overcoming the fear of reverting
>
> To some people, reverting the broken code feels like throwing work away and starting all over again, like it never happened. But this is a misconception of what developing systems is about. System development, and especially refactoring or restructuring, focuses mostly on learning about the system, the domain, the language, and the technology in use. Making the changes accounts for just a fragment of the total development time, and the great value of the Naive Approach is what you learn about the system. It enables you to see what actually stands in your way.
>
> The Mikado Graph then holds this information, and you can use it to decide exactly what you want to do at a later time. Hence, nothing much is lost when you revert your changes.
>
> If you still want to keep your changes, you could save a *patch*, a record of the changes made, using your version control system. When the prerequisites for the current change are in place, you can then reapply that patch, but often so many things have changed that the patch is invalid; with the prerequisites in place, it's usually easy to make the change anyway.

STEP 7: REPEAT THE PROCESS FOR EACH OF THE IMMEDIATE SOLUTIONS

For each of the prerequisites, *one at a time*, repeat the preceding steps starting with step 2. This means that for each of the prerequisites, start with a clean working system and try to implement the prerequisite naively. As before, find the errors (if any), come up with solutions to the errors, note them as prerequisites, revert the changes, and then continue with the next prerequisite. This will result in a graph that might look something like figure 1.7.

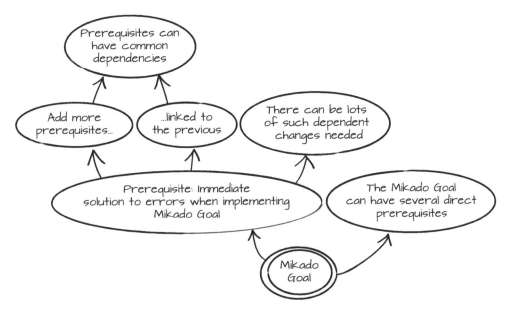

Figure 1.7 Repeat the steps for each prerequisite to build knowledge about the dependencies.

STEP 8: CHECK IN IF THERE ARE NO ERRORS

When you don't find any additional errors during the implementation of a prerequisite, you've come across a change that has no further prerequisites. When a prerequisite is implemented, you can note it in the graph with a check mark, as in figure 1.8.

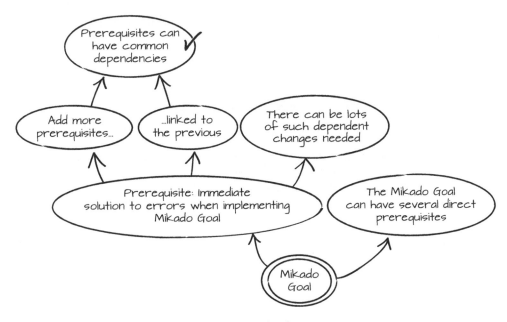

Figure 1.8 Check off the solutions as they are completed.

This is probably a good time to commit code to the main code repository to share it with your fellow developers. In general, commit if all the following are true:

- The code compiles.
- The tests run.
- The product is all good.
- The changes make sense to check in.

If the changes don't quite make sense, look at the graph and see if they should be accompanied by a few more changes to make a sensible commit. You can delay checking off prerequisites until you check in code.

Continue by selecting a new prerequisite to work with as the next iteration, and repeat the process from step 2.

STEP 9: IF THE MIKADO GOAL IS MET, YOU'RE DONE!

When you've finished and checked in all of the prerequisites and the Mikado Goal, you're done. Pat yourself, or your programming partner, or your team, on the back. Take a moment to reflect on what you've just accomplished. Now is probably a great time for some celebration.

1.3 Summary

We and others have used the Mikado Method in different situations and for different problems. In this book, our goal is to help you understand the method and the ecosystem surrounding it and to make use of it. The method will make your change efforts more focused, effective, and successful.

Are you ready for some code? Good, because the upcoming chapters will contain a mix of code, examples, and instructions about how to apply the Mikado Method to actual code.

Try this

- Set a timer for 15 minutes, refactor some code, and then *undo!* How did it feel?
- Create a branch in your version control system, and then delete it. Reflect on the effort.
- Imagine your smallest room, and then in your imagination try to fit a large bookshelf in the back of the room. Now draw a Mikado Graph of the changes/moves you need to perform. What surprised you?

Hello, Mikado Method!

2

This chapter covers

- Two tiny Mikado Method examples
- Baby steps and safe refactorings
- How to soften a hard dependency

You probably picked up this book because you're in a tricky situation. Maybe you're facing a mess, a legacy system, or a big ball of mud. No matter what you call it, it's time to put the Mikado Method to the test and see what it can do for your code. After you've finished this chapter, you'll have a basic idea about how to improve code without breaking your system while doing so.

As a first example, we've chosen a small system so you won't have to wade through pages of code while learning the method. Our goal is to keep the amount of code to a minimum throughout this book so you can focus on the method, not on reading code.

You'll see two examples in this chapter. The first is a tiny example that will show you the mechanics of a change done the Mikado way. Then we'll get into a slightly more complicated example where we'll iterate and apply what you learned in the first example several times over, changing a bigger chunk of code, but still in a careful way.

For the rest of the book, we'll assume that you have a basic level of Java knowledge or are familiar with a C-like language and object-oriented programming. You'll need to know basic refactoring techniques like *rename* and *move method,* and basic version control concepts for reverting code to a previous state. If you need to refresh your memory about refactoring, we recommend picking up *Refactoring* by Martin Fowler (Addison-Wesley Professional, 1999). Now, let's get started!

2.1   *Your first Mikado Graph*

In this section, you'll get acquainted with a small part of a larger codebase. We'll revisit the process diagram from chapter 1, shown in figure 2.1, and apply it to the first example, step by step.

In this example, we want to change the way an application is launched. Right now, the application uses a hardcoded path to a user data file. That makes the system inflexible; for example, we can't change the path when we need to test our application. We want to change how the application is launched and make it more flexible. But before we do this, let's take a look and see what the launcher looks like now. run.sh is the script that launches the application:

```
#!/bin/sh
java -cp app.jar org.mikadomethod.app.Launcher
```

As you can see, we have a shell script that launches a Java application, and the class responsible for the application launch is called Launcher, shown in the following listing.

Listing 2.1   Launcher.java

```
package org.mikadomethod.app;

...

public class Launcher {

    public static void main(String[] argv) {
        try {
            App.setStorageFile("/opt/local/app/db.txt");      ←⎯  The location of the
            App app = new App();                                    file is hardcoded.
            app.launch();
        } catch (ApplicationException e) {
            System.err.println("Could not start application");
            e.printStackTrace();
        }
    }

}
```

We want to avoid the hardcoded path, and to get this result without breaking the code, we'll use the Mikado Method.

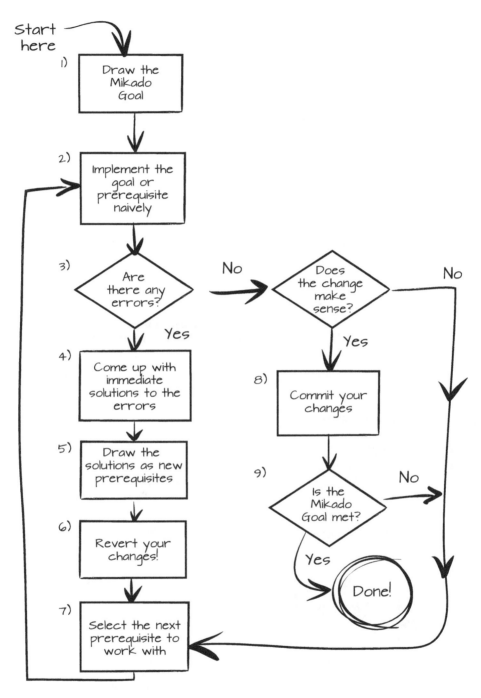

Figure 2.1 The Mikado Method process

2.1.1 *Making changes without breaking code*

Our goal is to change the way the application is launched. Maybe you've seen this kind of situation before and know that there's more than one way to solve the problem. You could configure the application via settings that are read from a file, or you could pass a parameter to the program at runtime, or something else. We try to avoid over-analyzing any change; we just try an idea and see what happens. When we have several ideas, we try the simplest first.

Let's try using command-line arguments passed to the main method. This is the starting point of the Mikado Method, so let's show it as a goal in a Mikado Graph.

DRAW THE GOAL

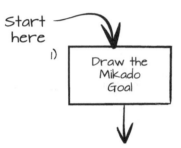

Figure 2.2   **Drawing the Mikado Goal will help us focus on the task at hand.**

Our goal is, "Use command-line arguments argv in Launcher.java to configure database file." In the Mikado Graph, it looks like figure 2.3.

Figure 2.3   **A clearly written goal makes it easy to know when it's accomplished.**

IMPLEMENT THE GOAL NAIVELY

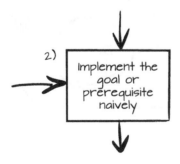

Figure 2.4   **Trying things can provide more feedback than hours of analysis.**

We have a clearly stated goal, and because it's possible to simply implement the goal, we can just do it, like in the next listing.

Listing 2.2 `Launcher.java` with parameterized `setStorageFile(..)`

```
package org.mikadomethod.app;
...

public class Launcher {

    public static void main(String[] argv) {
        try {

            App.setStorageFile(argv[0]);
            App app = new App();
            app.launch();
        } catch (ApplicationException e) {
            System.err.println("Could not start application");
            e.printStackTrace();
        }
    }

}
```

The file is now configured via an argument, and then the App class uses that file.

FIND ANY ERRORS

3)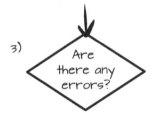

Figure 2.5 The compiler, tests, or running the system will help us find the errors quickly.

Now we try to find any errors. One of the fastest ways to find errors is to execute the application. Launching run.sh will result in an error:

```
Exception in thread "main" java.lang.ArrayIndexOutOfBoundsException: 0
  at org.mikadomethod.app.Launcher.main(Launcher.java:10)
```

The error is an `ArrayIndexOutOfBoundsException`, meaning that `String[] argv` doesn't contain even a single element, and especially not the database file path. This example is pretty small, and anticipating this result beforehand isn't that hard, but when you get into more complex examples, executing parts or all of the program is a good way to find errors.

COME UP WITH IMMEDIATE SOLUTIONS

4)

Figure 2.6 Don't think too hard about the consequences; just pick a solution that will pull the system in a good direction.

Now we need to come up with a solution that will prevent the previous error from occurring. The first option that springs to mind is editing the shell script, run.sh, and adding a file path there.

DRAW THE SOLUTION AS A PREREQUISITE

Figure 2.7   **We add the solutions to the graph as we come up with them.**

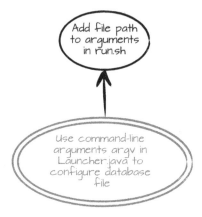

Figure 2.8   **Prerequisite added**

We can now go to our graph and add our solution as a prerequisite: "Add file path to arguments in run.sh" (see figure 2.8). A prerequisite at the outer edge of the graph is called a leaf. At this stage, it's easy to succumb to the temptation to just hack the next step from this broken state, and then the next, and the next..., but we won't do that, we'll just add the next step to the graph. Remember that what the Mikado Method helps you do is fix what needs to be changed without breaking the codebase; if you were to hack the next step, you'd be building on assumptions and guesswork.

REVERT THE CODE

Figure 2.9   **The most important, and yet unintuitive, step of the process: fix the broken system by reverting**

Before we go any further, we revert our changes, in this case the line App.setStorage-File(argv[0]);, because we don't know how much of the application we've affected. Remember, we don't want to build on assumptions. In this small example, it was only one line of code and we can see the impact of our change. For a larger, or more complex, change, stacking uncontrolled changes on top of each other is a big no-no. After reverting, the only visible trace from our change is some ink on a piece of paper.

SELECT THE NEXT LEAF PREREQUISITE TO WORK WITH

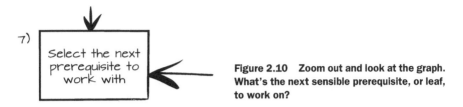

7)

Figure 2.10   Zoom out and look at the graph. What's the next sensible prerequisite, or leaf, to work on?

After reverting, we now take a look at the graph where we can see that our only leaf is the update of run.sh. A leaf is the only place where a change can be performed without possibly breaking code. The Mikado Goal isn't a leaf because it depends on "Add file path...," but "Add file path..." is a leaf because it has no further prerequisites. When implemented, you can see the slight change to run.sh:

```
#!/bin/sh
java -cp app.jar org.mikadomethod.app.Launcher 'db.txt'
```

After adding the file path to run.sh, we make sure that the application still works, and it does!

DOES THE CHANGE MAKE SENSE?

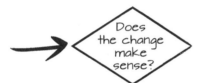

Figure 2.11   Checking in cohesive changes will make coworkers much happier.

The small change we made didn't actually do anything to our app; the added parameter isn't used in the application, so the change just prepared us for the next step. In that way, it doesn't make sense. In fact, adding an unused argument to a command will probably confuse anyone reading that piece of code. We have to add more to the solution before we check it in, and we should pick the next leaf prerequisite to work on.

Because the "Add file path..." prerequisite is implemented, the only leaf now is the actual Mikado Goal. Once again we can make the simple change we initially tried—changing the line back to App.setStorageFile(argv[0]);. We compile and run the application with run.sh again to find any errors. This time it all works, and we're satisfied with our changes. They make sense!

CHECK IN!

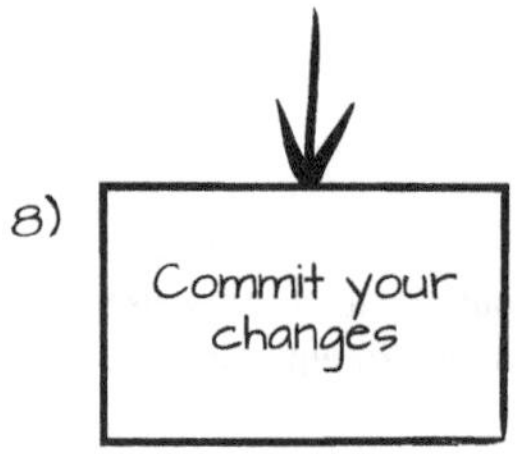

8)

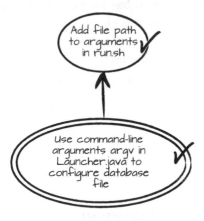

Commit your changes

Figure 2.12 Add the changes to the repository and have a small celebration.

Let's add the changes we made to our versioning system. When changes make sense, you want to share them with your teammates as quickly as possible. This is also a good time to check off the completed work in the Mikado Graph, as shown in figure 2.13.

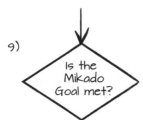

Add file path to arguments in run.sh

Use command-line arguments argv in Launcher.java to configure database file

Figure 2.13 Marking the completed work with check marks provides a sense of progress and closure.

IS THE GOAL MET? ARE WE DONE?

9)

Is the Mikado Goal met?

Figure 2.14 Are all the chart nodes taken care of? Is the goal met?

Our goal is met; we can change the database location from the start script. We're done!

When problems are this simple, you don't really need to use this much process. But when the problems are more complex, they're harder to analyze. In the next section, we'll continue with a slightly more complicated example that you might or might not be able to fit in your head. Don't worry though; we've tried to make it easy to follow.

> ### The Mikado Method is canned divide-and-conquer
> The examples in this book are tiny compared to any real system, but one of the real perks of the Mikado Method is that it's a divide-and-conquer approach. If you follow the method, most problems will, in the end, be rather small and manageable.

2.2 A slightly more complicated change

In the previous example, all we did was change the launcher so it locates the database file by using a parameter at runtime. We still have a hardcoded dependency on a specific type of database: the file-based database. This is cumbersome, because it puts constraints on the runtime and development environments. We want even more flexibility, so our aim is to replace the file-based database with something better, like a database that supports concurrency so that more than one person can use the system at the same time.

Figure 2.15 describes the system as it looks now. You can see that App is launched by Launcher, which in turn creates a UI that fetches login information from the FileDB. The "database" is a simple key-value store that uses a single file for persistence. If we were able to somehow configure where we store our data, we'd have more options. We could choose between different database vendors or have separate configurations for development, test, and production environments.

Figure 2.15 A schematic of the current system

Our aim is to be able to replace that database with something better. *Something better* can mean a lot of things, but in this case we're considering introducing a database abstraction to achieve more flexibility. By encapsulating the file-centered code, we hope to achieve enough flexibility to vary the database implementation at runtime. But before we make any changes, we'll get to know the code a bit better.

2.2.1 Getting to know the code

Let's browse the code for a while. Here are the three most important classes, one after the other.

Listing 2.3 Launcher.java

```
package org.mikadomethod.app;
...

public class Launcher {

    public static void main(String[] argv) {
        try {                                          Configure the
            App.setStorageFile(argv[0]);               storage ...
            App app = new App();
            app.launch();                              ... and then
        } catch (ApplicationException e) {             launch the
            System.err.println("Could not start application");   application.
            e.printStackTrace();
        }
    }

}
```

The Launcher sets up the system by configuring the storage, creating an App instance, and then launching the app.

Listing 2.4 App.java

```
package org.mikadomethod.app.ui;
...

public class App {

    private UI ui;
    private static String storePath;

    public void launch() throws ApplicationException {
        ui = new UI();
        ui.showLogin();                        Create a UI and show
    }                                          the login dialog.

    public static String getStorageFile() {
        return storePath;
    }
```

```
    public static void setStorageFile(String storePath) {
        App.storePath = storePath;
    }

}
```

The job of the App is to create a UI and then show a login dialog. App also has methods for configuring the path to the storage file.

Listing 2.5 The UI.java code, somewhat reduced

```
package org.mikadomethod.app.ui;

...

public class UI {

    private JFrame frame;
    private FileDB database;

    public UI() {
        frame = new JFrame();
        database = new FileDB();
        database.setStore(App.getStorageFile());     Load possible
    }                                                  roles and show
                                                       them in the UI.
    public void showLogin() {                    <───┘
        List<String> roles = database.load("roles");
        addLoginSelector(roles);
        addButtons();
        frame.setSize(800, 600);
        frame.setVisible(true);
    }

    private void addLoginSelector(List<String> roles) {
        JComboBox combo = new JComboBox(roles.toArray());
        frame.setLayout(new GridBagLayout());
        frame.add(combo);
    }

    private void addButtons() {
        ... a lot of GUI code ...
    }
}
```

The meat of the system is found in UI, and it has a lot of code. It's responsible for setting up the whole login dialog, complete with buttons, listeners, and all. We've spared you the details of all that and focused on the showLogin method, which does two important things:

1 Load roles from the database

2 Add roles to the login selector

The code here fetches the different roles that can be used with the system from a form of `FileDB`, which we know little about, via the `load(..)` method. Then it adds these roles to the GUI in the form of a login selector, `addLoginSelector(..)`.

Now that we've prepared ourselves by getting to know the code, another important task needs to be completed. We need to make sure we can return the code to a known, unaltered state.

2.2.2   *Reverting code*

Before we make any changes to our code, we must know that we can restore the code to our starting point. This is important for two reasons. One: if anything goes wrong or we lose track of what we're trying to achieve, we need to be able to start over to reduce the risk of messing things up. Two: we're going to experiment a lot, and starting from a known state is a must when you experiment.

If we're going to succeed, some sort of version control system (VCS) is a must. All VCSs we know of have a way to fetch a certain version of the code, which we'll make use of when we revert our changes.

> **REVERT, RESTORE, OR UNDO**   We'll use the word *revert* for restoring the code to a previously untouched state. You may be used to using some other term, like *undo checkout* or *reset*.

Choosing a VCS

All version control systems (VCSs) can revert your code. Get one that's easy to use and that can revert code within a matter of seconds. If it can create branches cheaply and handle merges without much hassle, that's a big bonus too. Sometimes you'll need to do some additional preparations in order to easily get back to your starting point, and in those cases a tag or a short-lived branch based on a specific version can help significantly. Our personal preference is Git.

Here's how you can revert in three different VCSs:

- Git: `git reset --hard`
- Mercurial: `hg revert`
- SVN: `svn revert`

We've now familiarized ourselves with the code so it doesn't feel totally new. Keep in mind that you can always return to the code if something is unclear.

It's now time to tackle the problem and put the Mikado Method to use.

2.3   *Making the code configurable*

Our objective with this code is to get rid of the hardcoded dependency to the database so we can enjoy the benefits of a more flexible design. We want to be able to configure, or at least easily change, the `FileDB` to something else, like a normal relational database. To do that, any code related to that file-based database will also need to be dealt with. Our plan is to introduce a database wrapper, or an abstraction, that we can use instead of the file-based database.

A common way to solve this type of problem is to encapsulate the class you want to change. We'll start by writing our goal on a piece of paper and circling it twice. Although it seems obvious at the moment, it's important to write it down so that you can remember what you're working toward. Here our goal is "Encapsulate `FileDB` to be able to switch database," as shown in figure 2.16.

Figure 2.16 After we figure out what our goal is, we write it down as our Mikado Goal.

> **Hard to decide on a goal?**
>
> If you find it hard to select a goal, this might be a hint that you don't have all the information you need to make that decision. Talk to people involved to see if you're missing something. If you need more input, spend a few minutes, hours, or days if it's a large change, and try a few different goals to see where they lead you.

2.3.1 Get going with the Naive Approach

By using the VCS, we know we can revert to a known initial state. This means that instead of worrying about keeping the system intact, we can focus on the problem at hand. Because the goal is open-ended, like a decision node (see section 3.2.3), we need to narrow down how we can achieve it with a few more specific prerequisites.

We might already have some ideas as to how the goal could be achieved, but instead of speculating too much, we'll try one of our ideas: "Replace `FileDB` with `Database` interface for `load(..)`/`store(..)`" ends up on our piece of paper, as shown in figure 2.17.

These two actions have a relationship, so we connect them with a simple arrow, meaning that "Encapsulate `FileDB` to be able to switch database" depends on us having completed "Replace `FileDB` with `Database` interface for `load(..)`/ `store(..)`" first.

Now, in the name of the Naive Approach, let's try something based on this. `FileDB` isn't used in a lot of places, so let's just type `Database` in all the places where the `FileDB` is declared and see what happens. No, there is no such class or interface in the codebase yet, but it's a good way to get feedback. And relax, this is only temporary. We *do* know how to revert the code.

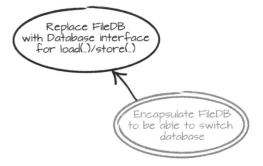

Figure 2.17 Adding a prerequisite that's a bit more explicit in its implementation details than the goal

Scratch refactorings

Play around, muck around, break things! Watch what happens, and then revert. Michael Feathers called this *scratch refactoring* in his book *Working Effectively with Legacy Code* (Prentice Hall, 2004). The Mikado Method uses that approach in a systematic way.

Listing 2.6   Changing `FileDB` to `Database`, with compilation errors in bold

```
package org.mikadomethod.app.ui;
...

public class UI {
  private JFrame frame;

  private Database database;                         ⟵┐ Changed FileDB
                                                       │ to Database
  public UI() {
    frame = new JFrame();

    database = new FileDB();
    database.setStore(App.getStorageFile());

  }

  public void showLogin() {

    List<String> users = database.load("users");

    addLoginSelector(users);
    addButtons();
    frame.setSize(800, 600);
    frame.setVisible(true);
  }
  ...
}
```

Now the code and the compiler are talking to us. Clearly the `Database` edit doesn't compile, so we can add "Create `Database` interface for `FileDB.load(..)/store(..)`" to the graph.

The business methods `load(..)` and `store(..)` should be in the interface, but the configuration method `setStore(..)` must be dealt with in another way. It would be best if we could initialize it in the constructor, so we can add "Configure file for `FileDB` in constructor" to the graph. Another prerequisite we can add is, "Use `Database` interface in `UI`." This results in the Mikado Graph in figure 2.18.

We got all of this information from just editing some code and quickly analyzing the errors. If you can't lean on a compiler, such as if you're working in a nonstatically typed language, you'll need to execute the code or the system, or go a bit further to analyze what your changes can reasonably affect, to get the feedback you need.

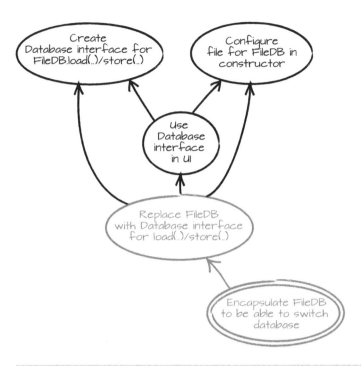

Figure 2.18
The information we've gathered from a naive edit

> ### Lean on the compiler
> Michael Feathers coined the phrase "lean on the compiler," meaning that you can make edits and see what, if anything, happens to the compilation results. This is one important source of feedback for the Mikado Method when using a statically typed language.

2.3.2 Revert when there are errors

We've tried some things, and we learned some important things about the code by breaking it. You might argue that you could forge ahead and continue the journey without reverting the code, and with a system of this size, chances are that you could pull it off. But you need to remember that this could be part of a bigger system. A central change like this usually ripples through large parts of the codebase, which means that if this piece is broken, it's going to affect several areas of the code.

The most important aspect of changing code the Mikado way is to reduce the side effects, mistakes, and unpleasant surprises, so it's imperative that you keep the code in working condition all the time. This means it should compile and all the tests should pass. If you don't have a test suite, we'll show you in chapter 5 how to add tests as a part of the Mikado Method. For now, you only need to remember that *revert* is a dear friend, and that you're learning about the system. Let's revert.

> **Tests and TDD**
> We strongly encourage the use of tests and test-driven development (TDD). We're also aware that when you work with structural changes, or you're trying to wrestle code into submission, you usually don't have the luxury of existing tests, nor are you likely to have suitable APIs to code against when testing. We suggest that you turn to Feathers' book *Working Effectively with Legacy Code* for more detailed advice on adding tests to a difficult-to-test codebase.

2.3.3   *Select the next prerequisite*

After we revert, we're now back where we started, except that we have a whole lot of new information in the form of the graph. When you have a graph, you can choose to take a depth-first approach, trying to implement one of the branches in the graph before taking on the next. You can alternatively take a breadth-first approach, meaning that you try to find all the prerequisites of the Mikado Goal first, and then take them on one after the other, building most of the graph before starting to implement parts of it. We have one branch in the graph now, so let's try the depth-first approach and implement our latest findings.

When we intend to implement things, we always start from a leaf. In this case, we have two leaves, and we can start from either one. Sometimes you can tell that a leaf will have further prerequisites just by looking at it, and in that situation it's usually a good idea to keep expanding the graph. In this case, both leaves look like leaves that we can implement without further leaves, so we'll just pick one of them: "Configure file for `FileDB` in constructor."

In this small example, we can just change the code by hand. But when you have a large codebase, and you're using a modern IDE, there's a neat trick you can use. First, create the default constructor in `FileDB`. Then you can use the IDE's Change Method Signature refactoring on that constructor. Add a `String` named `storageFile`, and give it the default value `App.getStorageFile()`. The IDE will then change the constructor and *all* calls to the original constructor to add `App.getStorageFile()` as a parameter. The changed call in this example is the call in the `UI` constructor, as can be seen in listings 2.7 and 2.8. This is often an extremely powerful way of changing code, but it changes all of the calls in the codebase, so you have to make sure that that's the outcome you want.

> **Automated refactorings**
> In the book *Refactoring*, Martin Fowler presents a catalog of refactorings—changes you can make to code that alter its internal structure without changing the observable behavior. These are usually fairly small changes, like extracting a method, renaming a method, or extracting an interface.

> **(continued)**
> Modern IDEs can perform these refactorings, and often more, on your code. You
> don't have to use them; you can make the same changes manually, but the auto-
> mation can speed up development a lot, and we use them heavily when we write
> and change code. We recommend getting to know your development environment
> and its automated refactorings.

We also have to start using the new parameter, so we'll assign the `field` in the constructor. Then we use another trick when we delete the call to the old `setStore(..)`
method: First, we make it an empty method. Then we remove it by using the IDE's
Inline (method) refactoring and selecting something along the lines of Inline All
Invocations—Delete Original Method. The refactoring replaces all calls to the
method with the body of the method, which in this case is nothing, and then deletes
the method.

Listing 2.7   The call to the `FileDB` constructor is changed.

```
public class FileDB {
  private File file;


  public FileDB(String storageFile) {          The constructor
    file = new File(storageFile);               takes the file
  }                                             argument.

                                                setStorage(..)
...                                             is deleted.
}
```

Listing 2.8   The call to the `FileDB` constructor is changed in `UI`.

```
public class UI {
  ...
  public UI() {                                The new constructor
    frame = new JFrame();                      is called instead of
    database = new FileDB(App.getStorageFile()); setStorage(..).
  }
  ...
}
```

Now, *does this change make sense?* Should we check it in? We could probably argue about
this, getting all philosophical, but let's just say that it's an improvement, it can be
understood, and it works, so there's really no good reason not to.

After we've checked it in, or committed the code, we can update the graph and
check off that prerequisite, as shown in figure 2.19.

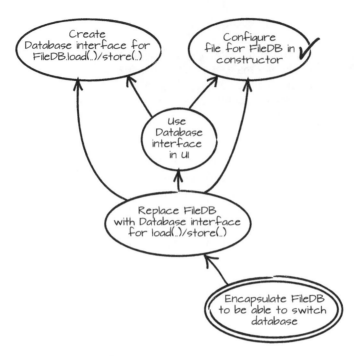

Figure 2.19   One leaf, or prerequisite, checked off and checked in

2.3.4   *Create an interface*

The next leaf in the graph is "Create `Database` interface for `FileDB.load(..)`/ `store(..)`." Often, when we use the Mikado Method, the things we implement are fairly simple. When they're not, there's usually a prerequisite that we still need to identify.

Let's create the interface `Database`, declare the methods in it, and let `FileDB` implement the interface.

Listing 2.9   `Database interface`

```
Database.java:
public interface Database {                          ⟵┐ The new
  List<String> load(String key);                        │ interface.
  void store(Map<String, Serializable> data);
}

FileDB.java:

public class FileDB implements Database {            ⟵┐ FileDB implements
                                                        │ the interface.
...
}
```

This is a change that makes some sense to check in, but we'd like to continue with the next small leaf as well: "Use `Database` interface in `UI`." This is also a very easy change: just change the declared type from `FileDB` to `Database`.

Listing 2.10 Use the interface in `UI`

```
public class UI {
  private JFrame frame;
  private Database database;          ⟵⎤ Change the
  ...                                     ⎦ declared type.
}
```

The IDE's automated refactoring, called Extract Interface, can usually replace the original type with the new interface in all places where such a change is possible, such as in the `UI` member declaration. If we had made the change using that automated refactoring, the process would have simply meant selecting the `FileDB` class, selecting Extract Interface from the refactoring menu, selecting `load(..)` and `store(..)` to be part of the interface, and selecting the option to replace all declarations where the new interface can be used instead of `FileDB`.

Now we definitely have a sensible change that we should check in. The "Replace `FileDB` with `Database` interface for `load(..)`/`store(..)`" prerequisite can also be checked off, because it's been implemented already. The graph now looks like figure 2.20.

2.3.5 *Restart from the goal*

Now that we've implemented a few things, the starting point of our refactoring has changed slightly, so the next time we have to revert, we'll end up with the current situation rather than the state the code was in originally. But we're still reaching for the same goal of encapsulating the `FileDB` and putting the related code in one place.

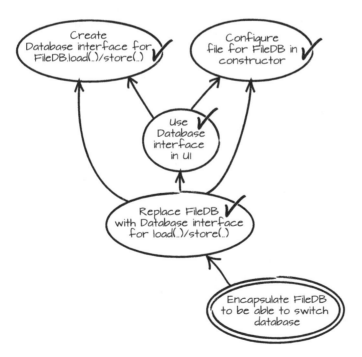

Figure 2.20   Database interface in use

And we're not done yet. We can see that it doesn't make sense to keep the `FileDB`-specific methods `App.setStorageFile(..)` and `getStorageFile()`. Let's remove them and see what we get. We'll add "Remove `App.setStorageFile(..)`/`getStorageFile()` methods" to the graph, and then remove the methods in the code to see if we get a few pointers to our next prerequisites.

Listing 2.11   Error in `Launcher`

```
public class Launcher {

  public static void main(String[] argv) {
      try {
        App.setStorageFile(argv[0]);                    ← Pull up creation
        App app = new App();                              of FileDB to here?
        app.launch();

  ...
}
```

Listing 2.12   Error in `UI`

```
public UI() {
  frame = new JFrame();                                 ← Or push down
  database = new FileDB(App.getStorageFile());            argv[0] to here?
}
```

We get two compiler errors, marked in bold in listings 2.11 and 2.12. From that information, and a look at the code, we can see two options: we can pull up the creation of the `FileDB` to `Launcher`, or we can push down the `argv[0]` string to the `FileDB` instantiation in `UI`. In general, it's better to keep the primitives at the edges of the application, and the object types further in, so we'll choose to pull up the creation of the `FileDB` to `Launcher`.

This decision also goes into the graph as "Pull up creation of `FileDB` to `Launcher`," so it looks like figure 2.21. With this information added to the graph, we can safely revert our broken changes and go for the new leaf from a working state.

OK, we have a clean slate once again. Pulling up an object through a call hierarchy is often a fairly straightforward task. We need to start in the `UI` constructor and then pull it via the `launch(..)` method of `App`. To implement this, we simply need to introduce a parameter of type `Database` to the constructor in `UI` as in listing 2.13, and all the callers have to create the `FileDB` object. The caller, in this case, is the `launch(..)` method of `App`, as in listing 2.14.

Listing 2.13   The `UI` is done

```
public class UI {
  ...
  public UI(Database database) {                        ← Taking a Database instead
    frame = new JFrame();                                 of constructing a FileDB
    this.database = database;
  }
  ...
}
```

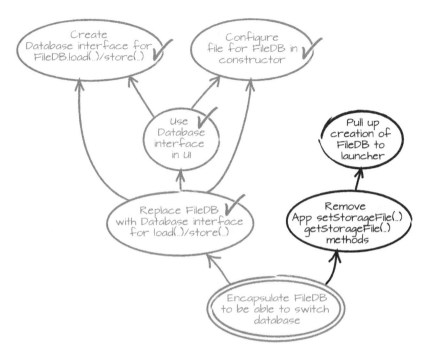

Figure 2.21 More prerequisites for our goal

```
public class App {
  ...
  public void launch() throws ApplicationException {        Intermediate place
    ui = new UI(new FileDB(App.getStorageFile()));    ◁──┘  of construction
    ui.showLogin();
  }
  ...
}
```

This process is then repeated in the launch(..) method to get the construction of FileDB to the Launcher.

For this type of task, there's also an automated refactoring in most IDEs called Introduce Parameter. Like the Inline Method and Change Method Signature refactorings, it will change all the places in the code where the method is called.

Whether the changes are made manually or are automated, the resulting code will look like the next listing

```
public class Launcher {
  public static void main(String[] argv) {
      try {
        App.setStorageFile(argv[0]);
```

```
      App app = new App();
      app.launch(new FileDB(App.getStorageFile())); 
    } catch (ApplicationException e) {
      ...
    }
  }
}
```

◁— **FileDB in place, and an unnecessary juggling of argv[0]**

Now the construction of FileDB is pulled up the call stack to Launcher. As you can see in the preceding listing, the argv[0] is set and then retrieved a couple of lines later. Let's simplify this and set the file directly in the FileDB constructor.

The prerequisite for deleting the file methods from App is now in place, but this isn't really a good time to commit any code because there are two now-unused methods in App. We can delete setStorageFile(..) and getStorageFile() from App, along with the field that holds the file parameter. The results can be seen in the following listings.

Listing 2.16 Launcher in final shape

```
public class Launcher {
  public static void main(String[] argv) {
    try {
      App app = new App();
      app.launch(new FileDB(argv[0]));
    } catch (ApplicationException e) {
      System.err.println("Could not start application");
      e.printStackTrace();
    }
  }
}
```

Listing 2.17 App in final shape

```
public class App {
  private UI ui;

  public void launch(Database database) throws ApplicationException {
    ui = new UI(database);
    ui.showLogin();
  }
}
```

Now when you look at the code, you can see that the Database, in the shape of a FileDB, is configured in one place with the command-line variable. All the other code is using the Database interface, and we've met our goal. We can check it in, and check it all off the graph (see figure 2.22). We're done!!

2.4 Summary

This is a small example of how to change code. We tried some rather straightforward edits that some would probably say were trivial, but what we learned from them was essential for solving the problem in a controlled way.

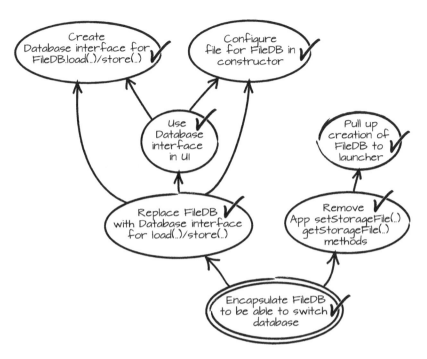

Figure 2.22 We're done!!

Now that you've seen a somewhat realistic example, we hope you've begun to grasp how to perform changes the Mikado way. This hands-on, empirical technique mixes small, safe experiments with note-taking, visualization, and reverts. By taking notes, you create your refactoring map, the Mikado Graph, as you go.

The biggest take-away from this chapter should be the process of trying things, learning, and then reverting the code to a working condition.

In the next chapter, we'll begin to introduce terminology for the Mikado Method and the code changes we make. In addition to that, we'll touch on some of the philosophy and the underlying processes that make the Mikado Method so effective.

Try this
- Perform a small restructuring using the Mikado Method. Draw the graph using pen and paper.
- Perform the same restructuring as above, but this time use a computer-based tool, like FreeMind, Visio, or maybe even a presentation application like Power-Point, to draw your graph. Notice what feels different this time.
- Compare two different VCSs in terms of speed when it comes to creating branches, reverting changes, and removing branches.

Goals, graphs, and guidelines

3

This chapter covers

- The Mikado Method guidelines
- The components of the Mikado Graph
- Variations when using the method and creating the graph
- Important properties of the method
- Relation to other thinking models

So far we've covered basic Mikado Method concepts and mechanics with the intention of teaching you enough to solve basic problems. To take you to the next level of understanding, we'll now get to the roots of the method and cover some new ground. It's time talk about the underpinnings of the method and touch on the theoretical aspects. After you've read this chapter, you'll be able to evolve and adapt the method and apply it to situations other than those described in this book.

3.1 The Mikado Method guidelines

There are a few core things you need to keep in mind when you use the Mikado Method, because without them the method will quickly deteriorate:

- Always start with the goal
- Use experiments
- Revert—the key to safe refactorings
- Focus on the leaves

We'll discuss these guidelines in the following sections, and they're here to remind you about the process if you decide to tweak it.

3.1.1 Always start with the goal

Whenever you work with complex problems, such as programming and systems design, you want to maximize your thinking capacity and direct it to finding a solution. By taking notes on a piece of paper or a whiteboard, you immediately reduce the cognitive load on your brain, and that capacity can now be used to solve the problem. There's no longer any need to juggle obstacles and possible solutions in your mind, as they're now recorded on a piece of paper.

If you formulate the goal as an ideal future, it'll be easier to recognize when the goal is met. Writing down the goal forces you to put the idea, or feeling about what needs to be done, into words. This often serves as a reality check: once you formulate a goal, it's easier to determine its importance and the reasons for achieving it. If you can't present good reasons, maybe you really should be doing something else. A goal that has been written down can also serve as an external commitment, both to yourself and other interested parties; it's something that can be discussed and scrutinized.

First and foremost, a good goal must carry value—the more value the better, and if stakeholders agree it constitutes value, you have a winner. Consider the difference between "Update third-party API to version X" and "Customer address is retrieved using the latest version of the third-party API." They might mean the same thing to a person with a technical background, but the latter hints at some sort of business value.

Second, the goal should be concrete enough so that you know where to start and when you're done, even after a long weekend. We prefer "When a session times out, a login screen is shown" over "Timeouts don't affect the user experience."

Finally, the goal needs to be specific. Vague goals like "Use a faster XML parser" aren't going to help anyone. You should aim for something more specific, like "Loading <100 Mb XML configuration files can't take longer than 2 seconds."

3.1.2 Use experiments

When the goal is in place, it's time to find out what's preventing you from reaching it. In the previous chapters, we showed you how to do this by making small code changes. These small changes are micro experiments that manifest themselves as compilation errors. Any error or other problem, such as a test that doesn't pass, gives you the feedback you need to explore the system. All these micro experiments in combination result in the restructuring map. *Restructuring map* is a term we use interchangeably with Mikado Graph, especially when we talk to non-technical people.

We could spend time analyzing this map, but we strongly prefer the rapid feedback from compilers and test suites over analysis, which is why we act as straightforwardly as we do. It's our way of avoiding analysis paralysis. We take this course as long as we do our work in a safe environment. By *safe*, we mean that there are tests, compilers, or other means for quickly checking for errors. If you use a lot of reflective features or a dynamically typed language, you'll need to be a bit more analytical, at least before you decide to integrate your changes with the rest of the code.

> **LANGUAGES AND TYPE SYSTEMS** Programming languages are often categorized as *statically type-checked*, a.k.a. *statically typed*, or *dynamically type-checked*, a.k.a. *dynamically typed*. In statically typed languages, the types for variables, methods, and functions in a program are checked to be compatible by a compiler at compile time. In a dynamically typed language, these checks are made at runtime, often just enough to make sure all instructions can execute. Well-known statically typed languages include Java, C#, and C/C++, and common dynamically typed languages include JavaScript, Ruby, and Python.

Instead of enduring long periods of analysis, we aim for the simplest possible thing we can come up with, and we're often surprised by our progress and findings. Mucking around is normally more fruitful and produces results far more quickly than hours of analysis. This experimental style, the *Naive Approach*, was discussed in the first two chapters. Some trivial examples include removing methods, changing qualifiers (such as `public` to `private` or `static` to nonstatic), and then recompiling the code or just running the application or tests to see what happens.

When our experiments don't seem to contribute to the expected progress, we stop for a minute and analyze the situation. Our initial efforts still pay good interest because the information we've discovered up to that point is often very useful when the analysis starts.

The Naive Approach shouldn't be confused with changing things at random and then committing code if it compiles. The value from this approach comes from its directness, and it stands in stark contrast to long periods of analysis that in effect don't verify a thesis. The analytical approach can often feel safe and structured, but it's only when the rubber meets the road that you see whether or not your analysis was correct. We've found that shortening the analysis phase and sometimes skipping it entirely produces the results we want a lot more quickly than thinking about a change.

There is, of course, room for both experimentation and analysis, but our experience tells us that the first is underutilized and the latter is overvalued.

3.1.3 *Revert—the key to safe refactorings*

The most fundamental concept or guideline of the Mikado Method, and of sensible software development as a whole, is to limit changes and additions to situations where the system is in a working and known state. Then, little by little, you can start tweaking the code and immediately confirm that it still works as expected. If it doesn't, you revert to the last known working state.

Making improvements and additions to broken code is problematic because when you make another change and the code wasn't working to start with, you don't know if the broken state comes from the initially broken state, the new change, or a combination of the two. In addition, you don't know if your change actually fixed the initial problem. Sometimes you end up lucky and fix everything in one sweep, but that's a rare case indeed. If instead of depending on luck, you make a change that takes you from a working state to a nonworking state, you can be quite sure that it was your change that broke the code. In a complex system, other things can affect the state, but if you revert and the problem is gone, that supports the theory that it was your change that caused the problem. (If not, you have another problem you need to take care of before making your change.)

This is exactly the same as the red-green-refactor cycle in test-driven development. You write a test that fails (red). You write code that makes the test, and all other tests, pass (green). Then you can refactor, making changes to your code as long as all the tests pass. If a refactoring breaks any test (red), you back out of that change (green), and try another refactoring.

Your Mikado Graph isn't only a refactoring map; it also works as a simple reminder that you should experiment and revert when things break. Look at it and update it frequently. If nothing happens in the graph, chances are you've been working in a broken state for too long.

If you're using a dynamically typed language, it's harder to know when the code is broken, and you need to be a lot more careful. The system must be executed in some way to verify its condition, preferably by using automated tests. If you're working without automated tests, you need to be extra careful and verify some other way that the system works. An alternative to using compilers and automated tests for finding problems is to build the system after each change and test the system manually to make sure, to some reasonable degree, that nothing is broken. This is a tedious process, but if you can build, install, and launch your system with a single command, you'll improve your situation.

It's never too late to turn back

Every once in a while, you'll be up against a change that doesn't feel big at first, but then it snowballs, and before you know it your change has spiraled out of control. When we initially came up with the Mikado Method, we walked into a situation like that, but that happens less often these days. Knowing about the method not only makes it possible for us to perform big restructurings; we can also sense a big change earlier. Turning back at moments like that is what we recommend.

One way to avoid derailing your changes is having some sort of reminder that asks, "Is it time to check in, or is it time to revert?" That reminder could be a timer set for 25 minutes, an agreement with a colleague, or something else that happens at a given point. Decide how much time you feel you can lose, and set up your working environment accordingly.

3.1.4 *Focus on the leaves*

Your hard work will eventually lead you to code that can be changed without introducing additional errors, but you have to be patient in getting there. Big redesigns and restructurings can touch on hundreds or even thousands of files, depending on how bad the condition of the system is, and how things are coupled. Sometimes exploring the graph's breadth first, one level at a time for all the nodes (leaves), feels like the natural choice. Sometimes going depth-first, where you explore all the levels in one branch, is best. Whichever you choose, exploration is always done by focusing on the leaves. The leaves are nodes that have no prerequisites yet, and they're usually found at the periphery of the drawn graph.

The Mikado Method is a bit like a dance, and it often goes like this in exploration mode: start (with a goal), experiment, note the results, revert, experiment, note the results, revert, experiment, note the results, revert, and so on. If you go depth-first, you try an experiment, note the results, revert, and continue to explore the graph in one direction until you can achieve something. This is the preferred approach if you have an idea about where you want to take the code. If you don't have a clear idea, or you want to get a sense of the size of the problem, try a breadth-first approach and make sure you find all the prerequisites for one leaf before moving on to the next interesting leaf. In either case, you'll eventually find leaves that are true leaves, and then the dance changes to execution mode: implement a leaf, check it into your versioning system, check it off the graph, implement the next leaf, check it in, check it off, and so on. Depending on your problem and your depth tactics, the two dancing modes may be interleaved.

> **Two different modes**
>
> When you use the Mikado Method, there are two more or less distinct modes when it comes to the graph and adding nodes: the exploration mode and the checking-nodes (or execution) mode. There's no clear definition of either, but you know you're in the latter phase when you get the feeling of having crested the hill. You know you're in the former when you're adding more to the graph than you're checking off.

3.2 *The Mikado Graph*

As you might have noticed, the Mikado Graph is a *directed acyclic graph* (DAG). All graphs consists of *nodes* (the "bubbles") and of *edges* (the connections between the bubbles). A graph that is *directed* means that the edges have a direction—they go only in one way. *Acyclic* means that you can never get back to the same point by following the directed edges. In this book, we call the directed edges *dependency arrows*.

If Mikado Graphs weren't DAGs and instead were directed cyclic graphs (DCGs), it would be possible to end up in a loop during the exploration phase. Fortunately, this isn't the case. But sometimes when you explore the code, you might think you have a cycle in the graph—this is what we call a *false cycle*. There's always a way to break a false cycle, usually by breaking the refactoring into smaller refactorings that can be executed step by step.

The full graph represents the body of knowledge you've gathered about a particular restructuring or redesign. Let's take a look at the individual parts of the graph for a while and deepen your knowledge about each different component.

3.2.1 The goal—business or technical?

When you decide to make a change to your system, there's an underlying assumption that this is necessary and that it must be done in order to move the system forward. Your goal could be a wish for a more flexible design, which in turn enables faster testing, just like the first example in this book. Or it could be a desire to partition the system in order to allow a new or changed feature; you'll see this in the example in chapter 5. Faster testing is generally considered a technical goal, whereas preparation for a new feature is more of a business goal. There is, of course, a fuzzy line between the two.

Mikado Graphs with business goals can be used to communicate with non-technical people. You can, for instance, show a non-technical person the graph and simply say, "So far, this is how much we believe needs to change in order to accommodate this new feature you're asking for." If you use a graph to communicate the complexity of a change, it's the number of nodes that conveys that information. The problem is that initially you don't have all the nodes, and in that case the breadth is a better measure of complexity. Do keep in mind that this is tendentious information only, not an exact metric.

A technical goal is generally used within a team when a problem arises that isn't directly tied to a business goal, such as "Introduce a `Money` type." Both technical goals and business goals are important to pursue, but keep in mind that technical goals usually have an underlying business goal. Keep looking for the business goal, because it's much easier to motivate people to spend time on something that's directly connected to the interest of the stakeholders. Work to combine the technical goals with business value. Try to split them into smaller pieces that can be dealt with one at a time, in connection with a business goal.

3.2.2 The prerequisites

You already know that the prerequisites often manifest themselves as compilation errors or test failures, and that you shouldn't try to fix those errors immediately. Instead, analyze the situation just enough to decide on immediate solutions that will resolve the errors. Often, you won't know what the exact consequences of your change will be anyway, so choose a simple resolution to the problem to keep your momentum going. When you realize that there are things that aren't immediately shown by the compiler or the tests, write these down as prerequisites as well. This way, you can put all your available tools and knowledge to use when you decide what to do.

You'll save a lot of time by following the Naive Approach and avoiding unnecessary analysis. Be practical and direct when you can be, and smart and analytical when you must.

> **Don't think too long**
>
> Our rule of thumb on analysis: try something straightforward and practical if you've been analyzing for more than a couple of minutes.

3.2.3 *Prerequisite—step or decision?*

As you explore and evolve the graph, you'll discover more and more details that you'll note on your piece of paper. Many notes are tasks or detailed descriptions of what should happen, but sometimes you need to make decisions. So far we've been fairly detailed in our notes, but there are times when you'll want to postpone an implementation detail. In those cases, you can just write "Break circular dependency" or something that reminds you about what needs to happen instead of writing exactly how. You'll still have the note, but also the flexibility of going in several directions.

A note like that is what we call a *decision node*, and if you pay close attention you'll also notice that decisions look the same in all our Mikado Graphs. That's because we don't want the method to be encumbered with unnecessary ceremony or notation. If we introduce too many concepts or too much detail, we run the risk of creating a new Unbeatable Modeling Language with rules about everything. Or even worse, detailed rules about several versions of notation.

We want all our attention to be focused on solving the refactoring, not on deciding what symbols to draw in the graph. By reducing the number of concepts, we aim to minimize the risk of drawing the graph in the "wrong" way. In addition, this gives you, the Mikado Method practitioner, more flexibility to modify the graph notation to fit your current needs. If you have a strong desire to make the decisions or any other node stand out, feel free to draw them in a different shape or to spice up your graph with bright colors. From an execution perspective, it doesn't matter much. You'll have to implement all the prerequisites in due time.

And with that said, we do have a few informal variations we've used, and those can be seen in chapter 7.

3.2.4 *How big should a step be?*

So far, we've intentionally been very explicit in our note taking, and nothing has been left out of our Mikado Graphs because we believe it's important to show you how the process works. But big redesigns and large restructurings often result in big graphs with many nodes. If you get the feeling that the graph is growing too quickly, with too much detail, you can try to combine several steps or tasks into one node. That is, you can decrease the granularity.

Like any other process or methodology, you probably want the Mikado Method to support you rather than to be in your hair when you're working. If you can't make out where you're going because there are too many nodes, the process might be getting in your way. Whether it is *getting in your way* or *supporting you*, however, is highly dependent on the context.

Sometimes you'll want to be a bit more detailed, such as when you need to convey information to fellow developers or other interested parties. Sometimes you'll have a tricky problem and the graph gets big.

Other times, you won't need the same granularity because you and the other developers already have a common language and the same idea of how things should be accomplished. At times like that, you can choose to be a little less detailed in order to speed progress.

3.2.5 *More about the leaves*

All nodes in a graph except the leaves are inhibited by their prerequisites. The leaves in the Mikado Graph are the only places where a code change can actually be performed. If a node isn't a true leaf, the system will break when you execute the task in the node. Some nodes may looks like leaves at first, but they may reveal prerequisites when you try to implement them.

When all the prerequisites for a node have been taken care of, that node itself becomes a leaf, ready to be dealt with. Usually, you can start with any leaf, but sometimes multiple nodes point toward the same prerequisite. This happens rather often, as it did in our earlier example of removing the database dependency (in chapter 2), where almost everything depended on the creation of a FileDB at the top of the graph. Other times, the graph splits early on into streams and joins later. In all cases, start with a leaf that seems to have the potential to give the next complete committable change set, or a leaf that you think will give the best uninterrupted flow of refactorings. In our example of removing the database dependency, we had to explore the entire graph before we felt we could check in anything. That made sense in that case, but often you can check in changes that in retrospect turn out to be midgraph.

3.2.6 *The dependency arrows*

As you explore systems and expand graphs, you add new nodes and also the dependency arrows between them. The dependency arrows point from the original goal toward its prerequisites (see figure 3.1). You can compare the goal, your major change, to an explosion, where the force of the change is directed out from the center.

This might feel a bit awkward at first, because you often think of what needs to be done in a sequence and point the arrows in that order. In contrast, the arrows in the Mikado Graph represent dependencies. When you make the changes, you travel in the opposite direction of those dependencies, starting with the leaf prerequisites. You are trying to stop the explosion.

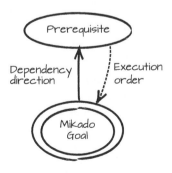

Figure 3.1 Notice that the dependency arrow points in one direction and that the graph mandates the opposite order of execution.

3.2.7   *The check marks*

To keep track of our progress, we check nodes as they're finished. Sometimes, we put a check mark by the leaves one by one as we complete them, and sometimes we check them off as a batch.

If we check them off one by one, we risk having to remove a check mark if we discover that we've missed something and must revert our changes, such as if we discover that a leaf wasn't a true leaf. A common strategy we use is to check off the nodes when a coherent change, a change that makes sense, is completed. When we check the nodes off the graph, we should also take the time to check our changes in to the versioning system.

Check in often

The simple mantra "check node, check in code" reminds us to check in code often. The VCS is there to help, so make good use of it.

We have few recommendations for tools other than pen and paper, but we do recommend using a VCS that supports short-lived branches, in which you can do several small commits, and do them really quickly. Distributed VCSs do this very well, because they enable you to make as many commits as you want, without affecting the main code repository. We can't stress enough how much we encourage frequent commits within a branch, at least when a coherent change is ready. That way you get several points to go back to, and that simplifies reaching a known state.

Checking the leaves off isn't just a good way of seeing what you've accomplished. It's also rewarding to check off one leaf after another, knowing that they are steps leading toward your goal.

Another way to put a leaf in a done state is by simply erasing it as it's completed. This frees up precious (whiteboard) space, and the finished nodes no longer clutter up your graph and thinking. The disadvantage of this approach manifests itself later if you want to analyze the path you took, or if you want to see each and every task you've finished. We suggest you take a photo, or copy your graph to a piece of paper if you believe you'll need it later. Usually you won't, though.

Erasing finished work from your graph is sometimes necessary if you have a limited amount of space, but putting a check mark beside a node as you finish a task is fast, and it also gives you a rough estimate of how much work you've completed and how much remains. Let your intuition guide you, and experiment with both approaches. You'll soon discover which is appropriate when.

3.3   *Tips for using the Mikado Method*

If you're going to use the Mikado Method in some novel situation or problem, the following tips we find helpful might also help you:

- Focus on the goal
- Follow the flow of the code
- Keep it simple
- Keep it visible
- Iterate, increment, and evolve
- Remember the state
- Reflect on your work

The Mikado Method is relatively easy to explain, and the body of knowledge needed to use it is fairly limited, but these points can help you when you're explaining the method to someone else or tweaking the method for yourself.

3.3.1 Focus on the goal

When you write down the Mikado Goal and do things that are connected to that goal, which is often a direct or indirect business goal, you automatically tackle the most important tasks first. Because you're trying to reach the goal by completing tasks in the leaf nodes, you're either getting closer to the goal or learning more about the system, and both are equally valuable. But that focus is easy to lose when pressure is added or distraction comes from a boss, customer, or someone else.

The clear, goal-oriented approach also doubles as a good basis for dialogue with business people who don't always understand how technical implementation details are tied to business changes. When you show them the goal and the graph, people who aren't responsible for the technical implementation can see how that work is directly connected to business needs. This can help disarm a common situation where developers are accused of delving into technology for technology's sake. It also avoids the reverse situation where business people are accused of not understanding the essential nature of technical improvements.

Defining a very specific and distinct goal makes the code easier to work with, not just because it can be discussed and related to, but also because it provides a clear focus and something tangible to work toward. At the same time, prerequisites are more easily identified and achieved along the way, and optional solutions to problems often present themselves in a totally different light when there's a plan.

The bigger decisions are best made when the whole picture is visible (in a zoomed-out mode), whereas the technical decisions are best made as the code is being written (in a zoomed-in mode). The graph is the plan, and it serves as a high-level strategy for reaching the goal. The nodes contain more detailed information and serve you better on a tactical level. You can zoom out for strategy and zoom in for tactical matters.

3.3.2 Follow the flow of the code

Before we discovered the Mikado Method, we used to work with to-do lists, which worked fine for small restructurings but not with some larger problems. We realized that to-do lists miss a very important aspect: the *transitive information*, or how things are connected to each other. To-do lists work when you need to keep track of work in one dimension, such as the breadth or the depth of a change, but not both at the same time.

The Mikado Graph can't be replaced with a simple list because the dependencies get lost and it's hard to remember what you need to do first. Furthermore, a single new dependency arrow can change the order of the entire execution. A list works for linear problems, but it's not a good model for the changes in a complex environment like a codebase.

The effectiveness of the Mikado Method comes from the fact that all the nodes in the graph are created from true prerequisites of the Mikado Goal, and that the goal has a transitive relationship to all the other nodes. That is, when the goal is met, all other prerequisite tasks have been taken care of. The reverse is also true: when all the prerequisites have been taken care of, the Mikado Goal is met.

Because you focus your attention on the leaves, there's no, or very little, extra work, and the work flows naturally. This means that you don't have to worry about not reaching your goal, because you always do, sooner or later. Sometimes, however, you reach a point where a decision has to be made. Should you go with solution A, or maybe choose solution B? Depending on which solution you choose, you might or might not run into other problems later.

Usually there's more than one way to solve a particular programming problem. This means that if you redo the same restructuring, you could end up with two quite different solutions. If you have options but aren't sure which one you should use, that's a good indication that a short design discussion or session is in order. In addition to that, we recommend that you consider trying out possible options and seeing where they take you. Remember, experiment-and-revert is your friend.

3.3.3 *Keep it simple*

The exploratory Naive Approach of revealing what's between you and your goal will point in the right general direction as you change code and try different solutions. It immediately shows you where the next problem is in the simplest way: an error. The graph is also the simplest possible tool you could come up with to record all the things you need to do in order to reach your goal.

The method isn't just simple, it's also pragmatic because it doesn't look for the optimal solution, just one that's sufficient. This is a great way to maintain focus and avoid *gold-plating*. You might think that sounds a bit rigid, but remember that the prerequisites allow you to fine-tune the solution to suit your needs.

Often engineers and developers want to be able to say, "This is the best way to do it!" The Mikado Method takes a different and more humble slant, saying, "This is one way to do it." We try to remember that "*perfect* is the worst enemy of *good enough*."

The goals of the examples in the previous chapters can actually be met in several different ways. Before we settled on the code that we presented in this book, we tried several different solutions, and they looked quite different. And our examples have been small; it's easy to see that a production system could have even more ways to meet a goal. There are, however, different ways to understand *simplicity* here. We mean it's simple to find a solution, not that the solution you find will be the simplest one to understand later. This is where your design skills come into play.

3.3.4 *Keep it visible*

Visual aids and information radiators such as whiteboards, flip charts, or a sheet of paper can provide an overall picture very quickly. These are what we use when we write down the goal and the nodes. This graph then guides us and reminds us where we're going and what we're currently working on. Using visible charts is also a great way to stimulate more parts of the brain, which is a good thing when it comes to problem solving.

3.3.5 *Iterate, increment, and evolve*

One step at a time is how we tackle big tasks, and big code changes are no different. When it comes to the process, the Mikado Method reminds us of an old joke:

Q: How do you eat an elephant?
A: One bite at a time.

Both in its exploration and execution phases, the Mikado Method is a one-step-at-a-time endeavor. This implies that the graph will continue to change as long as prerequisites and transient prerequisites are found on the journey to the goal.

Although the effects from the actual change effort come as small alterations and incremental improvements, the Mikado Method itself is an iterative process. This means that the system can evolve incrementally from work iterations, which makes it possible to select a good time for making critical changes or to spread out the work over time. It also means you can stop at any time, like at the end of an iteration, to make a release, if that's appropriate.

As opposed to producing a Big Bang change, like merging half a year's drastic refactoring work from a separate branch, the iterative nature of the Mikado Method and its incremental results produces an evolutionary, rather than a revolutionary, effect. No extensive merge work is needed; no long-lived branches with half-finished refactorings will be lying around with people wondering if they'll ever be used. And most importantly, code can be delivered and deployed at any time.

A Mikado refactoring can be stretched out over a long period of time, but you constantly merge the leaf changes back to the main branch. When the work is spread out over longer periods of time, it's likely that change will happen outside of the scope of the goal that was first addressed. If this happens, and it might if the goal is a major one, the graph needs to be revisited and updated. External changes could in extreme cases invalidate your refactoring and your graph, so try to coordinate and align other changes with yours to reap the synergistic benefits instead of bashing heads.

So, will I write better code?

The Mikado Method will not magically make anyone better at designing and writing software. Initially, it will just help you put existing skills to use in a more efficient and effective way. But in the long run, our experience tells us you'll learn to spot design problems more quickly, thus giving you more learning opportunities. Harnessing these learning opportunities is up to you.

We've also seen a shift in developer approach, toward making more fine-grained changes and more frequent check-ins, even when not using the Mikado Method. We believe this is an improvement in working habits that leads to better code.

3.3.6 *Remember the state*

Figure 3.2 **Simple things to the rescue**

Imagine a man walking in the countryside. It's a hot summer day, and he's getting thirsty. In the far distance, there's an old well, so he walks toward it.

The well is the old kind, with a crank and a bucket on a chain, but it looks like it's still in working condition. The man tosses the bucket down and hears a distant splash. He starts cranking it up, but the bucket's heavy and the well is deeper than he initially thought. The man's arms start aching and he feels the need to take a short break.

The person who built this well knew that hauling water is hard work, and he put a ratchet on the crank, so the bucket wouldn't fall back into the water when the crank is released. The man pauses, catches his breath, and is ready to go again. After some more cranking, the reward arrives, and the man tips the bucket and drinks the refreshing water.

Many big refactorings are like hauling water from a deep well; it's really hard work, and pauses are needed. We've done restructurings that have taken days, weeks, and even months in some cases, so we know that large restructurings benefit from pausing and reflecting.

Without some sort of "ratchet," this isn't possible. The Mikado Graph serves as *our* ratchet. It allows us to take a pause and leave our work for a while. When we're ready to pick up the work again, we can do so exactly where we left off. The graph keeps track of how far we've come, and it keeps us from having to backtrack and reexamine the codebase to figure out where we are. Just like a ratchet, the graph allows us to catch our breath, which in the end saves a lot of time and energy.

The graph is also a very fast way to refresh our memory. You can think of the graph as the *saved state* in a computer game, which can be loaded back into working memory. Just by looking at the graph, the priorities, thoughts, and goals are restored. The graph can lie untouched for a long time, but all it takes is a quick glance and work can be instantly picked up where it was left off. Compare this to reading a long list of to-dos hidden in the code, or a huge technical debt backlog. Not as compelling, right?

3.3.7 *Reflect on your work*

The Mikado Graph can also help when you reflect on previous refactorings, in discussions, and in learning. Even where a refactoring could be performed with a few small steps, the Mikado Graph can be useful. You can use it to reflect on the path taken to see if something could have been done differently, and what that might have been. Often just taking a short coffee break can put the Mikado Graph in a different light, and let you see it as if for the first time.

The graph is helpful if you need to practice and rehearse a refactoring, over and over, until it can be smoothly executed. This can be especially useful when you're up against a change that has a lot of steps that all need to be done to make sense before checking in. An example would be moving from one version of a framework to another, or some other case where the undo phase is time consuming or expensive. There are cases where the last critical steps that actually do the job or switch can be harmful if the timing isn't right. In cases like that, you can benefit a lot from rehearsing the steps and using the graph to reflect on the work ahead to maximize the odds of success.

3.4 *Relation to other thinking models*

No part of the Mikado Method is really new. Its novelty comes from the way it combines existing practices. We believe that as long as there's been software, there's been restructuring, starting over from the beginning, and visualizing dependencies. They're all concepts familiar to every software developer, if not to everyone who has tried to accomplish anything remotely complex.

Initially, we never thought much about how these concepts related to each other and just did what we needed to do to get the job done. After a while, we realized that the Mikado Method relates to other thinking models, and it gets its flow and rhythm from some vital properties of these models.

3.4.1   *Theory of Constraints*

The Theory of Constraints (ToC) was introduced by Eliyahu M. Goldratt in his novel, *The Goal: A Process of Ongoing Improvement* (North River Press, 1984). One part of the ToC is the *thinking processes*, where one tool is the *prerequisite tree*. The Mikado Graph represents a prerequisite tree for any given Mikado Goal.

The prerequisite tree has a goal called the *injection*. To reach that goal, *obstacles* need to be overcome. For each obstacle, there's an *intermediate objective* that overcomes each obstacle. The objectives can in turn have other obstacles that need to be overcome, in a transient manner.

The Mikado Graph contains the injection as the Mikado Goal, and the objectives, which are the prerequisites. The errors in the code that lead you to the prerequisites are the obstacles.

3.4.2   *Empirical control systems*

An empirical system can be defined as a system that's based on experiments and observation rather than on an exactly defined process. A common example of this is driving a car from one place to another. You could plan the whole trip ahead of time with the help of a map. Then, given your speed and the knowledge you gained from the map, you'd know when to shift gears and when to turn the wheel. The problem with this approach is that there are a lot more unknown variables in driving than just the directions and your speed. Even if you could gather and use data about normal traffic and weather conditions, chances are that something else would disturb your carefully crafted plan. This is why you need an empirical process to drive a car, where you adjust and learn over time and feed that information back into the system.

There's a whole body of science on how to control such systems, called Control Theory. Such empirical systems require feedback and corrective action in order to be controlled.

When the Mikado Graph is created using the Naive Approach, the compiler and the tests provide the feedback, and the Mikado Graph is then extended with the corrective action indicated. In Control Theory, fast feedback is important in order to minimize the errors in the process. With the Mikado Method, it's important to perform small experiments to get feedback instead of doing long sessions of analysis. Instead of sitting home and thinking about driving a car, you need to get out on the road and see and feel for yourself what it's like.

3.4.3   *Pull systems*

In Lean Software Development, one of the central concepts is that value should be pulled from the system, not pushed out of the system. Lean concepts originally come from the Toyota Production System and how they manufacture cars. In practice, this means that when a customer buys a car, the salesperson metaphorically pulls the car from the assembly line, which in turn pulls the engine, the chassis, the drive line, and the tires from their respective suppliers, and so on, all the way down to the nuts and bolts. As the nuts and bolts are delivered, the engine and chassis are assembled, and in turn the assembly line can put the car together and deliver it to the customer. This system has proven be very competitive in manufacturing and several other disciplines because it minimizes the amount of work in progress, storage costs, and the risk of not being sold.

The opposite, a push system, essentially creates something without establishing the need for it first. It could be a manager telling the employees in a factory to start manufacturing a certain number of cars, hoping that the sales staff can sell them. This approach introduces a greater risk into the system because you're relying on forecasts and predictions, and such guesswork is inherently more risky. The manager could, for instance, get the number of cars right but the color of the interiors wrong, or vice versa, which makes the cars harder to sell. As the number of properties that can vary goes up, the bigger the risk becomes with a push system.

A "push" refactoring is where you plan the steps needed in advance, using extended analysis, and then hope that you've covered everything and that the pieces will come together in the end. This is definitely possible—it *has* been done—but the risk is that things that don't need to change *will* be changed, and that essential things will be missed. The amount of work involved is likely to be greater than when using a "pull" approach.

The Mikado Method is a pull system, an approach with very little overhead, where the needed code changes are pulled from the codebase. The compiler and test failures resulting from the Naive Approach pull the next change, and so on, until the leaves are reached, which are the "nuts and bolts" of a code change. From there, the refactoring can be assembled by taking care of the leaves, one after another.

3.5   Summary

In this chapter, we dug a bit deeper into the Mikado world and explored some thinking tools that will prepare you to handle situations where the standard Mikado formula needs to be tweaked. In the next chapter, you'll get to know when it's a good time to start using the method—this depends on your code, your staffing, and your experience with the method.

Try this
- Have you used any of the other thinking models described in this chapter? How did it go?
- What values are most aligned with your beliefs?
- What values would you have a problem with in your current work environment? What could you do about those impediments?

Organizing your work 4

Imagine one day you're happily starting work on a part of the system you haven't looked at before. You have a new requirement for the user interface that shouldn't be too difficult to implement. But as you begin, you realize that there's an issue with the inheritance hierarchy in one of the core components you need to use. You call in a coworker and tackle this together. Digging a bit deeper, you find that the constructor of the base component is making assumptions and calling methods that might not be ready to call in the constructor. Making matters worse, there are dependencies going back to the very initialization of the entire application. You realize that fixing this will affect a substantial part of the system.

You and your colleague decide to bring the matter up at the team's morning meeting. The senior tech starts looking uncomfortable and says, "That code was written a long time ago by some guys who weren't very knowledgeable in object-oriented programming..." Your team has lived under the assumption that the code was in better shape than it actually was, but now you can't do that anymore, and it will affect the whole team's work. It's time to roll up your sleeves. But now comes the tricky part. Now you need to fix the problem and communicate what needs to be done to everyone who's affected, and do it as you're making the change.

There are a few ways in which the Mikado Method can help here:

- It can help you get an idea of how big the change is—we've already discussed how the Mikado Method can make changes of any size more manageable (even though it gives the most benefit when applied to medium- to large-scale improvements).
- It can help you communicate and keeping track of your work regardless of how many people are working on the project—whether you're working alone, in pairs, or in groups.
- It can help you decide where to put the development focus in a team setting—whether the workforce should focus on new features and restructure as needed, or focus only on structural improvements, or a combination of the two.

In this chapter, we'll look at how you can approach problems of different sizes, with different levels of staffing. Let's start with how you can get an idea of the scale of a problem.

4.1 The scope of a change

The single, most telling sign of the scope of a change is the size of the Mikado Graph. If the graph contains less than a dozen nodes, and the content of each node is relatively fine-grained, we consider that change to be small. Fine-grained means smaller refactorings, like "Introduce parameter," "Change method signature," and the like. If the graph contains more than a dozen nodes, or if the prerequisite nodes include more work than two to four refactorings each, it's a sign that the change is quite big. Coarse tasks or big graphs (or both) indicate a medium-to-large change and a lot of work.

Of course, when the graph doesn't grow anymore, you've found the prerequisites, which is the major part of the work. Hence, to estimate how large a change is before the entire graph is complete, you usually have to get a feeling for how much the graph is growing and assess your prerequisites, in order to guess how big the change is getting.

4.1.1 Changes at different scales

Different scales of changes require different approaches, but changes usually start small, and some continue to grow. If you compare graph sizes for small, medium, and large changes, you'll find that large changes take a disproportionally longer time—a graph with twice as many nodes is likely to take more than twice as long to work through. As a result, we structure our work somewhat differently when we tackle larger restructurings.

Let's take a look at changes at different scales so you can see how the Mikado Method fits in and see what the turning points between small, medium, and large problems look like.

SMALL-SCALE IMPROVEMENTS—MINOR ADJUSTMENTS

Small-scale improvements are those on the scale of a method or a class, where the consequences of making changes mostly stay within a handful of lines of code. You can make these changes continuously as the code is read, or before implementing new features. When readability is improved, benefit comes almost instantly, and others who follow will benefit too. The book *Clean Code* by Robert C. Martin (Prentice Hall, 2008) has plenty of advice for dealing with these situations, and the behavior we're describing is sometimes referred to as the Boy Scout Rule: "Leave the campground cleaner than you found it." In reference to code, that becomes "Leave the codebase in better shape than you found it."

Small improvements include improving naming, removing minor and obvious duplication, and deleting unnecessary code, to mention a few. These are the types of flaws that can be remedied in seconds with a modern IDE, usually by using an automated refactoring.

Unless you use a dynamic language or a dynamic feature like reflection, the compiler will tell you if something went wrong. Regardless, it's wise to have some sort of safety net while performing such changes, like a suite of automated tests. This suite should be so fast that you can run it after every change, no matter how small the change is. If it takes longer than a couple of seconds, the value of the test suite is reduced dramatically, and chances are that it becomes more of a straitjacket than a safety net. When you use a dynamic language or dynamic features, that safety net is a lot more essential.

Even if a change is tiny, like renaming variables and methods, you should make sure that it's backed up or checked in to a versioning system as soon as possible. This way, nothing is lost, and all those small improvements can be kept in the event that a rollback of something bigger is unavoidable.

Cleanups are more or less ad hoc and usually have few prerequisites, so the Mikado Method doesn't add much value at this low level. Small-scale refactorings have a lot to do with clarity, and problems tend to surface as the surroundings get less opaque. When you slowly remove dirt and mud from your code, the need for larger repairs becomes more apparent. It's almost as if the code talks to you, thanks to all these small refactorings. The discovery of medium-scale improvements often begins with small improvements, and this is a good reason for you to engage a lot in small-scale refactorings.

MEDIUM-SCALE IMPROVEMENTS

Medium-scale improvements typically involve a handful of classes. Some examples are replacing a wild-grown conditional with polymorphism, replacing an implicit tree with the composite design pattern, or splitting up a single class that has too many responsibilities into several classes. Another example would be fixing awkward usage of abstractions, or a part of a design that's disintegrating under changing requirements.

In addition to discoveries made when doing small-scale refactorings, medium-sized changes also come from the itchy feeling every time you visit a set of classes and think *there must be a better way of doing this*. Often there is.

Medium-sized changes usually take one or two developers anywhere from a couple of minutes to a day or two to perform, depending on the size and the number of classes or responsibilities involved.

This is where the Mikado Method starts to become more useful and adds value. If you're struggling to understand where you should start using the method, this is where we recommend you start. Here you can learn how to use the method and get real benefit from it at the same time. It can be quite powerful when interruptions are common and you want to get back to your train of thought quickly.

When you start pulling in medium-scale problems, and other problems keep popping up, and things get really messy, you've probably found a large-scale problem.

LARGE-SCALE IMPROVEMENTS—MAJOR OVERHAULS

A large-scale improvement will lead you to change several parts of a system. This is the true essence of a structural improvement, where you break up heavily entangled code and mazes of dependencies, extracting APIs from what weren't meant to be APIs, and dealing with the ripple effects of a large change.

Often, there's an external goal and a bigger vision connected to these kinds of changes, and that will result in a lot of work. Other times, large improvements are the result of a rotting design that has reached its breakdown point. In addition to the challenge of doing the work itself, it's also hard to estimate the complexity and size of large changes like these, so it can sometimes feel like you're never going to finish your improvement.

When large portions of the code are changed, your whole team and those around it who are affected will all have to be engaged. Everyone needs to know about the goals to be able to help out and understand. The team has to communicate outside of its immediate vicinity, especially when the change is because of an internal issue, such as an old design that has reached its breaking point.

All things considered, this is the perfect situation for the Mikado Method. As the code undergoes massive changes, work is generally spread out over several days, weeks, or months, and can benefit a lot from being carried out by several developers on a team. Putting the Mikado Graph on a whiteboard during this period of change is a great way to communicate that goal and the progress, and to spur conversations about the code design of the solution. External stakeholders, managers, and other people interested in the progress are also more likely to get involved if they can see what's happening.

The power of visualization

A picture is worth a thousand words, and a Mikado Graph is worth more than a thousand to-dos. We remember a project where the whiteboard with the graph was visible to everyone because we kept it in the team room. This sparked more questions about design and more action than the all the to-dos we had ever written in the codebase and all the design documents we composed.

4.1.2   *When do I start drawing my graph?*

As we said at the beginning of this chapter, it can be hard to know that you're getting into trouble when you start working on a problem. Small graphs don't take a lot of time to draw, but there's always a balance to strike between the overhead of the process and the benefits. For day-to-day work, we've developed a simple rule of thumb, which we call the *third-level tactic*.

The third-level tactic rule says that you can keep the dependencies in your head as long as there's only a goal and one level of prerequisites, which roughly translates to a to-do list of independent items. As soon as it gets more complicated than that, draw a graph on a piece of paper and continue working with the

Figure 4.1   Third-level tactic

graph until the problem is solved. If the graph stops expanding quickly after you've just drawn it, congratulations! You have a fairly simple restructuring ahead of you. If it doesn't stop expanding, that means you have a medium-sized or larger change ahead of you. In that case, be glad that you started drawing the graph early on. And by all means, if you want to draw a graph from the very start, please do. This approach is a bit more dogmatic, but it also gives you a nice representation of a to-do list, and you're all set if things turn rough.

In reality, taking on a big change is rarely something you'll decide to do on a whim. That decision usually comes after long and careful consideration. Sometimes the decision matures slowly after an insight about the codebase, such as if you realize there needs to be a type for `InterestRate` in the financial codebase, instead of just in a number in calculations. This requires the transactions to be in a certain format, thereby creating ripple effects through the codebase. At first, it might feel like a lot of work, but as the idea matures, and you see all the places that would benefit from the restructuring, the benefits might outweigh the effort.

Not only do all changes look different, they can also be approached differently. In the next section, we'll discuss using the Mikado Method as a single developer, as a pair of developers, and in a team.

4.2   *How to approach a change*

You already know the mechanics of the Mikado Method approach. Now it's time to learn how and when you can share your work to make it easier. Sometimes you'll have the luxury of working in a team, and sometimes you'll be on your own. Table 4.1 is a summary of the particular benefits of using the Mikado Method in some common constellations in software development. The following sections will explain this in more detail.

Table 4.1 Benefits of using the Mikado Method in different constellations

Single developer	Pair	Team
■ More easily remember changes that span days or weeks	■ Reach agreement with your coworker on the goal and how to get there	■ Enhance communication among team members
■ Zoom out to reflect on the entire graph; zoom in to focus on a specific problem	■ Solve complex and long-running tasks	■ Communicate how to solve long-running tasks that affect the whole team
■ Solve complex tasks that can't fit in your head	■ Separate the tasks of keeping track of graphics and strategy from the details of coding	■ Distribute work and share the current state between team members
■ Stay focused by having a clear process for how to work		

4.2.1 *Working in different constellations*

Let's say you've realized that you're up against a big change. You need to introduce that `InterestRate` concept after all, and it's all over the codebase. But should you make the change now, all at once, by yourself, or should you bring it up with the team (if you have one) and make it a team effort? Both could be valid approaches for a problem, depending on the circumstances.

DISTANCE YOURSELF USING THE GRAPH

Working as a single developer on a project has its advantages and disadvantages. The big advantage is that you *are* the team, and you make the decisions. On the other hand, no one will be there to critique your work or help you reflect on what you're doing. That's up to you, and the Mikado Graph can help you zoom in and zoom out on the problem. During and after your work, you can always take a step back to look at the graph. By doing so, you get a chance to reflect and possibly modify your strategy and tactics.

> **MAINTAINING YOUR GRAPH** Writing clearly in the nodes of the graph and being precise might not feel important at first, but coming back to a messy graph even after a short break can add significantly to the already cumbersome work of restructuring. When you're working alone, you should try to keep the graph in the same condition as you would if it was a shared one.

When you're on a team, you have the choice of working alone on a problem, but that should be a last resort. If you can, try to partner up when solving a problem that's large enough that you need the Mikado Method. You'll get the support, the different point of view, and the knowledge and experience of the people you work with.

PAIRING

Pair programming is a practice propagated by development methodologies such as Extreme Programming. Normally, when you pair program one person, the *driver*, is in charge of the mouse and the keyboard, and that person writes the code needed. The other person, the *co-driver*, helps the driver by keeping track of what they need to do next, proofreading the code, and being constantly alert and ready to take over driving when it's time to switch. Switching from driver to co-driver should occur fairly often, to keep you from getting stuck in a rut.

While the driver focuses on going from ideas to actual written code, the co-driver can stay at a higher level of abstraction, keeping the big picture in mind at all times. The abstraction level of future design is more aligned with the whole graph, and the tactical decisions of programming are closer to the single nodes of the graph. The driver focuses on *how* and the co-driver updates the graph and decides on the *what* and *when*.

Because the co-driver doesn't need to focus on the nitty-gritty details of the code and has both hands free to draw, the co-driver is best suited to update the graph. Because the roles switch back and forth during pairing, some extra effort is needed to make the Mikado Graph readable for the both the driver and co-driver. The graph needs to be explicit enough for either of the pair to continue the work where the other left off.

WORKING AS A TEAM

A team can also use the Mikado Method to coordinate ongoing redesigns and refactorings. When you do, you'll want the Mikado Graph to be put in a place where everyone can change it and see it, such as on a whiteboard in your team room.

Putting the graph on a whiteboard sends a signal to the team. There's a *visualized goal* and there's a path to get there. It's *collectively owned*, and anyone is allowed to change it and collaborate around it. This gives everyone the opportunity to contribute by expanding, changing, or questioning the graph.

When you have a visual representation of the goal in the form of a graph, it's easier to spot when a decision is in direct conflict with that goal, or if a decision is taking the code in the right direction. A collectively owned Mikado Graph can also double as a visual task board and bring the whole team closer to a mutual understanding of what they're doing. To increase its effectiveness, it's important that all team members be able to quickly understand what the essence of a node is, which makes an early agreement on the granularity of node content all the more important. Let your team decide how explicit and detailed the information in the nodes of the graph should be, and stick to that level of detail during the lifetime of the graph.

Large-scale restructurings or refactorings—the kind where the Mikado Method is especially helpful—should start by communicating within the team and then spreading this information to the rest of the organization. Because this kind of work often affects larger areas of the system, there may be conflicts with the work other people are doing. This is why large, unannounced, single-person refactoring raids scale poorly.

When you work as a team on a restructuring, you need to decide on how to split the team's focus between adding new functionality and embarking on structural improvements.

MOB PROGRAMMING

Mob programming is "all the brilliant people working at the same time, in the same space, at the same computer, on the same thing." (mobprogramming.org)

The easiest way to work with the Mikado Method and restructure a system in a team is by mob programming. Mob programming means having a single computer connected to a projector (or two), and everyone in the room watches the screen, helping out as you work on one thing at a time. The team members take turns at the keyboard, switching at regular intervals. The team jointly updates the Mikado Graph as the code reveals its secrets, and everyone in the room is as up to date as can be. The rest of the team can also contribute in other ways, such as searching for helpful information.

This is a very good way to get a common understanding of the problems in a system, to decide how to solve those problems, and to get acquainted with the Mikado Method or some other knowledge that might be unevenly distributed in the team. Some teams work in a mob all the time, on all of their development. You can take that approach, or you can use mob programming when you're starting out, to get a common point of view before splitting up to work in parallel. You can always resort to mob programming at a later stage if you run into a tricky problem, or if you have something that you want to share.

DISTRIBUTED TEAMS

Sometimes, your team isn't situated in a single room. On those occasions, try to find a tool that'll allow everyone to view and modify the Mikado Graph, preferably in real time, and that'll allow several users to simultaneously update the graph. In addition, it's good to have a teleconferencing system, or the like, in place for verbal communications. In the end, the needs of the team will determine what solution you choose. A good rule of thumb is to start with the simplest solution possible, and then update when there's a need to do so.

As always with distributed teams, more time and effort must be spent on communication, in this case around the creation and evolution of the Mikado Graph.

> **GRAPHVIZ—A LOW-KEY GRAPHING TOOL**   A very low-key, and free, graphing tool to use for sharing graphs is Graphviz (www.graphviz.org). Its simple text format makes it ideal for storing and sharing graphs in a versioning system, as opposed to binary image formats or other proprietary document formats that require a tool to edit. We used Graphviz to generate the initial drafts of the graphs for this book during writing.

GUIDE FOR PROBLEM SIZE AND CONSTELLATION

Your problems won't always be big ones. Table 4.2 illustrates some of the possible benefits of the Mikado Method in different constellations and for different sizes of problems.

Table 4.2   Main uses of the Mikado Method depending on constellation and problem size

Problem size	Single developer	Pair	Team or group
Small-scale problems	Use the Mikado Graph as to-do list so you're prepared if a task gets more complex.	Use the Mikado Goal as an agreement on what to develop, and the graph as a to-do list.	Not applicable—small problems can be handled by a single developer or a pair.

Table 4.2   Main uses of the Mikado Method depending on constellation and problem size *(continued)*

Problem size	Single developer	Pair	Team or group
Medium-scale problems	Use the Mikado Method for practice, or to get a better idea of the scope of a problem. Use the graph as a mnemonic to get started after a break.	Same as for a single developer. Use the Mikado Method for practice, or to get a better idea of the scope of a problem. Use the graph as a mnemonic.	Use the method to communicate what you've done, and how, to your team.
Large-scale problems	Use the Mikado Method to split up the complexity and scope into manageable pieces.	Let the co-driver manage the graph and the strategy so the programmer can focus on the code details.	Visualize scope and state with your team and stakeholders to agree on the goal and to share the workload among the team members.

4.2.2   *Where to put the focus in a team*

Now you have an idea of how and when to use the Mikado Method in different constellations and for different scales of problems. As you can see, when you work in a team, you have more ways of organizing yourself and the work around changes. Parts of a team can work on new features, improvements, bug fixes, performance optimizations—this is something that a single developer can't do without task switching.

With the option of having parts of a team work on different types of tasks comes more questions:

- Should we split the team?
- What should we focus on?

Figure 4.2   Selecting a goal

A very important step of the Mikado Method is to select the goal, or goals, you're going to work with (see figure 4.2). There are two main categories of goals to work with: new features and structural improvements. A new or augmented feature can be used as a goal, perhaps in the form of a use case or user story. Large features and the Mikado Method work best together if they're broken down into subcomponents as a first step, and then each of the subcomponents becomes a new goal. This way of working keeps the information about the features and the refactorings in one place, namely, the graph. Be careful, though, when you break up features; each goal must be able to stand on its own.

For new features or changes, the goal can be formulated as it normally is in a user story or requirement that ties it back to the business value of the work, so non-technical people can read the graph and get an idea of what's going on. For instance, "Replace hardcoded implementation with a pluggable architecture to add new services faster at lower risk," or "Replace XML configuration with code to simplify code navigation" speak to both the developer and the non-technical person.

For improvements that are mainly inward facing (very technical), we suggest reconsidering the outcome and looking at it from a business perspective. A goal that suggests replacing a custom-made framework, or an overhaul of the entire persistence architecture, isn't going to persuade non-techies, so formulating the goal in non-technical terms generally yields a better response. If you can explain how the organization benefits from an improvement in terms of an increased return on investment, a positive cost benefit, or a reduced risk, the discussions with the people who pay for the system will be a lot smoother. Still, taking on a large change that's the magnitude of an architectural overhaul as a single goal might be too much. Such large changes can require some additional planning and communication before they're started.

Now, how do you select tactics? Let's look at some different ways to focus your work in a team.

FOCUS ON NEW OR IMPROVED FEATURES

One way of working with a team is to focus on implementing new features, and to restructure parts of the code only if they pose an immediate problem. Imagine you have a server handling loan applications, with an apply service, a query service, and an approve service, but they're all mixed together in the same class. Let's say you have a feature request to move the apply service to a public server (this is the example you'll see in chapter 5), so you need to extract that part so it's deployable on a separate server. You could create a pluggable architecture and split out all the services, but in this case you can focus on doing only what is absolutely necessary. This makes it easier to get acceptance for structural improvements, because they're tied to a clear business value.

By using features as goals, growing the graph if need be, taking on as few goals as possible at a time, and trying to finish the goals as soon as possible, business value is maximized. This way of working greatly reduces the risk of spending time on things that won't get done, or that shouldn't be done in the first place.

So how much should you restructure? As a rule of thumb, you should be more eager to restructure when you have a good relationship with the people paying your salary, when you know it will pay back your efforts shortly, or when there's no other reasonable way out. Be less eager to restructure when there's an unusually important deadline approaching, when you need to build trust with your client, when you're uncertain about the benefits of restructuring, or when there's another solution within the current structure that isn't too unwieldy.

FOCUS ON STRUCTURAL IMPROVEMENTS

When your aim is to improve the internal structure of a system, such as introducing an `InterestRate` object instead of juggling doubles or integers, the graph is created with that improvement as the Mikado Goal. Everyone on the team should, in a coordinated way, build the graph and prune the leaves. Your focus should be on reaching the goal as quickly as possible.

This situation is rarely desirable from a non-technical point of view, because features aren't continuously delivered and it's hard to motivate further investment of time and money. Still, in the long run it may be crucial for the product. When the frequency of delivered functionality from developers to stakeholders drops, so does the level of trust, so you don't want to get stuck in this situation. But in spite of this, it can be useful to make an investment that will make it easier to get future features out the door.

When you're working with a system on a daily basis, you'll get a general feel for how well the system responds to change. This knowledge is internalized, and you'll consciously or unconsciously shy away from working on certain parts of the system. This is important information, because it probably affects both the spirit and productivity of the team. These parts of the system are good candidates to consider for a focused improvement effort.

In the loan server example, you might come to the decision that you'll be adding more services shortly, and putting time into a focused effort to make that as easy as possible would make sense. The goal would be to "Create a pluggable architecture to easily add more services." You would start by extracting the existing services, but you'd go on until all the services are extracted in the same pattern, with the same abstractions. All of those extracted services would be prerequisites for your goal. After finishing that restructuring, you'd be able to easily add new services, and you could return to normal feature development, adding the new services. Granted, some of the abstractions and the architecture might need to change slightly in the light of the new services you need to add, but the grunt work should be in place.

COMBINING STRUCTURAL IMPROVEMENTS AND IMPLEMENTING NEW FEATURES

Most of us are in situations where we need to make continuous structural improvements at the same time that we're developing new features. The difficulty is striking a balance between the two. Sometimes there's little or no need for structural improvement and everything seems to just flow. But as code becomes troublesome, there seems to be no end to the problems. At moments like that, you need to decide how to spread the work around. Should you do it over time or over people?

One way to find that balance is to split the team up and let some members work with new features, so the rest can focus solely on structural improvements. The Mikado Method lends itself very well to this sort of combined effort, because you're always making small, nonbreaking changes in the leaves of the graph that you generally should be able to check in to the main branch. Another way is to spend a certain amount of time on features and the rest on structural improvements, but this approach has the drawback of increasing the amount of work in progress across the team, and it creates context switching that might be interruptive.

In order to maintain a healthy balance between structural and feature goals, you should set up for collaboration and communication to keep everyone aware of the shape of the system and what the rest of the team is doing. One way to achieve this is to update everyone regularly, perhaps with a daily sync meeting. This works well if the team is split between structural and feature goals. If the whole team is working on the same Mikado Graph at the same time, we recommend that a short recap be done whenever someone checks in something to the VCS.

It's also possible for someone who's working on a feature to signal everyone else that they're about to touch code that's possibly involved with the prerequisites in the Mikado Graph. By signal, we mean telling everyone in a room, if you're co-located, that you're going to change a particular piece of code. If you're not co-located, an email or a Skype call might be more appropriate. This alerts the structure workers to pay close attention to that part of the graph, because the people working on the feature might change the prerequisites or close certain design possibilities. This signal is also a good opportunity to have a design discussion, and perhaps update the graph. There is, of course, a multitude of ways in which you can combine structural and feature work, and you'll have to find out what works best in your context. If you pay attention to your development process and adapt regularly, you can normally find the conditions that work best for your specific setting.

Splitting the focus between feature and structural work is especially suitable when you have longer-term refactorings, or refactorings that are very complex by nature. It's not unlikely that the system will need to be delivered several times before the improvements are done. One of the Mikado Method's better features is that it enables you to do this work in the main branch, because the system is always in a deliverable state.

PICKING THE RIGHT FOCUS

The following list summarizes the focus tactics you can use for different types of conditions:

- *Structural improvements*—You might want to focus on structural improvements when you have a technically neglected codebase or you need to make architectural changes.

- *New features*—You could focus on new features if fast delivery is crucial, or if you face low trust levels between the people responsible for delivery and the ones facing "business."
- *Combination*—You might choose a combination approach if you have a large or highly mature team or if you need to work on long-running restructurings and new features in parallel.

4.2.3 *Pain points when working as a team*

The hardest parts of working as a team are communication and synchronization, and this is true when you employ the Mikado Method as well. Even though a Mikado Graph is very visual and contains details about a restructuring, it doesn't replace the need to communicate actual implementation details and visions.

One common disagreement when it comes to implementation is the ambition level. At one point or another, someone will argue that the selected solution is too simplistic or that it barely solves the problem. If you ignore this concern, it'll resurface sooner or later. We believe everyone needs to be on board and agree about technical decisions.

Another aspect of teamwork is who should own the graph, and we believe the whole team should. Just like we believe that collective code ownership is superior to having areas that each developer is individually responsible for, we believe that collective graph ownership is better than having all graph updates going through one person.

To simplify collective graph ownership, we recommend that the graph be shared between the whole team and kept in a highly visible space. That makes it easy for anyone to see what problems you're currently facing and to dig in at any time. It also highlights the direction you're trying to take the code, and when someone checks off a task, that can serve as a prompt for discussion if the implementation wasn't obvious or should be discussed for some other reason.

When you work alone on a restructuring, you can do so either in isolation (using a refactoring branch), or you could do it in the trunk. Teamwork really makes you realize that restructurings should be done as close to the main delivery stream as possible. Synchronizing more version control branches makes all development more cumbersome, so try to avoid long-lived restructuring branches.

Having a homogeneous development environment simplifies your use of the Mikado Method, and it simplifies team-centric development overall. This is also true for homogeneous formatting of source code. If the code is structured slightly differently with inconsistent use of keywords or modifiers, merges will become a chore. Even things that seem like minor differences, such as the positioning of curly braces, spacing, and line breaks, can get in the way when you merge often. All formatting and code structure issues will become a lot more obvious because the rate of merges and how often you check in code will drastically increase. Frequent check-ins are, after all, one of the hallmarks of the Mikado Method. So before you plan a bigger restructuring in an area, we recommend that you format all code and check that in separately.

4.3 *Summary*

Small restructurings are possible without a detailed or carefully drawn graph. But as you get to medium- and large-sized restructurings, a well-kept graph is indispensable. A clue that you're working on a medium-sized change is a feeling that the code you're writing is a duplicate of already existing code—you may need to introduce an abstraction, or pull things out into a new module that can be used in several places. That feeling should prompt you to pull out a pen and paper, as restructurings like that can take a few days. If you realize, during your change effort, that every change is creating ripple effects throughout the system, or that your fixes are just opening up new cans of worms, you can be quite sure that you have a large-scale improvement ahead of you.

The Mikado Method can be used by a single developer, a pair, or a team. When you work as a team, you can start with features and handle restructurings as they appear, or you can have everyone working on restructurings. If the restructurings are significant, you'll probably have to split the work so the team can work on both features and restructurings simultaneously, and the Mikado Method is well suited for that. When you're learning the ins and outs of a system, you can start with small improvements, to clear away the "dirt" enough to see where the bigger structural improvements are needed. You can use the third-level tactic to grow into a larger change and see how the benefits of the method increase as the change becomes bigger and involves more classes.

This is the end of the first part of this book. You've learned how the Mikado Method works and in what situations it is best used. In the next part, we'll look more at the technical side of working with the Mikado Method, and offer some guidelines on where to take a system, and how.

Try this

- How would you use the Mikado Method? In a team, as a pair, or as a single developer? Why?
- What do you need to get started? Make a list of your prerequisites.
- Make a list of the problems you see in your codebase. Mark them as small-, medium-, or large-scale problems. Where is the Mikado Method a good fit?

Part 2

Principles and patterns for improving software

In this second part of the book, we'll start with a larger example that will show you how to break up a monolith by first adding tests and then restructuring the monolith into several packages. Following that, you'll get advice on how to let your class and package design emerge, and learn some common patterns for improving code and using the method. When you've finished reading this part, you'll have a better idea of where to take your code and how to take it there.

Breaking up a monolith

5

This chapter covers

- Getting to modularized code
- Unexplored nodes, decision nodes, and true leaves
- Tests that guide change

The most common questions we hear when we introduce the Mikado Method are, "What if I don't have any tests and want to refactor safely? Will the Mikado Method solve my problem?" We believe that these questions are somewhat misguided. The real question you should be asking yourself is, "At what point do I need to know if my changes broke anything?"

If the answer is, "immediately," then you need something (like automated tests) to validate that quickly. If you intend to wait and let your customers alert you to any problems, the answer is, "pretty late on." If you have a huge QA department, your answer might be, "during the test phase." If you asked us, we'd say, "as soon as possible." We believe in fast feedback, and the faster it is, the better it is. One way to get fast feedback is from tests. We want the majority of our tests to be automated and preferably to be very fast. This opens up the possibility for instant feedback, and that lays the groundwork for flexibility.

If you don't have any tests, you have two options: leave it that way and keep changing code without tests. This basically means that someone else, like a coworker or an end user, will figure out if the code works. Or you add tests as you go and try to cover as much of your code with tests as you can, and then modify the code. We like the latter approach and always try to cover our code with tests and then modify it.

You've had a first taste of the Mikado Method, and now we'll explore it further. We'll again use a code example to explain concepts, introduce terminology, and show how the method can be applied to move the code in the direction we see fit. This time we'll do it a bit differently, though. In the second example in chapter 2, we leaned on the compiler only; now we'll add tests, let them guide us a bit, and see how that changes our approach. When you've finished this chapter, you'll know how to split and partition code without causing an even bigger mess. The "cover (with tests) then modify" approach we'll discuss in this chapter is a truly nondestructive path to modular code.

5.1   *The code of an online loan institute*

The code we'll visit in this chapter is part of a big, back-office system used by a loan institute. Once again, we're facing software that needs to change, but this time the change was initiated by the market and the customers instead of by the developers.

To date, customers have had to apply for a loan at the bank with the assistance of the staff. The idea that has gained some traction lately is that customers could enter information about themselves and their desired loans in web forms and post them. Then staff could process the applications, make risk assessments, and approve and pay out the money if everything seemed to be in order.

The back-end web service already supports most of this, but the "approve" functionality is bundled together with the rest of the application logic. In order to make this workflow safe for customers and the bank, the approve logic needs to be separated so that customers can't approve their own loans, which would be bad for business. The idea is to set up two separate servers: one to handle applications, and the other to handle approvals. The loan application server is made accessible from the internet, and a web form is built for customers. The approval server is kept safe behind a firewall on the bank intranet. This makes it a lot harder for customers to approve their own applications, and bank officials can process the applications using a web form.

Before we start restructuring this piece of code, we'll show you how the system works and also peek quickly at the design. We always start by looking around in the code we're about to change, and we recommend you do that too, unless you're already very familiar with the code you'll be working with. This needn't take a long time—5 to 15 minutes is usually enough. Let's do that now, looking first at the API, then at the architecture, and finally at the actual code.

5.1.1 *The existing functionality*

At the moment, there's only one entry point to the server, from which all the calls are then dispatched using an action parameter. There are three actions that can be performed:

- Apply
- Fetch
- Approve

Each of these actions needs one or more parameters to function.

APPLY

The `apply` action needs two additional parameters: `amount` and `contact`. The first is the desired loan amount, and the second is an email address that can be used to contact the borrower. Here's an example of a loan application sent via an HTTP request:

```
http://localhost:8080/?action=apply&amount=10000&
contact=donald@ducks.burg
```

All HTTP requests sent to the server return a JSON (JavaScript Object Notation) string, and so does `apply`. If an application is successful, a ticket with an identifier is returned, which is used to retrieve information about the application. The JSON response to the previous `apply` call above would look like the following if it was the second loan application and it was successful (note the `id`):

```
{
    "id":2
}
```

> **JSON**
>
> JSON (JavaScript Object Notation) is a lightweight data interchange format commonly used with web apps. Computers can parse and generate JSON with ease, but it's also easy for humans to read and write.

FETCH

After an application request has been made, or if a bank official needs to retrieve information about an application, `fetch` is used. When `fetch` is used, the `id` parameter from the `apply` call is used as an identifier to retrieve information. Here's an example that fetches a previously made application via an HTTP request:

```
http://localhost:8080/?action=fetch&id=2
```

When `fetch` is called, it retrieves the application and returns all of the information that's available about it. The JSON response looks like this:

```
{
    "applicationNo":2,
    "amount":10000,
```

```
        "approved":false,
        "contact":"donald@ducks.burg"
}
```

APPROVE

After an application request has been made, and if everything seems to be in order, a bank official can approve the loan. This is done via the approve action, and once again the id from the apply response is used:

```
http://localhost:8080/?action=approve&id=2
```

The approve action returns the ticket id, just like apply does; in this case:

```
{id='2'}
```

In order to see the application's actual state, fetch must be used. If the application was approved, it'll look like this:

```
{
        "applicationNo":2,
        "amount":10000,
        "approved":true,
        "contact":"donald@ducks.burg"
}
```

5.1.2   *The architecture and the code*

The code of this server (the apply, fetch, and approve services) is organized in six classes: LoanServer, LoanHandler, LoanApplication, LoanRepository, Ticket, and ApplicationException. The latter is used whenever an error occurs and isn't included in the architecture diagram in figure 5.1.

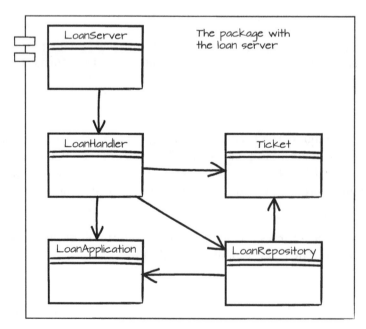

Figure 5.1   The LoanServer creates a LoanHandler, which creates a LoanApplication, which is passed to the LoanRepository, which returns a Ticket for the loan application.

The `LoanServer` class is the entry point of the server. It contains the server setup and launches the service at port 8080. When `start` is called, all incoming requests are handled by one dispatching class: the `LoanHandler`. The call to `join` just makes the main thread wait for the server thread to finish:

```java
public class LoanServer {
  public static void main(String[] args) throws Exception {
    Server server = new Server(8080);
    server.setHandler(new LoanHandler());
    server.start();
    server.join();
  }
}
```

In the example, we use parts of the Java Servlet API. If you don't know about that, you should be able to follow along nicely anyway. What you need to watch for is how we structure, move, and change the code rather than how we use the Servlet API. If you're more used to dynamically typed languages, then appendix C is for you.

The `LoanServer` uses a `LoanRepository` to store and fetch `LoanApplications`. Whenever an application is made, a new `LoanApplication` object is created and stored so it can be retrieved later. If an application is successfully stored, a `Ticket` is returned. The `id` of the ticket can be used to fetch information about loan applications.

Listing 5.1 The `handle` method in `LoanHandler.java`

```java
@Override
public void handle(String target, Request baseRequest,
HttpServletRequest request, HttpServletResponse response)
throws IOException, ServletException {
  response.setContentType("application/json;charset=utf-8");
  response.setStatus(HttpServletResponse.SC_OK);
  baseRequest.setHandled(true);
  PrintWriter writer = response.getWriter();


  try {
    if (isApplication(request)) {

      LoanApplication application = new LoanApplication();
      application.setAmount(amountFrom(request));
      application.setContact(contactFrom(request));
      Ticket ticket = LoanRepository.store(application);
      writer.println(new Gson().toJson(ticket));

    } else if (isStatusRequest(request)
         && idSpecified(request)) {

      writer.println(
        fetchLoanInfo(
          request.getParameter(TICKET_ID)));

    } else if (isApproval(request)
```

Sets correct encoding and response code and prepares response writer

Creates LoanApplication object from the request parameters and stores it using the LoanRepository

Retrieves a previous LoanApplication and returns the information found

```
                && idSpecified(request)) {

        writer.println(
            approveLoan(
                request.getParameter(TICKET_ID)));
```

> Approves the loan application by setting status to true and returns ticket number as a JSON string

```
    } else {
      writer.println("Incorrect parameters provided");
    }
  } catch (ApplicationException e) {
      writer.println(
          "Uh oh! Problem occurred: " + e.getMessage());
  }
}
```

In addition to the handle method, LoanHandler.java contains several helper methods, most of them one-liners that are self-explanatory. Some of them use a LoanRepository to store loan applications, and some use information from the request. The most complicated method is getNextId(), whose job is to come up with the next ticket and application ID.

Listing 5.2   Helper methods in `LoanHandler.java`

```java
private String contactFrom(HttpServletRequest request) {
    return request.getParameter("contact");
}

private long amountFrom(HttpServletRequest request) {
    return Long.parseLong(request.getParameter("amount"));
}

private String approveLoan(String parameter) {
    return new Gson().toJson(LoanRepository.approve(parameter));
}

private boolean isApproval(HttpServletRequest request) {
    return APPROVE.equals(request.getParameter("action"));
}

private boolean idSpecified(HttpServletRequest request) {
    return request.getParameter(TICKET_ID) != null &&
        validId(request) >= 0;
}

private long validId(HttpServletRequest request) {
    String ticketId = request.getParameter(TICKET_ID);
    try {
        return Long.parseLong(ticketId);
    } catch (NumberFormatException e) {
        return -1L;
    }
}

private boolean isStatusRequest(HttpServletRequest request) {
```

```
            return FETCH.equals(request.getParameter("action"));
    }

    private boolean isApplication(HttpServletRequest request) {
        return APPLICATION.equals(request.getParameter("action"));
    }

    private String fetchLoanInfo(String ticketId) {
        LoanApplication formerApplication = LoanRepository.fetch(ticketId);
        return new Gson().toJson(formerApplication);
    }

    public long getNextId() {
        File file = new File(LoanRepository.REPOSITORY_ROOT);
        File[] files = file.listFiles(new FileFilter() {
            @Override
            public boolean accept(File pathname) {
                return pathname.getName().
                    endsWith(LoanRepository.FILE_EXTENSION);
            }
        });

        return files == null ? 0 : files.length + 1;
    }
```

Our goal was to learn a bit more about the system—how it works and what the architecture looks like—and then to look at the code. We've done that and we won't linger any longer. The time has come to start changing code again.

5.2 Beheading the beast

Let's behead this code beast and separate the approve logic from the apply logic and put them into separate classes. If you're also thinking, "Let's get a fresh piece of paper and write down the goal," that's good, because that's exactly what we're going to do.

5.2.1 Set a goal

When we use the Mikado Method, we always start with the end in mind—the goal. Let's write that down now (see figure 5.2).

Now we have the goal written down and we're familiar with the code, so it's time to start work. This time, however, we won't try to achieve our goal directly. Instead, we'll start by adding some tests. After our initial poking around in the code, we came to the conclusion that the best place we can safely start our testing is in the LoanHandler. If we start there, we won't need to change anything before we cover the code with tests. We can just instantiate a LoanHandler and call the handle method. Sometimes we aren't this lucky and need to modify code before we can test it. Testing can be sort of a catch-22; to safely change something, you want verifying tests, but to be able to

Figure 5.2 This is the Mikado Goal. When we've achieved this, we're done.

add tests you need to change code. This time, however, we can add tests without modifying anything.

Adding tests will, however, be a fair amount of work, because the `handle` method takes no less than four arguments: a `String`, a `Request`, an `HttpServletRequest`, and an `HttpServletResponse`. There are several ways of controlling the input to this method, and we've decided to take the approach that we believe involves the least amount of work. We'll pass `null` and three stubbed classes.

The `StubbedResponse` implements the `HttpServletResponse`, mostly with empty methods. To make things easier to test, we'll also add a method to retrieve the response that's written to the writer.

Listing 5.3   The stubbed response

```
public class ResponseStub implements HttpServletResponse {

    private final ByteArrayOutputStream out = new ByteArrayOutputStream();
    private final PrintWriter writer = new PrintWriter(output);


    public String responseAsText() {                    ◁─── responseAsText is used by
        return new String(out.toByteArray());                tests to retrieve what's
    }                                                        written by the writer.

    @Override
    public PrintWriter getWriter() throws IOException {
        return writer;
    }
    .
    .
    .

}
```

To be able to control how the `StubbedHttpServletRequest` behaves, we create a constructor that uses a `Map` of parameters' responses. What's injected in the constructor is later used by the `getParameter` method.

Listing 5.4   The stubbed `HttpServletRequest`

```
public class ServletRequestStub implements HttpServletRequest {

    private final Map<String, String> params;

    public StubbedServletRequest(Map<String, String> params) {    ◁───
        this.params = params;
    }
                                                        By injecting a map of
    @Override                                          parameters, we can control
    public String getParameter(String key) {              the response from the
        return params.get(key);                           getParameter method.
    }
    .
```

```
     .
     .
     .
}
```

The `RequestStub` that we create extends `Request`, so we can override methods if we need to.

Listing 5.5 The stubbed `Request`

```
public class RequestStub extends Request {
}
```

Listing 5.6 The tests

```
public class LoanHandlerTest {

    LoanHandler loanHandler;
    RequestStub baseRequest;
    ResponseStub response;

    @Before
    public void setUp() {
        loanHandler = new LoanHandler();
        baseRequest = new RequestStub();
        response = new ResponseStub();
    }

    @Test
    public void incompleteRequest() throws Exception {        ◄──┤ Verifies that an
        Map<String, String> params = Collections                    incomplete call yields
                .<String, String> emptyMap();                        an error message
        ServletRequestStub request = new ServletRequestStub(params);
        loanHandler.handle(null, baseRequest, request, response);
        response.getWriter().flush();
        String actual = response.responseAsText();
        assertEquals("Incorrect parameters provided\n", actual);
    }
                                                              Asserts that an id is
    @Test                                                       returned upon a
    public void completeApplication() throws Exception {            complete
        ServletRequestStub request =                          application request
            new ServletRequestStub(applyParams());
        loanHandler.handle(null, baseRequest, request, response);
        response.getWriter().flush();

        assertEquals("{\"id\":1}\n", response.responseAsText());  ◄──┘
    }

    @Test
    public void givenAnIdTheStatusOfLoanIsReturned() throws Exception {
        ServletRequestStub request =
            new ServletRequestStub(fetchParams());
        loanHandler.handle(null, baseRequest, request, response);
        response.getWriter().flush();
```

```
        assertEquals("{\"applicationNo\":4," + "\"amount\":100,"        ◁─────┐
                + "\"contact\":\"a@ducks.burg\",\"approved\":true}\n",
                response.responseAsText());
    }
```

**Fetches a whole
application and returns
information about it**

```
    @Test
    public void loanApplicationsCanBeApproved() throws Exception {
        ServletRequestStub request = new ServletRequestStub(
                approveParams());
        loanHandler.handle(null, baseRequest, request, response);
        response.getWriter().flush();

        assertEquals("{\"id\":3}\n", response.responseAsText());        ◁─────┐
    }
```

**Ensures an approval returns
an id, if no error occurs**

```
    private HashMap<String, String> approveParams() {
        HashMap<String, String> params = new HashMap<String, String>();
        params.put("action", LoanHandler.APPROVE);
        params.put("ticketId", "3");
        return params;
    }

    private HashMap<String, String> applyParams() {
        HashMap<String, String> params = new HashMap<String, String>();
        params.put("action", LoanHandler.APPLICATION);
        params.put("amount", "100");
        params.put("contact", "donald@ducks.burg");
        return params;
    }

    private HashMap<String, String> fetchParams() {
        HashMap<String, String> params = new HashMap<String, String>();
        params.put("action", LoanHandler.FETCH);
        params.put("ticketId", "4");
        return params;
    }
}
```

We covered this code with tests, but we realize as they run that the code is depending on the filesystem. The LoanRepository persists applications to a certain path, and we don't have full control over that process. This makes it harder to test the Loan-Handler. Just like the example in chapter 2, this situation suggests that we need to take control of the repository before we continue splitting approvals and applications into separate servers.

5.2.2   *Create an abstraction*

Our first decision is that the LoanRepository really should be named FileBasedLoan-Repository and that we should extract an interface named LoanRepository. We won't dive into the details around that redesign; instead, we'll just show you the graph of that change and the result. See figure 5.3.

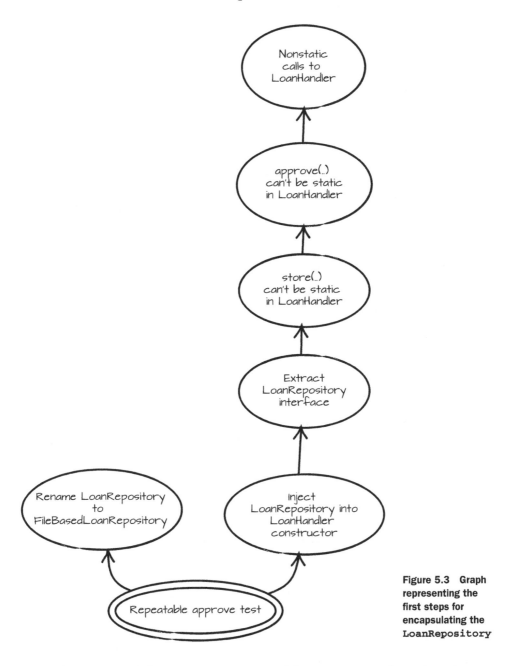

Figure 5.3 Graph representing the first steps for encapsulating the `LoanRepository`

To be able to control the `LoanRepository`, we inject a `LoanRepository` into the `Loan-Handler` constructor and assign it to the variable `repo`. That variable is used later in the `handle` method.

> **Listing 5.7   The slightly changed `LoanHandler.java`**

```
public LoanHandler(LoanRepository loanRepository) {
    repo = loanRepository;              ◄─── Inject the LoanRepository
}                                            in the constructor.

@Override
public void handle(String target, Request baseRequest,
        HttpServletRequest request, HttpServletResponse response)
        throws IOException, ServletException {
    response.setContentType("application/json;charset=utf-8");
    response.setStatus(HttpServletResponse.SC_OK);
    baseRequest.setHandled(true);
    PrintWriter writer = response.getWriter();
    try {
        if (isApplication(request)) {
            LoanApplication application = new LoanApplication();     Use the
            application.setAmount(amountFrom(request));              repository
            application.setContact(contactFrom(request));           injected in the
            Ticket ticket = repo.store(application);         ◄───── constructor.

            writer.println(new Gson().toJson(ticket));
        } else if (isStatusRequest(request) && idSpecified(request)) {
            writer.println(fetchLoanInfo(request
                    .getParameter(TICKET_ID)));
        } else if (isApproval(request) && idSpecified(request)) {
            writer.println(approveLoan(request
                    .getParameter(TICKET_ID)));
        } else {
            writer.println("Incorrect parameters provided");
        }
    } catch (ApplicationException e) {
        writer.println("Uh oh! Problem occurred: " + e.getMessage());
    }
}

.
.
.
                                                              Use the
                                                              repository
private String approveLoan(String parameter) {                here as well.
    return new Gson().toJson(repo.approve(parameter));  ◄─────
}
```

With the `LoanRepository` abstraction in place, we can start taking advantage of that in our tests.

> **Listing 5.8   The slightly changed `setUp()` in `LoanHandlerTest.java`**

```
@Before
public void setUp() {
    loanHandler = new LoanHandler(new MemoryLoanRepository());  ◄───
    baseRequest = new StubbedRequest();
    response = new StubbedResponse();             A MemoryLoanRepository
}                                                 is used for test purposes.
```

5.2.3 More LoanRepository duties

Despite our efforts to encapsulate the `LoanRepository` responsibilities, we failed to notice that we aren't quite done. Only after running the tests do we find that we don't have full control over the generation of new applications. They get an ID based on the number of applications already on the filesystem. The ID comes from the `LoanHandler`:

```
public LoanApplication() {
    applicationNo = LoanHandler.getNextId();
}
```

This needs to stop; we must control the ID generation.

We can't allow IDs that are generated outside of the `LoanRepository` implementation, so before we go any further, we'll change that. Once again, we present the graph (figure 5.4) and the resulting code, but not the whole process of getting there.

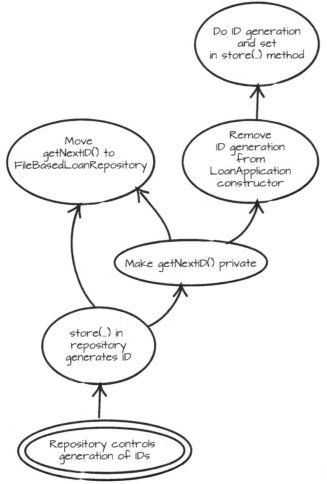

Figure 5.4 Graph representing the final steps to encapsulate

5.2.4   *Back to the business goal*

After that slight detour, we're now in a position to lean on the compiler, and we also have a safety net in the form of lightning-fast unit tests. This makes our task a lot easier, because fast feedback like that is a great foundation for quick and controlled experiments.

The major advantage of tests and the Naive Approach, compared to analyzing the code, is the comparatively shallow learning curve. By trying things, you learn more about the code and what the actual change is going to look like, instead of learning unnecessary details about your code. You also don't need to worry about the cost of starting at the wrong end, or even worse—changing the wrong things.

With this in mind, we'll simply try to create a new server. Here's the Approve-Server with the new ApproveHandler:

```java
public class ApproveServer {
  public static void main(String[] args) throws Exception {

    Server server = new Server(8081);                       ◁──┐ The server runs on
                                                               │ a different port.
    server.setHandler(new ApproveHandler());            ◁──┐
    server.start();                                        │
    server.join();                                      The new
  }                                                     handler.
}
```

With the new server code in place, we discover that we need an ApproveHandler to handle the approvals (obviously). This is what we're talking about: the Naive Approach in action. Just do it, and see where it leads.

Because we want the approve code to be on a separate server, we decide to put it in a separate project as well. In Java land, putting things in a separate project usually means a separate .jar, .ear, or .war file; in .NET land it means a separate assembly. This new project has no dependencies on the existing project, and the existing project doesn't depend on this new project. This is useful information that we want to hold on to.

5.2.5   *Update the graph*

Keeping information for later means updating the graph, rather than trying to remember it, so before we write any more code, we'll add a circle to the Mikado Graph to record what we'll do, in case we need to revert and start over.

We're pretty confident that the Mikado Method is a bit more familiar to you now, so we'll move along slightly slower than during the encapsulation of the LoanRepository but a bit faster than in chapter 2. We'll take notes without explaining every step in detail and generally focus on improving the code. You'll also notice that as the code becomes more complex, so will the route to our goal.

In the graph in figure 5.5, we've added several new circles to remind us of the things we need to take care of.

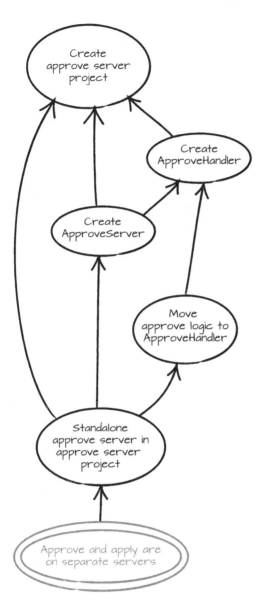

Figure 5.5 To finish separating the different responsibilities, we need an approve server.

Now we can look at the graph to see what we need to do. ApproveHandler is an empty class at the moment, and the first real step toward separating the code is moving the approval logic from LoanHandler to ApproveHandler. The first code to be moved is the actual approval and the conditional surrounding it. We'll assume that all third-party libraries are added to the new projects, such as Request, HttpServletRequest/ Response, and so on.

Here's the new `ApproveHandler` with compiler errors in bold:

```
public void handle(String target, Request baseRequest,
  HttpServletRequest request, HttpServletResponse response)
    throws IOException, ServletException {
  if (isApproval(request) && idSpecified(request)) {
     response.getWriter().println(
        approveLoan(request.getParameter(TICKET_ID)));
  }
}
```

Adding the preceding code produces an `ApproveHandler` that contains compiler errors, because none of the methods `isApproval`, `idSpecified`, and `approveLoan`, nor the constant `TICKET_ID` exist in our new class. When we try to remedy the error by moving them to `ApproveHandler`, we get compiler errors in `LoanHandler` instead. We find that we need to move `isApproval` and `approveLoan` to `Approve-Handler`, and make `idSpecified` and `TICKET_ID` available for both `LoanHandler` and `ApproveHandler`.

Remember, compiler warnings and other errors are exactly what we want. They contain lots of useful information. We note that `isApproval`, `idSpecified`, `approve-Loan`, and `TICKET_ID` need to be moved, and then we revert again. This gives us a clean slate to work with and a diagram that looks like figure 5.6.

5.2.6   *Revert and restart from a clean slate*

Reverting and working with compiling code, and successful tests if you have any, is one of the hallmarks of the Mikado Method. You should always try to start from a known state.

In this case, we have one new leaf in the graph: "`idSpecified` and `TICKET_ID` available for `ApproveHandler` and `LoanHandler`." That node is a *decision node*—a node that doesn't say how to do something, but only what you need to accomplish. This is a great tactic when you're not quite sure how to solve the problem, and you want to defer that commitment. Decision nodes will you help keep your mind and your options open.

> **Decision nodes**
>
> Special nodes (like goals, decision nodes, and any other node that has a special meaning) could possibly have a special notation. The only node we've given a special notation is the goal. Whether or not the others need a special notation is up to you to decide.

In this case, we have a method and a constant that we want to use in two different projects, so placing them in a helper class seems appropriate. Because this is code we want to share, the new class, the `RequestHelper` class, should live in a shared project in order to be available for both handler projects. We decide to create the new class in a

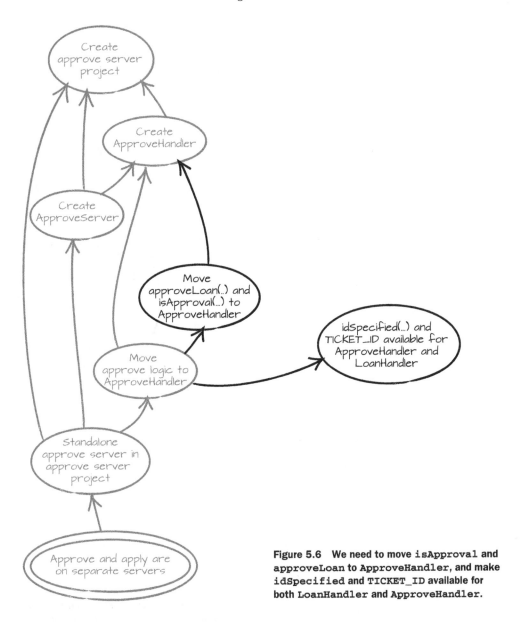

Figure 5.6 We need to move `isApproval` and `approveLoan` to `ApproveHandler`, and make `idSpecified` and `TICKET_ID` available for both `LoanHandler` and `ApproveHandler`.

new project, the loan core project. Then we move `idSpecified` and `TICKET_ID` to `RequestHelper`, but this causes compiler errors—the `validId` method also needs to move to `RequestHelper`. As usual, we jot down what we've learned in the Mikado Graph before we revert (the new nodes are the darker ones). See figure 5.7.

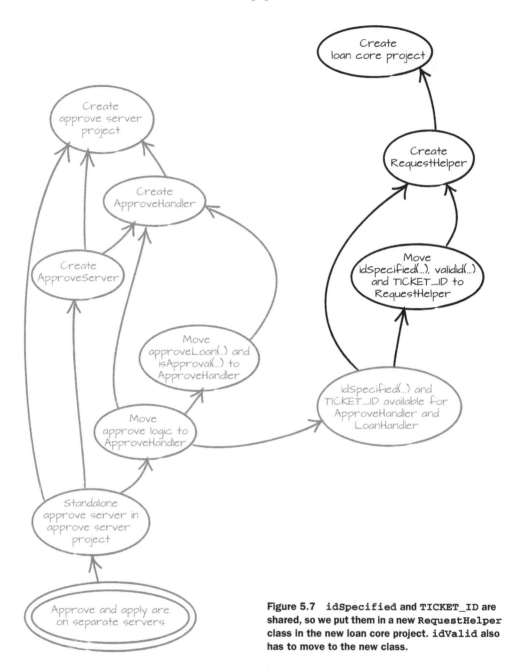

Figure 5.7 `idSpecified` and `TICKET_ID` are shared, so we put them in a new `RequestHelper` class in the new loan core project. `idValid` also has to move to the new class.

The RequestHelper now looks like the following listing.

Listing 5.9   Contents of the RequestHelper class

```
public static final String TICKET_ID = "ticketId";

static boolean idSpecified(HttpServletRequest request) {
```

```
        return request.getParameter(RequestHelper.TICKET_ID) != null
            && RequestHelper.validId(request) >= 0;
}

static long validId(HttpServletRequest request) {
    String ticketId = request.getParameter(RequestHelper.TICKET_ID);
    try {
        return Long.parseLong(ticketId);
    } catch (NumberFormatException e) {
        return -1L;
    }
}
```

We've just moved `idSpecified` and `validId` to the new `RequestHelper`, and the code looks fine. Because we reverted earlier, we need to recreate the approve project and the `ApproveHandler` before we can get to "Move approveLoan and isApproval to ApproveHandler," which is the next unexplored node. You might think it's unnecessary work to re-create these things, and you're partially right. Sometimes you can get away with stashing away your changes as a patch in your versioning system, and later reapplying them. Sometimes it's easier to just redo the changes, because the code your stashed code relies on might have changed.

> ### Stashing, shelving, creating a patch
>
> Many VCSs have a function that allows an edited state to be saved, giving you the option to later reapply the change to the code. This functionality goes by different names, such as stashing, shelving, or creating a patch. In the Mikado Method, you can create such a saved state with the changes that broke the system, and then when the prerequisites are in place you can reapply the change. Sometimes this works, but sometimes the codebase has changed enough that the base of the saved state doesn't exist anymore, and the patch fails.

When we move `approveLoan`, we get another error (yay!). The error hints that we also need to move the `LoanRepository` to the new loan core project. We do a quick revert, move `isApproval`, and get a new error that tells us we also need to move the `APPROVE` constant to the new `ApproveHandler`. Time to add some more nodes to the graph and revert again (see figure 5.8).

After our revert, we have a clean slate again. Does that mean we're back where we started? No. We know a lot more about the system and the changes we need to make. Looking at the graph, we can see that the unexplored node is "Move `LoanRepository` to loan core," but first we need to re-create the loan core project. We're working with a clean slate, remember?

When we try to move `LoanRepository`, all hell breaks loose and nothing seems to compile anymore. Apparently that wasn't a leaf either. More likely, all hell breaking loose is a sign that we've come across a central concept. After a quick look around, it seems like the repository is coupled to `LoanApplication`, `Ticket`, and `ApplicationException`.

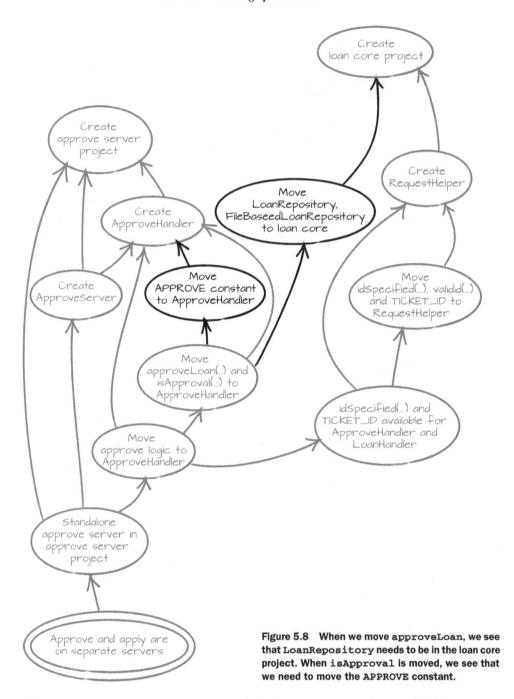

Figure 5.8   When we move `approveLoan`, we see that `LoanRepository` needs to be in the loan core project. When `isApproval` is moved, we see that we need to move the `APPROVE` constant.

Once again, we make use of the VCS and revert. When we see the code compile, we start by moving `Ticket`, `LoanApplication`, and `ApplicationException`, and then `Loan-Repository`, to the loan core project. This is also noted in our graph, shown in figure 5.9.

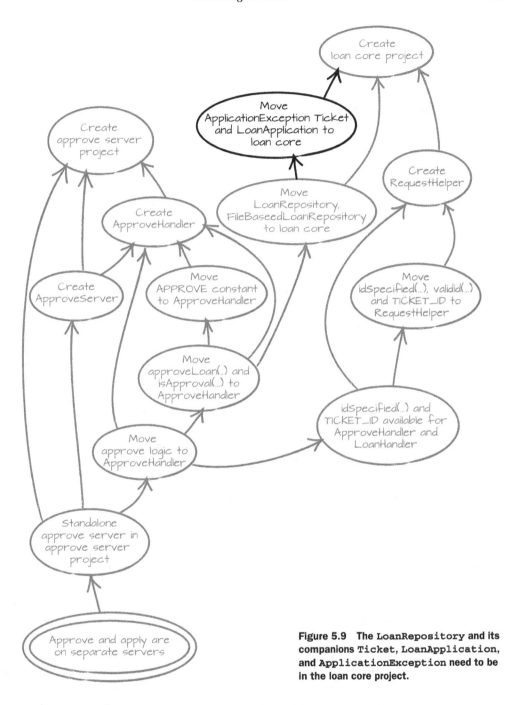

Figure 5.9 The LoanRepository and its companions Ticket, LoanApplication, and ApplicationException need to be in the loan core project.

This restructuring is starting to feel almost too safe, on the verge of boring. This is *exactly* the point of the Mikado Method. It takes code changes that might range from "tricky" to "nightmare" and turns them into a rather dull sequence of making a change, finding the problems, appending solutions to the graph, and reverting.

But are we *ever* going to get to a point where we can actually *do* something? Of course.

5.3   *Getting to the true leaves of the graph*

In every Mikado restructuring journey, there comes a time when things fall into place, and you can actually implement changes instead of just updating the graph and reverting. The transition isn't always easy to spot; you rarely know when it happens until after the fact.

When you reach the peak and travel over the hump, the nature of the work shifts from exploration to repetition. When this happens, you may wish you'd stored the changes somehow, so you don't have to redo them. We've felt this as well and we've experimented some with different version-control techniques, but so far it's been easier to stick to the "revert and redo later" technique. We're sure, however, that someone will eventually come up with a clever trick for an existing VCS or will invent something that makes it easier to apply old changes.

In our example, we're just about to make this transition and switch from exploration to repetition. In other words, we won't be doing much more to the graph but adding check marks.

5.3.1   *The first steps on the way back*

We glance at our graph and see that once we've created the loan core project, a new leaf is revealed. We go after our new leaf: "Move `LoanApplication`, `Ticket`, and `ApplicationException`" and try to move the code. To our great satisfaction, it works! The next no-brainer is to move `LoanRepository`, and that also works.

We take another look at the graph and spot our next step, "Create `RequestHelper`." It looks like a leaf, so we declare that the next natural step. It works, and so does moving `idSpecified`, `idValid`, and `TICKET_ID` from `LoanHandler` to `RequestHelper`. That means we've also fulfilled the decision node to make those available to both `ApproveHandler` and `LoanHandler`. From the look of the graph, we're humming along nicely (see figure 5.10), and our loan core project has formed and taken shape. We're not facing any resistance from the code as we make our changes.

Now that we have the loan core project in place, it's time to move the approval code to the approve project. We start by creating the new approve project, creating the empty `ApproveHandler` in that project, and then creating the `ApproveServer`. We make this project depend on the loan core project, to get the shared code in there. Then we move the `APPROVE` constant and the `approveLoan` and `isApproval` methods to the new `ApproveHandler`. As we move the approve logic to the new handler, the `ApproveServer` is indeed implemented. Figure 5.11 proves it—we're done!

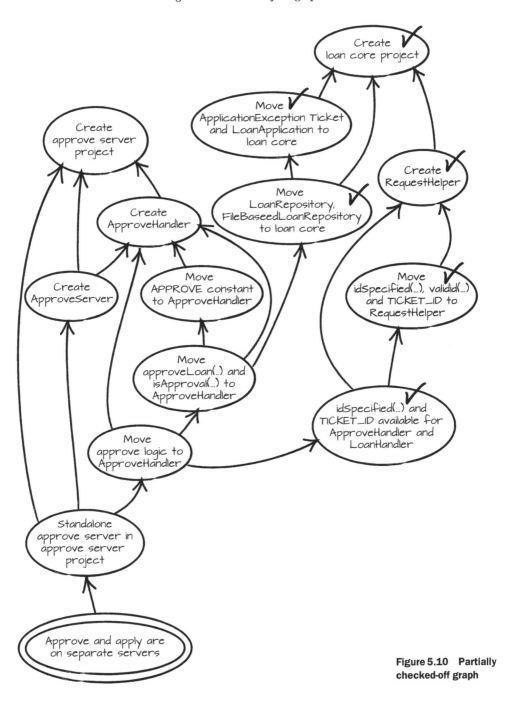

Figure 5.10 Partially
checked-off graph

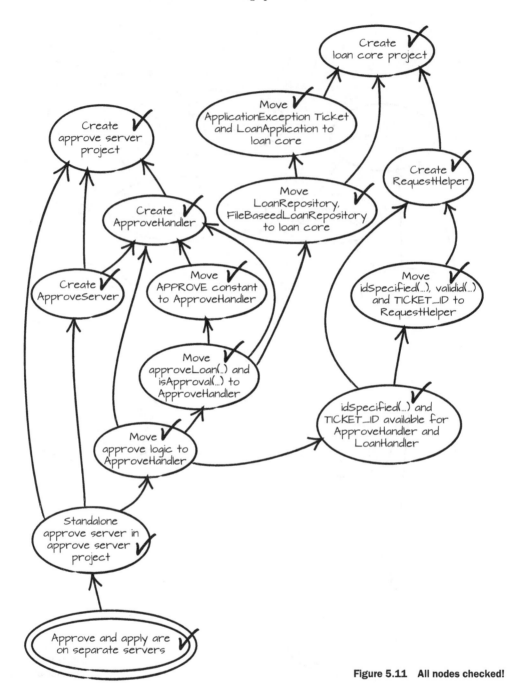

Figure 5.11   All nodes checked!

The resulting UML diagram is shown in figure 5.12.

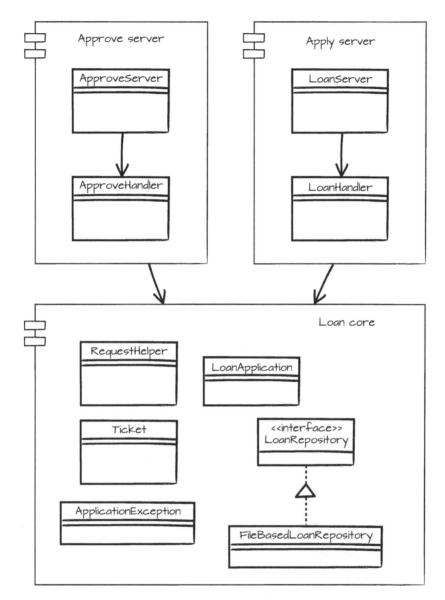

Figure 5.12   The result of restructuring the code. At the top are the server parts, and at the bottom is the shared loan core project.

If you're observant, you're probably now asking, "What about the tests?" Yes, that's right, the code doesn't really work. We need to move the stubs and `MemoryRepository` to the loan core project as well. After that, the test that verifies the approve functionality, `loanApplicationsCanBeApproved()`, should be extracted from `LoanHandlerTest` and inserted in `ApproveHandlerTest` in the approval project. Only then are we truly finished.

The final version of the more interesting classes can be found in listings 5.10, 5.11, 5.12, and 5.13.

Listing 5.10   Contents of the `ApproveHandler` class

```
package org.mikadomethod.approveserver;
import ...
...

public class ApproveHandler extends AbstractHandler {
  public static final String APPROVE = "approve";
  private final LoanRepository repo;
  public ApproveHandler(LoanRepository loanRepository) {
    this.repo = loanRepository;
  }
  @Override
  public void handle(String target, Request baseRequest,
    HttpServletRequest request, HttpServletResponse response)
      throws IOException, ServletException {
    response.setContentType("application/json;charset=utf-8");
    response.setStatus(HttpServletResponse.SC_OK);
    baseRequest.setHandled(true);
    PrintWriter writer = response.getWriter();
    if (isApproval(request) &&
          RequestHelper.idSpecified(request)) {
      writer.println(approveLoan(
          request.getParameter(RequestHelper.TICKET_ID)));
      } else {
        writer.println("Incorrect parameters provided");
      }
  }
  private String approveLoan(String parameter) {
     return new Gson().toJson(repo.approve(parameter));
  }
  private boolean isApproval(HttpServletRequest request) {
     return APPROVE.equals(request.getParameter("action"));
  }
}
```

Listing 5.11   Contents of the `LoanHandler` class

```
package org.mikadomethod.loanserver;

import ...
...

public class LoanHandler extends AbstractHandler {
    public static final String APPLICATION = "apply";
    public static final String FETCH = "fetch";

    private final LoanRepository repo;

    public LoanHandler(LoanRepository loanRepository) {
      repo = loanRepository;
```

```
    }

    @Override
    public void handle(String target, Request baseRequest,
      HttpServletRequest request, HttpServletResponse response)
          throws IOException, ServletException {
        response.setContentType("application/json;charset=utf-8");
        response.setStatus(HttpServletResponse.SC_OK);
        baseRequest.setHandled(true);
        PrintWriter writer = response.getWriter();
        try {
            if (isApplication(request)) {
                LoanApplication application = new LoanApplication();
                application.setAmount(amountFrom(request));
                application.setContact(contactFrom(request));
                Ticket ticket = repo.store(application);
                writer.println(new Gson().toJson(ticket));
            } else if (isStatusRequest(request) &&
              RequestHelper.idSpecified(request)) {
                writer.println(fetchLoanInfo(
                  request.getParameter(RequestHelper.TICKET_ID)));
            } else {
                writer.println("Incorrect parameters provided");
            }
        } catch (ApplicationException e) {
            writer.println("Uh oh! Problem occurred: "+e.getMessage());
        }
    }

    private String contactFrom(HttpServletRequest request) {
        return request.getParameter("contact");
    }

    private long amountFrom(HttpServletRequest request) {
        return Long.parseLong(request.getParameter("amount"));
    }

    private boolean isStatusRequest(HttpServletRequest request) {
        return FETCH.equals(request.getParameter("action"));
    }

    private boolean isApplication(HttpServletRequest request) {
        return APPLICATION.equals(request.getParameter("action"));
    }

    private String fetchLoanInfo(String ticketId) {
        LoanApplication formerApplication = repo.fetch(ticketId);
        return new Gson().toJson(formerApplication);
    }
}
```

Listing 5.12 Contents of the `LoanRepository` interface

```
package org.mikadomethod.loanserver;

public interface LoanRepository {
```

```
LoanApplication fetch(String ticketId);
Ticket store(LoanApplication application);
Ticket approve(String ticketId);
}
```

Listing 5.13   Contents of the `ApproveHandlerTest` class

```
package org.mikadomethod.approveserver;

import ...
...

public class ApproveHandlerTest {
    ApproveHandler approveHandler;
    RequestStub baseRequest;
    ResponseStub response;
    private MemoryLoanRepository loanRepository;

    @Before
    public void setUp() {
        loanRepository = new MemoryLoanRepository();
        approveHandler = new ApproveHandler(loanRepository);
        baseRequest = new RequestStub();
        response = new ResponseStub();
    }

    @Test
    public void loanApplicationsCanBeApproved() throws Exception {
        LoanApplication loanApplication = new LoanApplication();
        loanApplication.setAmount(100);
        loanRepository.store(loanApplication);
        ServletRequestStub request = new ServletRequestStub(
            approveParams());
        approveHandler.handle(null, baseRequest, request, response);
        response.getWriter().flush();
        assertEquals("{\"id\":1}\n", response.responseAsText());
    }

    private HashMap<String, String> approveParams() {
        HashMap<String, String> params =
          new HashMap<String, String>();
        params.put("action", ApproveHandler.APPROVE);
        params.put("ticketId", "1");
        return params;
    }

}
```

5.3.2   Side effect–free programming

You just saw us spend a lot of energy figuring out how to navigate the dependencies of an application in order to make a change. When you use the Mikado Method, dealing with dependencies is mainly what you'll do, and you'll start to see them everywhere. After a while you'll start to think, "Isn't there a way to avoid all these dependencies?"

No, you can't avoid dependencies, and there will always be a need to restructure code. You can't disregard the importance of how you structure your code, but you can structure it differently.

We've found that code with few or no side effects is much easier to restructure and move around. Mutable state creates dependencies that aren't directly seen in a dependency graph, but that are temporal and depend on the order of execution at runtime. In a multithreaded environment, this gets even more complicated, and even the best test suite might not be able to alert you about errors caused when you change code. This complicates the exploratory nature of the Naive Approach because finding errors can be much more difficult than locating functional errors or compilation problems.

When you stumble across code that has mutable state, you need to change your strategy and try to make the methods pure and the data objects immutable. This can feel wasteful and will probably mean you need to take the restructuring on a small detour. But when you think it's a detour, remember this: it's well worth the effort.

Keeping functions pure and having immutable objects make code easier to move around, which reduces the pain substantially when you refactor and restructure it. Hence, the more side effect–free code you have, the smoother your current and future refactorings will be.

5.4   Summary

In this chapter, you saw that a restructuring done the Mikado way is a long sequence of making an edit, finding problems, updating the graph with desired solutions, and then reverting. This goes on until you can actually implement something, and then the scene changes. From then on, it's a rather straightforward chore of implementing leaf after leaf until you reach the goal. Sometimes the two phases are more interleaved and mixed, but the general idea is the same.

You've also seen that you can approach a change a bit differently by covering your code with tests before changing it. Adding tests is sometimes necessary in order to give you the extra courage it takes to tackle extra-difficult code. This can feel like a detour, but it saves you time in the long run.

We've looked at a lot of code, so now let's become a bit more general and look at how we can abstract what we've learned so far. In the next chapter, we'll look at how design principles can help us while we change difficult code.

Try this
- Try to restructure your code with automated refactorings only.
- Look for a place to add tests without changing the code. Reflect over how that's different from being allowed to change code to add tests.
- Try changing a piece of code in different ways, with the same goal in mind. What happens to your graph when you do that?

Emergent design

This chapter covers

- Emergent design that's robust in the face of change
- Redesigning classes
- Morphing the code to a good package structure
- How to let the Mikado Method guide you in a redesign

We deliberately started describing and explaining the Mikado Method from the practical end of things, letting you get your hands dirty and actually change code. We did this because we know how easy it is to get stuck analyzing things and going nowhere.

The Mikado Method is all about changing code, but you don't want to change the same code over and over again. The trick is to pull the code toward a state where changes don't create ripple effects, forcing other changes. If you think back, you can probably identify several situations where you've tried a lot of things and felt like you were going in circles, or when you reached the goal but didn't feel that you improved the system very much. If so, you know that just trying *random* things to reach your goal isn't enough. You also need a *direction*.

In previous chapters, we showed you how to get on top of a restructuring by starting with a clear goal and then systematically trying to change code and reverting. What we didn't tell you was that we also applied several *design principles*. These design principles are always on our minds when we use the Mikado Method. They give us guidance and direction regarding *how* and *why* we move things around, pull things apart, or merge things. The design principles we'll talk about have been created by different people in software development, but they're very well and holistically described in the book *Agile Software Development, Principles, Patterns, and Practices* by Robert C. Martin (Prentice Hall, 2002).

We'll take a look at these principles from the perspective of the Mikado Method, at the problems that arise when developing, and at the decisions you need to make as you change your code. By the end of the chapter, you'll be able to let your new and better design emerge as you restructure your application with the Mikado Method.

6.1 Designing classes

When we use the Mikado Method, we use design principles to guide us regarding what methods to put in what classes, what abstractions to create, and what dependencies between classes we should pursue. Instead of just rambling on about the principles in this section, we'll discuss them in the context of problems that often arise when we use the Mikado Method, and we'll look at how design principles can help solve those problems.

6.1.1 Code that does too many things

PROBLEM

When you design a software program from scratch, you can control reasonably well what goes into a class or a function. But if you're not careful, changes upon changes combined with bad judgment can add up and make the code bloated, with each method or class doing too many things. It's very common to come across code like this when restructuring with the Mikado Method. Usually, there's a piece of functionality in the bloated part that you want to reuse, and you need to move it to a method or a class where reuse is possible.

Take a look at the `Login` class in the following listing, where the `login` method is handling too many responsibilities.

Listing 6.1 A piece of code that does too much

```java
public class Login {

  public static void main(String[] args) throws Exception {
     login();
  }

  private static void login() throws Exception {
     Class.forName("com.mysql.jdbc.Driver");
     String connectionString = "jdbc:mysql://localhost/ssem";
```

❶ Establish database connection

```
        String dbUser = "dbu";
        String dbPwd = "";
        Connection conn = DriverManager.getConnection(connectionString,
                dbUser, dbPwd);
        Connection connection = conn;
        JOptionPane.showMessageDialog(null, "Trying to login");        ❷ Create login
        JPanel panel = new JPanel();                                      dialog
        JLabel label = new JLabel("Enter a password:");
        JPasswordField pass = new JPasswordField(10);
        panel.add(label);
        panel.add(pass);
        String[] options = new String[] { "OK", "Cancel" };
        int option = JOptionPane.showOptionDialog(null, panel,
                "Please login", JOptionPane.NO_OPTION,
                JOptionPane.PLAIN_MESSAGE, null, options, options[1]);
        if (option == JOptionPane.OK_OPTION) {
            String password = new String(pass.getPassword());

            String sql = "select username from users where "
                    + "username = 'admin' and password = ?";
            try {
                PreparedStatement pst = connection
                        .prepareStatement(sql);
                pst.setString(1, password);
                ResultSet rs = pst.executeQuery();
                                                                  ❸ Verify user
                if (rs.next()) {                                     credentials
                    JOptionPane.showMessageDialog(null,
                            "Login succeded");
                    JFrame main = new JFrame();                        Create
                    main.add(new JButton(new AbstractAction("Stop") {  application
                                                                   ❹ frame
                        @Override
                        public void actionPerformed(ActionEvent arg0) {
                            System.exit(0);
                        }

                    }));
                    main.setVisible(true);
                } else {                                           ❺ Handle
                    JOptionPane.showMessageDialog(null,              errors
                            "Username or password incorrect");
                }
            } catch (Exception e) {
                JOptionPane.showMessageDialog(null, e);
            }
        }
    }
}
```

This code does a handful of things. It establishes a database connection ❶, creates a login dialog ❷, verifies user credentials ❸, creates an application ❹, and does some error handling ❺. When you see a long method or a big class, it's often an indication that the method has several responsibilities.

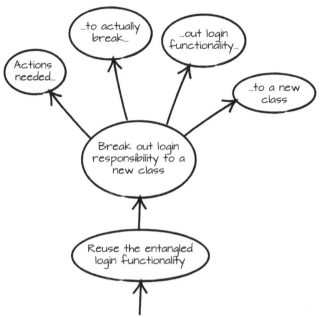

Figure 6.1 A typical Mikado graph for extracting a

SOLUTION

Possible ways to refactor this code include putting the database behind an interface, placing the GUI code in a separate package, moving the error handling to a more general solution, or just using the login functionality in more places. If you wanted to separate the login from the other logic, you'd create a graph that looks something like figure 6.1.

Depending on the time you have, you can either extract just the functionality you need or move out all the different responsibilities to new classes. A solution where all incidental responsibilities are moved to separate classes could look like the next listing.

Listing 6.2 Responsibilities distributed

```
public static void main(String[] args) throws Exception {
    SsemConnection ssem = new SsemConnection();          Establish
    login(ssem);                                          database
}                                                         connection

private static void login(SsemConnection ssem) {
    JOptionPane.showMessageDialog(null, "Trying to login");
    Application application = new Application();
    if (application.login()) {                            Create
        SystemUser systemUser = new SystemUser(ssem);     login
        if (systemUser.verify(application.getPassword())) {  dialog
            application.createMainScreen();
        }else {
            application.deny();                           Handle
        }                                                 errors
    }
}
```

Verify user credentials →

Create application frame →

The restructured example in listing 6.2 does the same things as listing 6.1, with the main difference being that the responsibilities have been distributed in smaller classes with expressive names. Why is this a good idea?

CREATING SEAMS IN A CODEBASE In *Working Effectively With Legacy Code*, Michael Feathers defines a seam as a place where you can alter a program's behavior without editing in that place. Typically, a seam is a method call or function call where the callee can be changed without changing the caller. If your code lacks a seam where you need one, the usual solution is to extract a method containing the code you want to alter. Then you can either extend the class and override the method, or move the method to a separate class or interface, and provide the caller with the class or interface. Depending on your programming language, there might be other options such as passing a function or changing the extracted method at runtime.

THE SINGLE RESPONSIBILITY PRINCIPLE

In the previous example, we moved the different responsibilities to separate classes. The guiding principle in this case is the *Single Responsibility Principle* (SRP): "A class should have one, and only one, reason to change." Separating responsibilities in your code has the following advantages:

- Makes it easier to read the code.
- Makes it easier to move code around.
- Code that isn't changed is unlikely to suddenly break.
- Decreases the risk of creating unnecessary dependencies between the implementation details in the different responsibilities.
- Makes reuse more likely due to both the singled-out responsibility and the lower probability of implementation dependencies between responsibilities (see the previous point).

Determining just what a responsibility is can sometimes be a bit difficult. For example, should a User class validate the user name, or should that be extracted to a UserName class? If the *user* concept changes for other reasons than the *user name* concept, the answer is yes. But initially in an application, the User may have only a user name, and then at some point the *user* concept might be extended to mean more than just the user name, or the *user name* concept might be extended to include responsibilities that go beyond those of the user. Determining when that line is crossed in a complex codebase is the tricky part. As a rule of thumb, you can start by splitting out the code representing the responsibilities you are absolutely sure don't belong where they currently reside. Later, when you find more evidence for code representing misplaced responsibilities, that code can be extracted as well.

WHAT DO PROBLEMS WITH SRP LOOK LIKE? Problems with SRP are pretty easy to find. Just look for long methods—methods with more than 25 lines. Some would even say more than 10 lines. Whenever you find them, extract additional methods, and after a while you'll have a class with several extracted methods. Maybe the new methods belong in a new class, or maybe they need to go into an existing one. If you pay attention and try to come up with descriptive names for the methods, the code will start *talking to you* and tell you where it needs to go.

6.1.2 Code that isn't stable in the face of change

PROBLEM

When you do the work of changing code with the Mikado Method, you don't want to change the same code over and over again if you can avoid it at an affordable cost. Bearing that in mind, have a look at the following simplified card game application, and see if you can spot the problem.

Listing 6.3 What will happen if you add another game?

```
. . .
public static final int FIVE_CARD_POKER = 0;
public static final int INDIAN_POKER = 1;
. . .
public class CardGameEngine {
    . . .
    public void deal(Game game, User user, Dealer dealer) {
        if(game.getType() == FIVE_CARD_POKER) {
            user.setCards(dealer.deal(5));
        } else if(game.getType() == INDIAN_POKER) {
            user.setCards(dealer.deal(1));
        } else {
            // else what?
        }
    }
}
```

In the deal method, the two constants and the if-else statements are good indicators that something is wrong. For every new game that's added, a new constant and a new conditional have to be added, in every part of the code where a variation of the behavior is needed. This type of code *isn't stable in the face of change*. Even worse, if other variations are needed, there will be a conditional mess that needs to be updated every time something changes. This type of programming is a common problem in legacy code. Granted, in procedural languages this how you do it, but in most languages there are other constructs that are much more appropriate.

SOLUTION

The solution is to create structures and abstractions in the code that support adding new features without changing the existing code. A Mikado Graph for adding a whist game to the previous code would typically look like figure 6.2.

Whist

Whist is a classic, English, trick-taking card game that was played widely in the eighteenth and nineteenth centuries.

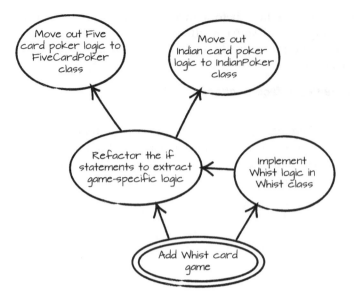

Figure 6.2   Adding the game of whist to the `CardGameEngine`

The refactored code before adding the whist game would look something like the following.

Listing 6.4   Refactored code

```
interface Game {
    void deal(User user, Dealer dealer);
}
public class FiveCardPoker implements Game {
    . . .
    public void deal(User user, Dealer dealer) {
        return user.setCards(dealer.nextCards(5));
    }
}
public class IndianPoker implements Game {
    . . .
    public void deal(User user, Dealer dealer) {
        return user.setCards(dealer.nextCards(1));
    }
}
. . .
public class CardGameEngine {
    . . .
    public void deal(Game game, User user, Dealer dealer) {
        game.deal(user, dealer);
    }
    . . .
}
```

The logic of these games is encapsulated behind the Game interface, in the different implementations of the interface. The CardGameEngine only knows how to connect the Game, the User, and the Dealer. It knows nothing about the specific games. Adding the Whist game would only involve creating a new implementation of the Game interface. The deal logic wouldn't have to change in any of the existing classes. The code is *stable in the face of (the anticipated) change.*

Refactor before adding new functionality

Let's say you wanted to add a new game, whist, to the first version of the code in listing 6.3. You *could* alter all the if statements across the codebase, but a better way is to first make the CardGameEngine stable in the face of change, and then add the new game. In our experience, the former approach is error-prone and time-consuming, and it makes the situation even worse because of the increased complexity of more conditionals. We find that first stabilizing the code and then adding the new game is less error-prone, and it yields faster results in general. This is a refactoring-in-advance step, where you first refactor the code and then implement the new logic.

With this approach, you're not tempted to leave the code immediately after you've added the new if statements and skip the refactoring step entirely. It's very important to complete the refactoring step to avoid building up complexity, and doing it first is good insurance.

At times when you can't see any good abstraction or generalization of behavior in advance, you might have to wait until after the new functionality (a game, in this case) is implemented. These are usually cases where there isn't too much complexity built up anyway, and another if statement won't make the transformation significantly harder.

The code in listing 6.3 was improved by using a common refactoring called "Replace conditional with polymorphism" (a.k.a. "Replace conditional with strategy"), as described in Martin Fowler's book *Refactoring*. In order to stabilize the code in listing 6.3, you need to extract the code in the blocks in the if statements into new methods, move those methods into classes that implement the Game interface, and then call them on the provided game, instead of having the conditional statement.

THE OPEN-CLOSED PRINCIPLE

The guiding principle when going from the code in listing 6.3 to the code in listing 6.4 is the *Open-Closed Principle* (OCP): "A class's behavior should be extendable without having to modify it." In its purest form, the OCP says that when you add a feature to a codebase, you shouldn't have to alter any existing code; you should be able to just add new code.

As you can see in listing 6.4, by moving specific game behavior to the different implementations, the generic Game engine can be kept stable in the face of change. As a byproduct, it also becomes a whole lot cleaner.

In general, it's hard to make all code OCP-compliant because it's hard to know what changes the future will require. But you do want your code to allow you to add new features of the same type that you already have without modifying the existing code very much.

AVOID CONDITIONALS   The OCP effectively rules out programming variations using conditionals, such as if statements, because adding a new conditional is modifying existing code. Conditional-free code requires some effort and thinking, but it's often worth it. Misused if statements are usually a big hurdle when it comes to improving large and unwieldy codebases, because they make the code harder to understand and follow. When you make changes to large codebases, strive to remove variations coded with conditionals if the code is on the critical path of your current change. The goal should be to push all conditionals to the edges of your applications.

6.1.3   *Code that violates its contract*

PROBLEM

Another common scenario when restructuring code is that you find a class that implements the contract of an abstraction or a base class, but when you make assumptions based on this, you get runtime or compiler errors. This is likely because the contract of the abstraction is broken in some way.

There are several ways to break a contract, and a common example is the Square-Rectangle problem. For example, here's a Rectangle class:

```
public class Rectangle {
    public Rectangle(int height, int width) { . . . }
    public void setHeight(int height) { . . . }
    public int getHeight() { . . . }
    public void setWidth(int width) { . . . }
    public int getWidth() { . . . }
}
```

Then you find a use for a Square object, and want to add that. A square is a special case of a rectangle, so subclassing Rectangle might seem like a good idea. Here's a Square that extends the Rectangle:

```
public class Square extends Rectangle {
    public Square(int side) {
        super(side, side);
    }
    public void setHeight(int height) {
        super.setHeight(height);
        super.setWidth(height);
    }
    public void setWidth(int width) {
        super.setWidth(width);
        super.setHeight(width);
    }
}
```

The problem here is that the contract of the Rectangle says you can change the sides independently. If a method takes a Rectangle and then changes its height, it would expect the width to be unaltered—that's part of the contract of the Rectangle. In the case of the square, the *derived class is not substitutable for the base class* because it breaks the contract of the base class.

SOLUTION

Consider the difference between the inheritance approach of the previous `Square` class (where the `Square` is a `Rectangle`) with the following approach.

Listing 6.5   Composition approach for `Square` with a new interface

```
public interface TwoDimensionalObject {
    int getWidth();
    int getHeight();
}
public class Square implements TwoDimensionalObject {
    private Rectangle internalRect;
    public Square(int side) {
        internalRect = new Rectangle(side, side);
    }
    public void setHeight(int height) {
        internalRect.setHeight(height);
        internalRect.setWidth(height);
    }
    public void setWidth(int width) {
        internalRect.setWidth(width);
        internalRect.setHeight(width);
    }
    public int getWidth() {
        return internalRect.getWidth();
    }
    public int getHeight() {
        return internalRect.getHeight();
    }
}
```

In listing 6.6, you can see the `Rectangle` class that implements the `TwoDimensional-Object` interface. (Note that the interface only specifies the getter methods.) You already know that the `Square` and the `Rectangle` can't have their dimensions altered in the same way, so the interface can't have any dimension setter methods.

Listing 6.6   `Rectangle` should also implement the new interface

```
public class Rectangle implements TwoDimensionalObject {
    public Rectangle(int height, int width) { . . . }
    public void setHeight(int height) { . . . }
    public int getHeight() { . . . }
    public void setWidth(int width) { . . . }
    public int getWidth() { . . . }
}
```

The code in these two examples is similar, but there's one important difference: the inheritance. The APIs of the `Square` and the `Rectangle` are still the same, but in the first case the `Square` *is* a `Rectangle`, and in the latter case it *uses* a `Rectangle`. The new `TwoDimensionalObject` interface creates a new contract that doesn't say anything about the relation between width and height, and this interface can be used across the application.

When you find such a problem, the related part of the Mikado Graph often has a node with something like "Square does not extend Rectangle," or if you figured out how to implement it, "Square implements TwoDimensionalObject instead of Rectangle." By just removing extends Rectangle from the code, the compiler, should you have one, will identify a lot of the places that you need to fix. For any runtime tricks, such as casting an object to another object, you'll need an automated test suite or manual testing. Often you can't just remove the existing inheritance, and instead you'll need to replace it with interfaces and new base classes that are better suited to the way you use the abstraction, as in the Square-Rectangle case.

A REFACTORING TRICK   In cases where the inheritance is extensive and intertwined, a good trick is to first use the "Push down methods to subclass" refactoring. This refactoring duplicates the superclass's methods in all its subclasses, creating their own implementations of all the methods needed. After this, it's easier to remove the inheritance and replace it with an interface or a new base class. Sometimes inserting an empty class in the inheritance hierarchy can help you move methods to the right classes.

This problem isn't always limited to the functionality inside the classes, but often extends to the consumers of the poor abstraction. A common telltale of bad abstractions is code like the following, where the type is checked at runtime, and different paths are taken based on the implementing type:

```
public class GraphicsManager {
    ...
    public void handleObject(Rectangle rectangle) {
        if(rectangle instanceof Square) {
            Square square = (Square)rectangle;
            ...
        } else {
            ...
        }
    }
    ...
}
```

There are several ways of breaking the contract:

- Using the wrong abstraction or extending an unsuitable class, which was the case with the Rectangle-Square example.
- Overriding a subclass method in a way that's inconsistent with the protocol of the abstraction. This often happens in complex inheritance hierarchies.
- Having a method take a superclass as an argument, and then perform completely different actions depending on the implementing subclass, as in the preceding GraphicsManager.

THE LISKOV SUBSTITUTION PRINCIPLE

In the solutions in listings 6.7 and 6.6, you change the contract to better accommodate the properties you're interested in. The guiding principle is the *Liskov Substitution*

Principle (LSP): "Derived classes must be substitutable for their base classes." In other words, it should be possible to use a subclass to an abstraction anywhere the abstraction is used. Adhering to the LSP makes programs easier to read, reason about, and change.

Inheritance and LSP go hand in hand, and whenever there's a problem with an inheritance hierarchy, like in the Square-Rectangle case, you should stop and ask yourself a simple but very relevant question: "*Is* this Square class a Rectangle, or should we just *use* a Rectangle in the Square class?"

When in doubt, use *composition over inheritance*, just like we did when we made Square use a Rectangle. Our simple advice is to start with composition and then consider inheritance if that makes more sense. It's a lot easier to move to stronger dependencies, like inheritance, than to move the other way.

6.1.4 *Bulky interfaces*

PROBLEM

Often, interfaces are used in code to separate the contract from the implementation. If the interface is large, the chances are that it accidentally serves several purposes, or several consumers. When you want to move certain functionality to a new place, such as for a specific consumer, you can't just do that. For example, in the left part of figure 6.3, you can't just move one of the users and the parts of the interface it uses to a new project or solution, should you need to. As you probably know by now, moving code is a common consequence of using the Mikado Method on nontrivial code, and bulky interfaces are common obstacles when moving code.

SOLUTION

Problems with too extensive interfaces are often discovered when you try to split functionality, such as when moving parts to separate packages. By extracting smaller client-specific interfaces, like in figure 6.3, the application gets a better structure, and the users and their interfaces can be put in different packages.

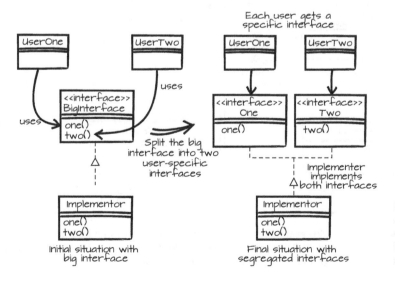

Figure 6.3 **Create a codebase that's easier to change by creating user-specific interfaces.**

Depending on the size of the interface, it can be split and combined in many ways. The division in figure 6.4 is the simplest case. A variation could have one of the users using both methods, and in that case the division would look a bit different.

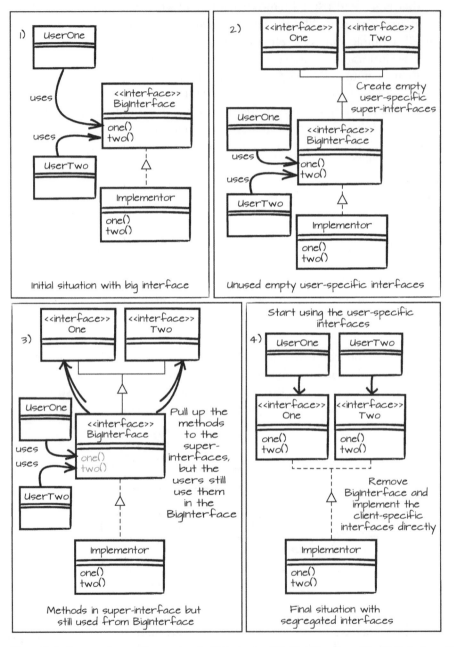

Figure 6.4   Process for creating segregated interfaces: 1) Initial situation with a big interface. 2) Create empty user-specific interfaces. 3) Pull up one method at a time to the new interfaces. 4) When the new interfaces are defined, change the users' references to the new interfaces.

With more methods and users, it gets more complicated. In a compiling language, to find the methods to be extracted to a specific user interface, you can use the Naive Approach. If you just remove or comment out one method at a time from `BigInterface`, you can see where the different methods are missed in the code, and thereby build your knowledge about what methods go where. You can also start using empty interfaces where you would like to, see where the code breaks, and then grow the graph with what methods you must pull up based on the feedback you get from the broken code. If your IDE can find method usages, you can use that to find candidates for methods to move into the new interfaces, or you can find them by doing relevant regular expression searches. Keep on extracting different user-specific super-interfaces until you can do what you set out to do, possibly until the original `BigInterface` is empty and can be removed.

> **IDE SUPPORT** The automated refactorings of some IDEs, like Eclipse and IntelliJ, can help extract new super-interfaces from an existing interface, and pull up or push down methods in the interface hierarchy. You have to decide how to divide the methods among the interfaces, but you can get significant help with the boilerplate coding from an IDE. To avoid unnecessary manual labor, get to know the capabilities of your IDE before you do these types of refactorings.

THE INTERFACE SEGREGATION PRINCIPLE

When splitting the preceding interfaces, we used the *Interface Segregation Principle* (ISP) as our guiding principle: "Interfaces should be fine-grained and client-specific." Breaking the ISP creates implicit dependencies between the unused members of the interface class and its users, which adds to the complexity of the codebase and decreases stability.

You don't want to expose more functionality than necessary to a client. All clients should be on a need-to-know basis, and when you have several clients with different needs, you should create one interface for each type of client. If a client needs more information at some later point in time, you can extend the interface at that time. Try to find seams in the code where the connecting interfaces can be kept to a minimum. This minimizes the risk of having inappropriate relations between the parts of the system.

6.1.5 *Code with rigid call-dependency chains*

PROBLEM

The core problem when changing code is the troublesome dependencies in the code. These are what the Mikado Method is there to help you find, but if you don't do anything about them, not much improvement will happen. To illustrate this, let's look at the following very simple piece of code, which looks quite ordinary:

```
public class Door {
    private final CylinderLock lock;

    public Door(CylinderLock lock) {
```

```
        this.lock = lock;
    }

    public void open() {
        lock.unlock();
        ...
    }
}
public class CylinderLock {
    public void lock() {
        ...
    }
    public void unlock() {
        ...
    }
}
```

In this code, the Door uses an injected CylinderLock, which introduces a problematic dependency. The door is depending on an implementation detail—what type of lock is used.

Granted, if this is the only code you'll ever need, it's probably fine. But it's rarely this simple. The CylinderLock depends on a lot of code that's specific to the CylinderLock, and the Door transiently depends on that code as well, as the left part of figure 6.5 shows. Now, if you want to move the Door to a new package, you'll have to make sure that the entire tail of dependencies from CylinderLock is also reachable. This could be OK, but it's often a problem when restructuring code.

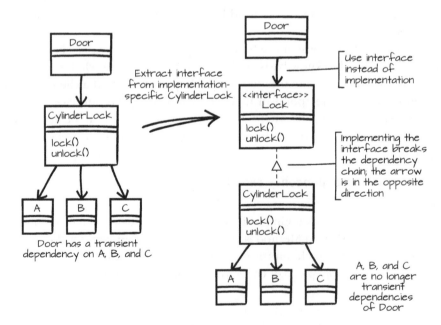

Figure 6.5 By extracting an interface between a client and a provider, a troublesome dependency chain can be broken.

SOLUTION

If you extract an interface from CylinderLock, a Lock interface, with the conceptual functionality that Door needs, the chain is broken. This is what's illustrated in figure 6.5. Note that the *implements* arrow points to the interface, as does the *using* arrow. This is a dependency barrier, where all dependency arrows point toward an object, and none point out. The code with the barrier, where the Door knows nothing about the type of lock, looks like this:

```
public interface Lock {
    public void lock();
    public void unlock();
}

public class Door {
    private final Lock lock;

    public Door(Lock lock) {
        this.lock = lock;
    }

    public void open() {
        lock.unlock();
        ...
    }
}

public class CylinderLock implements Lock {
    public void lock() {
        ...
    }
    public void unlock() {
        ...
    }
}
```

This code is much less fragile with regard to changes in the lock implementations because the Door doesn't implicitly depend on any of the code that the CylinderLock uses. You could now move the Door class and the Lock interfaces to a separate package, and as long as any lock implements the protocol of Lock, all is fine. Another benefit is that adding another lock is just a matter of implementing the Lock interface.

Abstractions, like interfaces or abstract/virtual classes, are usually the more stable points in a codebase. That's partly because they contain less or no code and therefore have fewer dependencies and change less than concrete implementations, and partly because they usually represent concepts one level above the implementation—concepts that don't change as much as the implementation details. The Lock interface in the preceding code won't change as much as the Lock implementations. In addition, the abstractions can be used to break dependency chains, like we did with the Lock previously. This provides even more stability to your codebase by isolating the users of an interface from changes in the implementers of the interface.

DEPENDENCY INJECTION Troublesome dependencies in object-oriented programming are often related to the instantiation of objects, because that ties the instantiating class to the instantiated class by a call to its constructor. This is a rather strong dependency, which makes it difficult or impossible to use another class in a flexible manner. By depending on abstractions that are provided to a class, the decision of what implementation to use is deferred to the calling class. This often increases the flexibility of an application, but it has to be balanced against the increased complexity.

THE DEPENDENCY INVERSION PRINCIPLE

In the preceding examples, we strove to depend on interfaces and classes higher up in the inheritance hierarchy, guided by the *Dependency Inversion Principle* (DIP): "Depend on abstractions, not on concretions." Doing so, and at the same time adhering to the other class design principles, makes the code more robust in the face of further changes.

The principles guide you on a fairly granular level, and they remind you of how you should design classes to increase the chances of ending up with code that's easy to maintain. But there's a little more to maintainable code than just class design. You also need something to tell you how you should organize your classes in packages.

6.2   *Designing packages*

Even seemingly simple Mikado goals can require you to move classes between packages, create new packages, or even reorganize the overall packaging structure. The Mikado Method will often have you move code around, and you need to know what to put where. Just as there are principles for class design, there are principles for designing packages to make your codebase more robust in the face of change.

In the following sections, we'll look at some of the packaging problems that can occur when evolving an application with the Mikado Method, and also at some common

---

What's a package?

The term *package* is a bit ambiguous and overloaded in software development, so let's define what we mean.

A *package* in this chapter refers to a UML *component*. A UML component is *a deployable or executable component*, which can be anything from a single class to an arbitrary amount of code packaged for deployment. This usually equates to a project in your IDE.

Note that the term *package* in UML and Java corresponds to the *package declaration*, which in Java also means a folder in the filesystem where the class files and other resources reside. To complicate matters, in other environments such as .NET or Ruby, the equivalent of a Java or UML package is the *namespace*.

The packaging principles we'll describe in this chapter are much more important when dealing with UML components, or projects, than with UML packages. They're still relevant to UML packages, though, because we sometimes break out a package that becomes a new component.

solutions to those problems and the principles they're based on. We'll look at how a package structure could evolve in an application like chapter 5's loan application. We'll leave out a lot of details to keep our focus on structuring the packages.

6.2.1 What to put in a package

An application often starts with one single package, for one single deployment. This is the simple life, as shown in figure 6.6.

Then you realize you want to have two different versions of the application, such as the public application and back-office approval versions from the loan application in chapter 5. You start a new Mikado Graph with "Create approve server to simplify loan applications" and realize that there's some common code that you need in both applications, so you add a prerequisite, "Create loan core package," as in figure 6.7. You create the loan core package and start moving the common code there. As usual, you can see what you need to change by using the compiler or tests, or by analyzing the moved code.

By releasing the shared code in a separate package, you can start reusing it in an orderly way. This is an example of the *Reuse-Release Equivalence Principle* (REP): "The granule of release is the granule of reuse." Regardless of your intentions, you have to consider all accessible code in the package as reused. In figure 6.8 you can see the two deployments with a shared code package.

One reason to split up code into packages is that it communicates that the code within a given package should be used together. This is the *Common Reuse Principle* (CRP): "Classes that are used together are packaged together."

Back in the development of loan application, you realize that you have to change a detail regarding the rate ticker in the common package, but this change ripples

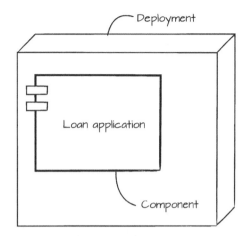

Figure 6.6 The simple life: a single loan application package deployed on a server

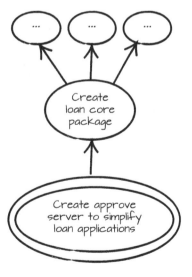

Figure 6.7 When you want to create the new approve server, you realize that there's some loan core code you want to use in both places.

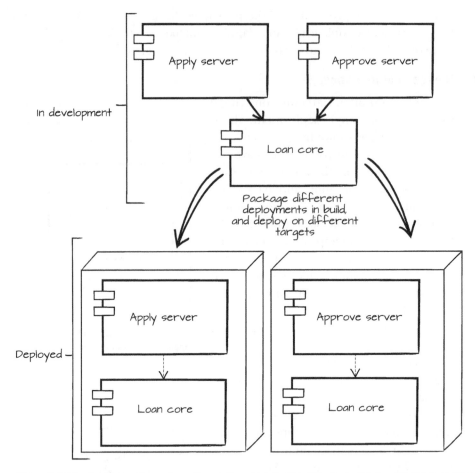

Figure 6.8 In development, you have the apply package, the approve package, and the loan core package. In the deployment step, they're bundled in two deployables and each is placed on one server.

up into both apps, and it's a mess. The loan core package is obviously not yet properly partitioned; there were some pieces missing in the shared code package. This could mean that you have a problem with the *Common Closure Principle* (CCP): "Classes that change together are packaged together." In this case, you had to change the code in all packages to complete a single change. You can't mitigate all possible types of changes in advance, but you should be able to do so for anticipated changes. If you make a change and get a problem, that's an anticipated change from then on.

THE COHESION PRINCIPLES The Reuse-Release Equivalence Principle, the Common Reuse Principle, and the Common Closure Principle are often called *cohesion principles* because they strive for packages that are as highly cohesive as possible. This means that when you create a package of code, the code in it should be used together and changed together.

6.2.2 *Dependencies between packages*

In the previous section, we failed to contain a change in the common package. Let's revert the failing changes and add a node to the existing, or possibly new, Mikado Graph: "Make loan core package self-contained and cohesive," as in figure 6.9.

When you go to move the code to the right place, there's a messy `RateFeed` class that should be moved to the loan core package, but when you move it there, the loan core package has a dependency back to the presentation code in the application packages. This is a violation of the *Acyclic Dependencies Principle* (ADP): "The dependency graph of packages must have no cycles." This isn't an acceptable solution, and in many environments it won't even compile. We've tried to illustrate that in figure 6.10.

Luckily, you learned about the Dependency Inversion Principle earlier (see section 6.1.5), and

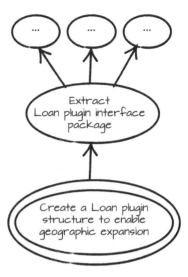

Figure 6.9 When moving the `RateFeed` class to the loan core package, the circular dependency must first be broken.

you can use this here. Let's revert the code again and add "Break circular dependency by creating `RateFeedConsumer` interface" to the Mikado Graph. The new interface

Cyclic dependencies in the wild

Cyclic dependencies are easier to avoid between packages than within them. In fact, they can't exist between projects in IDEs like Eclipse, IntelliJ, or Visual Studio. So as long as you structure and build your applications in a standard manner, this shouldn't pose a problem.

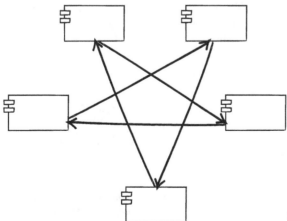

Figure 6.10 Cyclic dependencies are evil

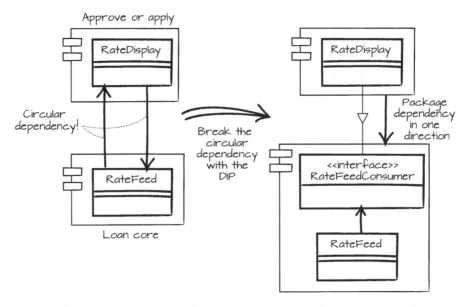

Figure 6.11 Moving the `RateFeed` class to the loan core package creates a circular dependency because of the interaction with the `RateDisplay` class. By breaking the circular dependency with an interface, the packages can comply with the Acyclic Dependencies Principle.

and the rate feed functionality go into the loan core package, and by implementing the interface in the applications, the applications can create rate tickers that are automatically updated, as described in figure 6.11. Now you can move the last pieces of code to make the loan core package more robust in the face of change, following the cohesion principles.

The development of the application moves on, and after a while you realize that if you could plug in different types of loans for different countries, your business could grow a lot. A common way to create a plugin architecture is to create a plugin interface package, and then plug in packages that implement that interface package. Start a fresh Mikado Graph with the goal, "Create a `Loan` plugin structure to enable geographic expansion" like in figure 6.12. One of the first prerequisites will be "Extract `Loan` plugin interface package."

By building the application with different plugin implementations, different behaviors can be achieved. More behaviors can be added subsequently, still without changing a single line of code in the existing packages. The package structure is illustrated in figure 6.13.

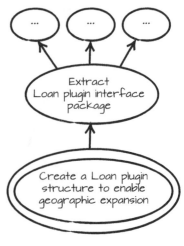

Figure 6.12 The initial Mikado Graph for creating a plugin structure

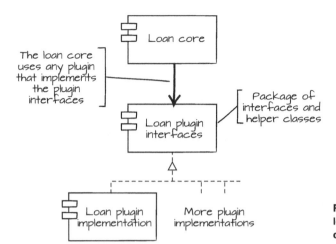

Figure 6.13 The loan core accepts loan plugins that implement the contents of the loan interface

The stability of the solution can be attributed to two principles. First, you used the *Stable Abstractions Principle* (SAP): "Abstractness increases with stability." The plugin interface package contains mostly abstractions such as interfaces, making it more stable due to fewer moving parts in the shape of implementation details, and hence fewer outgoing dependencies. Then, there's the *Stable Dependencies Principle* (SDP): "Depend in the direction of stability." This one can be seen in figure 6.13, where both the dependency arrow and the extension arrow point toward the abstract interface package. In reality, packages don't implement other packages, but the *classes* in the implementing package implement the interfaces and abstractions in the interface package.

THE COUPLING PRINCIPLES   The Acyclic Dependencies Principle, Stable Abstractions Principle, and Stable Dependencies Principle are often referred to as *coupling principles*. They tell you what dependencies to create between packages. In general, you should strive for low coupling and high cohesion, and the couplings you make should be toward stable, abstract packages.

A system has to change somewhere in order to evolve, so not all packages can be stable. The key is to move the more stable interfaces and abstract classes to their own packages. After that, you put their volatile implementers in implementation packages that depend on the interface packages.

JUST-IN-TIME EXTRACTION   Creating a new package and defining a release process (and then sticking to it) is tedious work. In addition, crossing package boundaries when you're restructuring code can be problematic due to the constraints of the interpackage dependencies. When you need to extract a new package, as we described in this chapter, do it *just in time*, when you need it, and not *just in case* you might need it in the future. Use the Mikado Method to make sure you have all the structure in place and all the dependencies right so that the extraction can be made without errors.

As the application is developed further, more candidates for package extraction will be discovered. In time, you'll probably also have to merge packages, or merge and restructure along another axis. By using the principles for both package and class design, your application design will emerge from what you have, and from what you want to do next.

6.3 Summary

Keep your methods and classes focused, keep the system extensible without editing existing code, follow the contracts of the code, keep interfaces sufficiently small, and avoid long dependency chains.

Here are the same points expressed as class design principles, often referred to as the *SOLID principles* based on their initial letters:

- Single Responsibility Principle
- Open-Closed Principle
- Liskov Substitution Principle
- Interface Segregation Principle
- Dependency Inversion Principle

When you create a package of code, the code in it should be used together and changed together. And here are the same points listed as cohesion package design principles:

- The Reuse-Release Equivalence Principle
- The Common Reuse Principle
- The Common Closure Principle

In addition to high cohesion, your packages should also strive for low coupling. The couplings you make should be toward stable, abstract packages. These are the coupling package design principles:

- The Acyclic Dependencies Principle
- The Stable Abstractions Principle
- The Stable Dependencies Principle

These names are really just mnemonic devices. It's much more important to know what they stand for than to know what their names are.

Changes are an intrinsic part of the Mikado Method. In this chapter, we looked at how you can make classes and packages more robust in the face of change. By practicing and applying the same kind of thinking in your own development, you can let your designs emerge from what you already have, and from what you want to do. By moving your designs in increments instead of big bangs, you can continuously improve, extend, and deliver your software.

> **Try this**
> - See if you can find any part of your codebase that could be improved after the lessons of this chapter. Try to improve it.
> - Try to find code that looks good given what you just learned. Was it easier or more difficult than finding code that looks bad? Could you write more of the good-looking stuff?

Common
restructuring patterns

Your Mikado Graphs will likely never be exactly the same, but often you'll get the feeling that you've seen something similar before, or that you're doing a chain of refactorings you've done previously. When you see such a form recurring or see yourself repeating almost the same thing you did last week, it's possibly a pattern. We call them patterns because they're more or less prepackaged solutions that can be applied to similar situations. With a little bit of mapping to your problem domain, patterns are good tools to have in your toolbox.

The patterns included in this book are ones that have helped us; they're not by any means an exhaustive list. We encourage you to observe your behavior when it comes to restructuring and programming and to find your own patterns.

In this chapter, we'll show you some patterns for moving and grouping code that's been scattered in different packages in a codebase, a central task when working with legacy code. In addition, we'll show you some code tricks we've used. But we'll start out easy with some graph patterns for drawing clearer graphs.

7.1   *Graph patterns*

When we use the Mikado Method to draw a graph and restructure software, the graph sometimes becomes a bit cluttered or unclear in different ways. We don't want to create too many rules about how to draw the graph, but we also want to have clear graphs, and there's a balance to strike. In the following sections, you'll read about some patterns that make graphs easier to draw, work with, and understand. You'll come across patterns that deal with exploring options, splitting graphs, concurrent goals, and other issues.

7.1.1   *Group common prerequisites in a grouping node*

SITUATION

You have a group of nodes that depend on the same other node, or nodes.

SOLUTION

Gather the group of nodes in a *grouping node* and draw arrows to or from that grouping node (see figure 7.1).

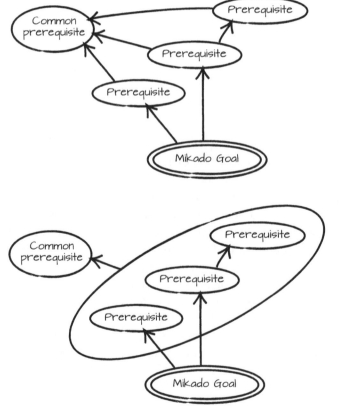

Figure 7.1 Two equivalent graphs; the second one groups nodes with common dependencies

SCENARIO

The need to group nodes often arises when several changes depend on one and the same prerequisite. For example, when classes need to be moved to a new project, you need to set up that project before any classes can be moved. Figure 7.1 could describe such a case where three actions are grouped. If there are only three actions that depend on the same prerequisite, the graph isn't very cluttered, but if you come across a case where 10 changes depend on the same prerequisite, the need to group nodes becomes more compelling.

7.1.2 *Extract preparatory prerequisites*

SITUATION

You have a set of tasks that need to be carried out before starting on a goal, but the tasks aren't directly related to the goal.

SOLUTION

Extract the preparatory prerequisites to a separate Mikado Graph, and complete them before you start.

SCENARIO

You want to complete some preparations before you even start to explore the code and work the Mikado Method. If you add those preparatory prerequisites to the graph, all the other nodes will point to them, wasting space and cluttering the paper or whiteboard. Examples of such changes are general code cleanup (like removing unnecessary or unused code), commented out code, or applying a formatting template on all the code.

> **CLEANUPS** Remember to put cleanups, formatting, and the like in separate commits. That way it becomes a lot easier to find the relevant differences between commits.

7.1.3 *Group a repeated set of prerequisites as a templated change*

SITUATION

You have a common set of prerequisites to perform at different places in the code, and repeating these prerequisites at all the different places in the graph creates too many nodes, cluttering the graph.

SOLUTION

Draw the prerequisites in a separate template bubble, and annotate the bubble with the items for which you need to repeat the template.

The template change also becomes a *grouping node* that itself can have prerequisites, as in figure 7.2.

SCENARIO

If you decide to change a method signature, the callers of that method will need to be updated in several places and you can record that information in a templated change. When you work with a dynamically typed language, or if your development environment

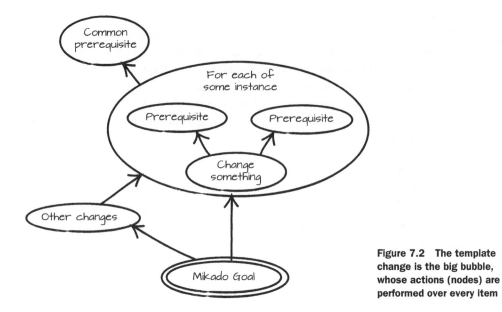

Figure 7.2 The template change is the big bubble, whose actions (nodes) are performed over every item

doesn't have automated refactorings that can perform a change across the entire code-base, you'll need to do this more frequently.

7.1.4   Graph concurrent goals with common prerequisites together

SITUATION

You have different Mikado Goals that need to be dealt with simultaneously.

SOLUTION

Draw the goals in the same graph and let them share common prerequisites.

SCENARIO

If you have two goals, it might look like the graph in figure 7.3. We had a similar scenario in chapter 5 where we wanted to separate the loan applications from loan approvals. If, after the restructuring in that chapter, we wanted to put the query part of the application on a separate server for performance reasons, those two goals would have had some common refactorings, such as moving the LoanApplication classes to the common project we created in that same chapter. When the graphs for the different goals are set side by side, the common hot spots are easier to identify and deal with, their importance is elevated, and you have more information about how that piece of software should be restructured. Figure 7.3 represents an abstract version of such a graph.

7.1.5   Split the graph

SITUATION

You need to distribute work from one graph to a separate graph. This can be because you need to spawn the work to another working unit, or perhaps you just ran out of whiteboard space.

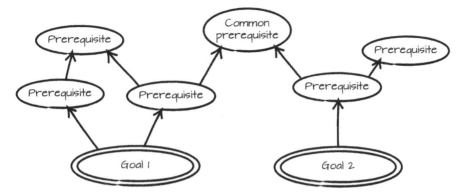

Figure 7.3 Two goals with common prerequisites

SOLUTION

Create another graph that's really a subgraph, and then draw a node that contains a clear reference to where the subgraph is (see figure 7.4, where the subgraph is named *XYZ graph*). Preferably the broken-out part shouldn't have any arrows back to the original drawing.

SCENARIO

When you're doing larger restructurings and improvements, splitting a graph can be a way of limiting the scope. You might want to focus on a smaller part of the graph because you don't have time or you don't have enough develop-

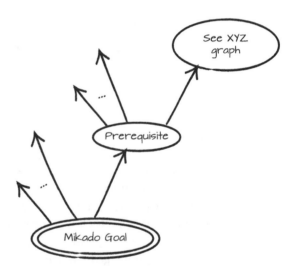

Figure 7.4 Splitting a Mikado Graph

ers. A smaller portion of the work can often be completed in a shorter time, and splitting the graph makes it easier to distribute the work. If you split it into several parts, multiple people or teams can help complete the work.

7.1.6 *Explore options*

SITUATION

You have a problem that can be solved in more than one way, and you don't know which is the best solution.

SOLUTION

Draw a split-dependency arrow to the options you have. Explore each option as far as you need to get sufficient information and to understand reasonably well what the consequences are for choosing each option. See the graph in figure 7.5 for an example.

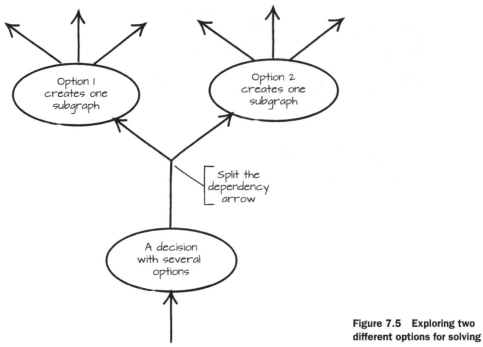

Figure 7.5 Exploring two different options for solving

SCENARIO

A common example of choosing between options is breaking circular dependencies. Imagine a scenario where class A depends on B, B on C, and C in turn on A. Circular dependencies can effectively be broken by introducing abstractions. In Java or C#, you can extract an interface, and then use a class that implements that interface. But before you decide which class you're going to use, you can experiment with two or maybe all three of them, as in figure 7.5.

Exploring options gives you more information, and more information makes it easier to resolve design discussions if you're uncertain which solution is superior. This is especially important when you can't predict the consequences properly. Seeing what an implementation actually looks like is a lot more powerful than imagining it.

If you can complete other parts of the restructuring, we suggest you do them first and delay the parts where you're not sure which path to take. Working with the system and the Mikado Method will help you build more knowledge about the system. When you've taken care of the other paths, you might find you've gained enough knowledge about the options to know which to choose. Occasionally the problems you want to solve with one of your options may have already been resolved, but don't count on it.

Once you've decided on an option, the options not chosen and the prerequisites it doesn't share with the rest of the graph can be removed from the graph.

7.2 Scattered-code patterns

Packages, or projects, and their dependencies create restrictions on what code can reference what other code. This can be used to your advantage, but in the face of change it may also pose a problem if you can't move or access code as you want to.

A common scenario we face when we deal with legacy code is that applications have been split into packages, but little care has been put into what goes in what part, resulting in a mess of dependencies. Code that should be together is scattered across the codebase, rather than cohesively placed behind a service or an API.

> **WHAT'S A PACKAGE?** When we talk about *packages*, it's the UML component concept we mean. Java developers can think of *projects*, and .NET programmers can think of *assemblies*.

The packaging principles described in section 6.2 are usually violated in these scenarios, and when these principles are broken, problems usually manifest themselves in a couple of different ways:

- You might have difficulty finding the code you're looking for, because the package names don't clearly identify what's in them.
- You might discover dependency problems between libraries and other packages when you move things around, typically when you use the Naive Approach. When logic is spread across the codebase, a nasty web of dependencies forms and keeps everything entangled.

A common Mikado scenario is extracting a piece of code from such a codebase to create a library that can be used in several places. In the following sections, you'll see a few powerful ways to move code around, remove code, or put parts of your code into new packages.

7.2.1 Merge, reorganize, split

SITUATION

You have code that isn't partitioned in the right packages, and you need to rearrange them in a new structure.

SOLUTION

Merge the relevant packages, reorganize the code, and then extract the new libraries to new packages, as illustrated in figure 7.6.

> **ISN'T MERGING PACKAGES JUST A WAY TO HIDE THE DEPENDENCY PROBLEMS?** Well, yes, in a way. This is often not the permanent solution, but a stepping stone to something better. But if you can make this move and avoid having these dependency problems block critical paths, you could just leave them there until they enter your critical path again.

SCENARIO

When you deal with scattered code, it's often beneficial to merge the affected packages to temporarily avoid any blocking dependencies, and thereby get more flexibility

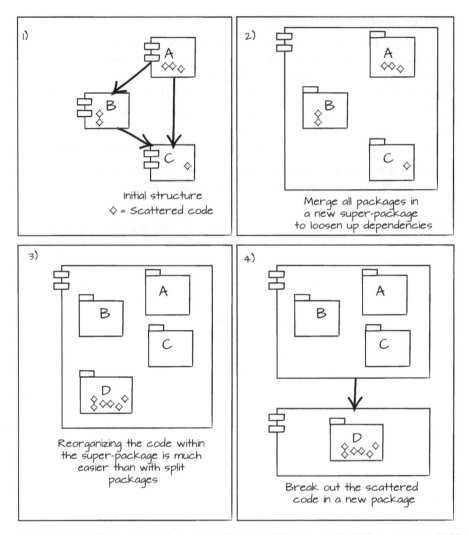

Figure 7.6   Merging code to split it out another way: 1) Code is scattered in a structure. 2) Merge all the code into a single super-package. 3) Reorganize the code within the super-package and gather the scattered code into a new package. 4) Extract the new package containing the formerly scattered code.

to implement the changes you want. You can often start by merging packages, reorganizing them, and then extracting a new library, as illustrated in figure 7.6. After you've merged the packages, you can group the scattered code and, following the Naive Approach, move it to the new package. The compiler, analysis, or your tests will then show if you missed any dependencies that you need to take care of first.

In most cases, it's fairly straightforward to merge two packages. There's rarely more to it than moving the contents of one package into the other, which then becomes the union of both. After that, you just make all other packages that depended on either of them depend on the newly created union package. If you run into trouble, it's typically with dependencies that reference parts of a package (such as A, B, or C, as described in figure 7.6) and can't reference back to the newly created A-B-C package, because that would create a cyclical dependency. The usual solution is to use the Dependency Inversion Principle, and insert an interface.

If you remember the door-and-lock DIP example from chapter 6 (section 6.1.5), this is the same thing. Use an abstraction to break and invert a dependency, create an interface, and put that with the scattered code in the newly created package, D.

After such a change, there's more information available on how you can structure the software. If you need to extract more functionality from the A, B, or C packages, you can do that by following the same procedure. If the packages don't have to be split for any reason, then keep them together.

The resulting Mikado Graph can vary in appearance, but a typical graph might look like figure 7.7.

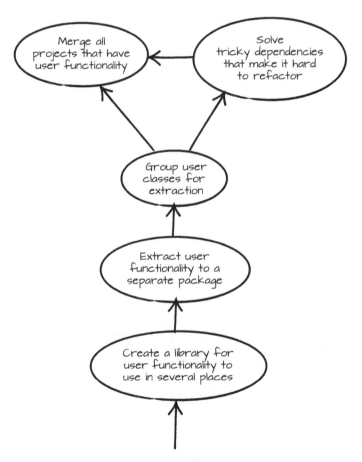

Figure 7.7   Extracting a library containing user functionality

TRANSFORMING PROBLEMS   One way to look at this merge-move is as a common trick in mathematics: transforming a problem into another coordinate system where solving it is easy, and then transforming the result back to the original coordinate system. Merging packages is a little bit like transforming a problem to another coordinate system, and then transforming it back into a better solution by extracting the packages you need.

Sometimes the packages can't be merged. Then you have to use another tactic to extract the new package.

7.2.2 *Move code directly to a new package*

SITUATION
You need to regroup scattered code into a new package, but for some reason you can't merge the code before splitting out the new package, as in the merge-reorganize-split pattern.

SOLUTION
Create a new package that all concerned packages depend on, and move the scattered code directly to the new package, as shown in figure 7.8.

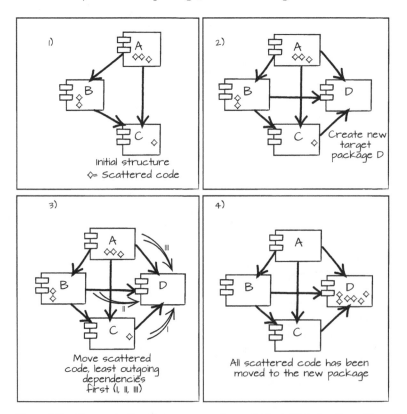

Figure 7.8   Move code directly to a new package: 1) The initial situation with scattered code in several packages. 2) Create a new package for the scattered code. 3) Move the scattered code into the new package, starting with the package with the least number of outgoing dependencies. 4) The result with all scattered code gathered in one package.

As you can see in the figure, you start out with packages that have scattered code (1). Then you create the new empty package and add that package as a dependency for the other packages (2). Next, you move the scattered code from the package with the least number of outgoing dependencies first, which in this example is package C, and then in turn B and A (3). By doing so, the risk of breaking dependencies by moving code is minimized, although not eliminated. You end up with the scattered code gathered in the new package (4).

SCENARIO

In the loan server example from chapter 5, you wouldn't want to merge the public application and administrative approval services in order to extract common code from those packages, because that would cause significant security issues. In that case, moving code directly to a new package would be a better strategy.

By following the Naive Approach and just moving the code to the new package, you'll quickly find dependencies that have to be taken care of. As always, that information needs to go into the Mikado Graph. In the example in figure 7.8, the package dependencies are rather simple, but in reality, dependencies can be much more extensive. Analyzing the dependencies to find the leaves can be helpful, but tedious. Instead, you can use the Naive Approach to narrow down what parts of the code you need to analyze more closely to figure out what you need to do. This pattern generally requires you to take care of more accidental dependency problems than the merge-reorganize-split pattern does.

7.2.3 *Move code gradually to a new package*

SITUATION

You want to gather scattered code, but you can't, or don't want to, merge the packages or extract a new package immediately. It's also possible that the moved code could benefit from some intermediate processing as you extract and move it between packages in the codebase.

SOLUTION

Accumulate the new package as you move the code throughout the system, as shown in figure 7.9. In some cases, it's possible to just move scattered code in the dependency direction, and then extract a new package. In other cases, the code needs some preparation in order to be moveable. The Naive Approach can help you narrow down what analysis and refactoring needs to be performed.

> **MOVING CODE AND DEPENDENCY DIRECTIONS**   When you move code through a system, it's always easier to move it in the dependency direction. If package A depends on package B, it's generally easier to move code from package A to package B than in the opposite direction. For moving code in the opposite direction, you need to use the tricks from the Dependency Inversion Principle to make sure the dependencies are going exclusively from the moving code to the code left in package B. This can be tedious work, and it almost always requires changing larger parts of the package structure.

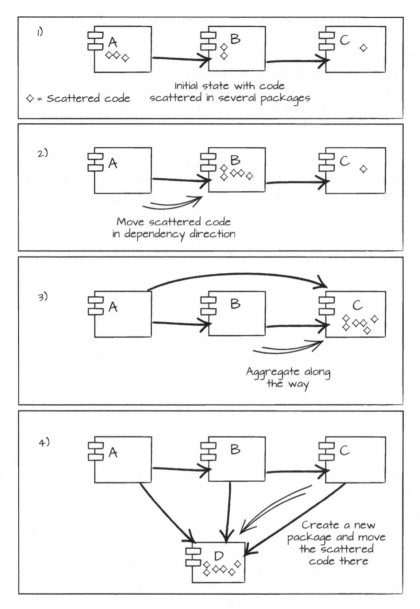

Figure 7.9   Move code gradually to a new package: 1) Initial state with code scattered in dependent packages. 2) Move the scattered code in the dependency direction to minimize problems. 3) Aggregate along the way; the A package acquired a dependency to C, in order to be able to use the scattered code there. 4) Create the destination package and gather the scattered code there; all packages depend on this new package because they all use the scattered code's functionality.

In this figure, the first step is the original situation, and each subsequent step moves scattered code along the dependency direction until it's all in one package. After that, it's possible to move the scattered code to a separate package altogether.

SCENARIO

This pattern has the least impact on existing code of all the scattered-code patterns, especially when you can move the code in the dependency direction. This pattern is also a little bit more stealthy than the previous patterns. Creating new packages communicates an intent, and this pattern can be a good option if you don't want to expose that intent at an early stage.

7.2.4 Create an API

SITUATION

You need to hide implementation details from the consumer of a package.

SOLUTION

Create an API by extracting interfaces and types wrapping the implementation details, and move the API code to a separate package.

SCENARIO

Breaking out functionality as described in the previous examples may make your code comply with cohesion principles or enable you to do what you want, but there might still be some work left to do. Maybe the extracted code contains too many classes or too much information for the consumer of that library. Maybe parts of the implementation shouldn't, or couldn't, be provided. Maybe the implementation of the package changes a lot, but the API of that package is rather stable. Maybe there are to be several implementations of that API.

> **API—APPLICATION PROGRAMMING INTERFACE** An API is part of a program that's exposed to the consumer of the program. It's the interface used to separate the *what* from the *how* of the program, and it's often a good complexity reducer. We prefer APIs that are self-explanatory, that guide the user toward correct usage, and that require no additional documentation to be used correctly. Any error messages should clearly state the detailed cause of the problem and the measures required to correct the error.

In these cases, it might be a good idea to create an interface package for the API and an implementation package as an example or default implementation of the API. This works a bit like the Dependency Inversion Principle, but for packages. The consumers of the package create their program using the interface package, or use the default implementation, or provide an implementation of their own at runtime. By separating the *what* from the *how*, the packages adhere to the Stable Dependencies Principle and the Stable Abstractions Principle.

Use the Naive Approach to try moving out the implementation part to see where it breaks, and use that information in the Mikado Graph. Try to separate, or extract, the necessary interfaces and classes. When they're the only ones used directly, you can move the implementation part to a separate package. A typical Mikado Graph might look like figure 7.10.

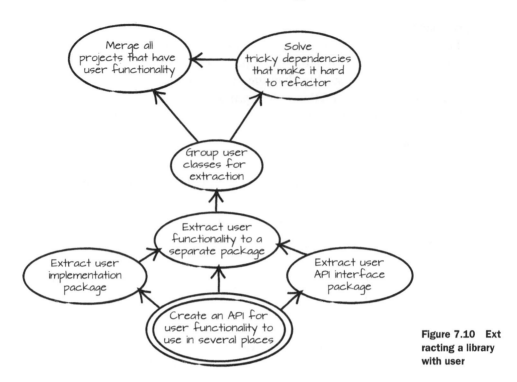

Figure 7.10 Ext racting a library with user

7.2.5   *Use a temporary shelter*

SITUATION

You have code for a concept—maybe single methods or even blocks of code—that's scattered across the codebase, and you can't decide in advance how to partition the code for the concept.

SOLUTION

Gather the pieces in a *temporary shelter*—a class, or possibly a module—where you can get an overview of what functionality you have for the concept. From there, it's often easier to get an overview, remove duplication, and see the patterns for repartitioning the code.

SCENARIO

One type of problematic code is duplication on the domain level. It usually manifests itself as related code scattered all over the codebase. The preceding examples relate to scattered classes, but sometimes code is scattered on a more fine-grained level, with methods here and there, or even blocks of code within methods. This scattered code is usually copy-paste parts, as in listing 7.1, or methods that do almost the same thing, as in listing 7.2.

Listing 7.1   Plain old copy-paste

```
...
public boolean isParent() {
    return isValid() && isActive();
```

```
}

public boolean canHaveSubComponent() {
    return isValid() && isActive();
}
...
```

Listing 7.2 Subtle domain-level duplication

```
class Customer {
    List accounts;
    ...
    public boolean isActive(Date date) {
        return accounts.size() > 0 &&
            !transactionsWithinPeriod(0, date).isEmpty();
    }
    public boolean canTerminateAllAccounts(Date today) {
        return !accounts.isEmpty() &&
            futureTransactions(today).size() == 0 ();
    }
    ...
}
```

The duplication in the copy-paste example is easy to spot. In the second example, it's much harder to spot. The `accounts.size() > 0` expression is actually the same as `!accounts.isEmpty()`. The `futureTransactions()` could be the same as `transactionsWithinPeriod()` because they sort of suggest that you're looking at transactions within a period. At some point, someone decided that the `isActive()` method and the `canTerminate-AllAccounts()` method should go down separate paths.

Instead of continuing down the same path or scattering code even more, try to find a couple of core ideas behind the scattered code. Examples of this can be `User` or `Payment`—something that fits the domain at hand. Choose an existing class or create a new one for these core areas—these classes will be *temporary shelters* for the functionality. Then try to move all related functionality to the temporary shelter. This might be ugly, but it's a stepping stone. Figure 7.11 shows what this might look like in a Mikado Graph.

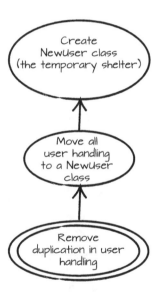

Figure 7.11 Move functionality to a temporary shelter before performing a change.

After a while, you're likely to see patterns of similar code in those rather ugly temporary shelters. At that point, it's time to remove the duplication by extracting common sections. Sometimes this is best done with a base class and variations in subclasses or in separate functions. Sometimes it's better to break out separate concerns to new classes and delegate to those classes. It's the old composition versus inheritance decision again.

With some effort, the previously scattered blocks of code can end up in a comprehensive and cohesive structure, and the temporary shelter is gone.

The Mikado Method in the real world

Even though it's desirable, sometimes it isn't feasible to reach a goal by taking small steps that can be committed to a versioning system continuously. It could be that other developers are working on the code, and your changes would result in merge conflicts that are very tedious and disruptive to resolve. It could also be that making half a change would introduce a pending state where there are two ways of doing things, which might be confusing at best and error-prone at worst.

We've used the Mikado Method in such situations. We practiced our refactoring over and over again until we felt confident that we could perform the change in the time slot available. This included heavy use of automated refactorings and refactoring scripts to speed up the process and relieve the drudgery of doing the same refactorings over and over again.

We particularly remember a time when we performed a large, single-step refactoring where the objective was to replace an old XML configuration with pure code. The XML glued together business logic and caused some serious problems for the developers. The XML had been a big concern for about five years, but no one had dared touch it.

The major reason for the change was to simplify code navigation and enable further refactorings, which was almost impossible due to the fact that the XML configuration was so intertwined with the code. Wherever we turned, the XML was buried deep in the code. To make matters worse, there were only a few tests in place, partly because the framework made it hard to test at a good level, and partly because of historical neglect. There was no time to cover the application in tests, so the change had to be made in a single step or development of the project would grind to a halt during the change. This was not an option at the time.

We created a Mikado Graph for the change and started the Mikado dance. Make a change, see what breaks, extend the graph, and revert. After almost every revert, we synced the code with the main repository so we were working with the latest version from the other developer.

Some of the prerequisites in the Mikado Graph were running scripts that generated code from existing XML. Other prerequisites were regular expression replacements that could be performed in the IDE. There were also the standard refactorings that the IDE usually provides, like move method, change method signature, and extract method.

Some of the prerequisites were leaves that could be checked in and marked as ready in the Mikado Graph, but most of the changes required replacing all the XML with code before they were complete. This could not be checked into the common code repository until it all worked and all XML files were replaced.

(continued)

To perform such a change without serious merge conflicts, it was necessary to have everyone check in their code. In this case, the development couldn't be halted because the majority of the team wasn't working with the XML replacement. The switch from XML configuration to the new solution needed to be performed one evening, and everyone had to check in the code before 5 p.m. that afternoon.

In the days before, we practiced and refined the Mikado Graph so we could perform the change as swiftly as possible. We probably rehearsed parts of the graph 20 or 30 times before it was time to actually perform the change.

At 5 p.m. the refactorings began, this time for real. Scripts were run, code was generated, and refactorings were performed across the codebase. At 7 p.m. we realized that we had, after all, missed a special case, and we had to revert the code and start over. After an additional couple of hours, and no further mishaps, we had performed the refactorings and all the XML code was gone. We verified the solution by running the few scenario test cases that existed, and then we checked the code into the VCS. At about 1 a.m. we could leave the building.

In spite of the size of this massive change, there were just a couple of minor problems reported over the next six months from the refactoring. This result would have been hard to achieve in such a short time in any other way.

7.3 Code tricks

When we've restructured code, we've used a few other tricks that have eased the burden. These tricks aren't quite patterns, but they're still useful in different situations.

7.3.1 Update all references to a field or method

When the need to change a field or a method implementation arises, you need to update all the references as well. For example, if you have a `private` field that's accessed directly in a class, but you want to move that field into a `Person` object instead, you can follow a fairly simple process:

1 Encapsulate the field.
2 Change the implementation within the encapsulation method.
3 Inline the contents of the encapsulation method.

This makes the whole refactoring safer. In code, it would look like this:

```
public class Employee {
    private String name;
    public Employee(String name) {
        this.name = name;
    }
    public String greet() {
        return "Hello "+name;
    }
}
```

First, you use the Introduce Indirection refactoring to encapsulate the member name, resulting in the following:

```
public class Employee {
    private String name;
    public Employee(String name) {
        this.name = name;
    }
    private String getName() {
        return name;
    }
    public String greet() {
        return "Hello "+getName();
    }
}
```

Then you change the one usage of name to use an introduced Person object instead:

```
public class Employee {
    private Person person;
    public Employee(String name) {
        this.person = new Person(name);
    }
    private String getName() {
        return person.getName();
    }
    public String greet() {
        return "Hello "+getName();
    }
}
```

After that, do the Inline Method refactoring on the Employee.getName() method:

```
public class Employee {
    private Person person;
    public Employee(String name) {
        this.person = new Person(name);
    }
    public String greet() {
        return "Hello "+person.getName();
    }
}
```

Granted, for this simple code, the process may seem wasteful, but often members and properties are used in several places in a class or across the codebase. In those cases, getting consistent help from automated refactorings can be crucial.

The same technique can be used when you need to change calls to a method. Use the Introduce Indirection refactoring on the original method to wrap it in a new method, and call the new method in all places the original method is used. Then change the implementation in the new wrapping method. After that, you can use the Inline Method refactoring as previously to introduce the change of the wrapping method in all places it's called from. Remember to make sure that any objects referenced in the new wrapping object are also available from the calling places. Use the

Naive Approach and inline the new wrapper immediately to see what objects are missing and where they're missing.

> **EXTRACT METHOD AND INLINE METHOD AUTOMATED REFACTORINGS** Extract Method is a powerful automated refactoring in IDEs for simplifying long methods or heavy duplicated code. But its counterpart, Inline Method, can be equally powerful when it comes to refactoring and restructuring code. If you don't use both, you're missing an important tool. Play around with them and see how creative you can be.

7.3.2 Freeze a partition

When you have external users, like developers in another project or customers that use an API you've created, you need to stay backwards compatible, and you can't change the code in whatever way you like. The users expect certain parts of the code to be stable. To avoid changes in those parts, you can *freeze* them.

The more code you change, the likelier it is that you'll accidentally change an API or some implementation that external developers depend on. People downstream of yourself who rely on the product of your work aren't as interested in your refactorings as you are. While automated refactoring is a powerful tool, sometimes it can affect too much of the code, changing parts that shouldn't change.

Sometimes, being aware of what can't change is enough, but sometimes a more structured approach is needed. When you need to be extra careful, you can move parts of the code into a special project or directory, and watch that area closely. That way you can quickly see if the frozen parts are changed when you check what files have changed before checking in.

Another useful strategy is to write reflective API tests that aren't affected by refactorings whose sole purpose is to verify signatures, classes, and interfaces that can't change. A variation on this approach is placing the API tests in a project that isn't affected by automated refactorings. This will also provide excellent documentation for anyone who uses the API regarding what parts will be more stable.

7.3.3 Develop a mimic replacement

Every now and then you need to introduce an indirection around an entire framework that's used in your application. The reason could be that you want to replace it, or that you want to be able to test without calling the actual framework, but the problem is that the framework is used almost everywhere in the codebase. This makes it very tedious and difficult to implement detailed changes in all the places where the framework is used. Instead of changing the users of the framework to fit the replacement, you can change the replacement to fit the users.

In this situation you can develop a *mimic replacement* of the framework you want to replace. This mimicking version won't have all the functionality of the framework. Only the functionality that's actually used in the application is implemented.

When the mimic is implemented, a switch is made from the old framework classes to the new mimic classes in one of two ways. You can give the mimic exactly the same class names and package names, or namespaces, as the old mimicked framework. Or you can give it the same class names except for the package name. When you switch, you change the import or usage statements, just linking in the new framework instead of the old. This way the framework can be replaced without changing any of the code that uses the framework. The mimicking version must, of course, also do the work that the framework did, possibly by relaying to a new framework or the old framework.

A variant of this is when you're pleased with the existing framework, but you need an interception point to be able to alter behavior for testing or to introduce alternative implementations. The mimic version can have the option of just forwarding to the old framework, almost in a one-to-one mapping, or of having mocked or stubbed responses.

7.3.4 *Replace configuration with code*

Basically, there are two types of things that end up in configuration files: configuration of behavior and configuration of environment. The former doesn't change after the code is built, and the latter must be editable before, during, and after the program is executed.

Many software developers, and others too, believe that applications should be extensively configurable from within the application or with configuration files, thus minimizing changes to source code. The reason usually offered is that it's better to have a flexible application. The real reason is more likely that no one knows how the software will be used, or no one dares make the decision. This usually leads to complex code and extensive configuration files that are sometimes equally complex.

These configuration files often stand in the way of navigating, understanding, and changing a codebase. They also add another layer of complexity when it comes to testing code and testing configuration options that aren't allowed. This tedious work adds little value, because most of the possible configurations are often left unused.

Because the type of flexibility that developers hope to achieve with behavioral configuration parameters rarely changes at runtime, you can either skip them entirely or build a separate product or distribution for those cases. In the following example of customer-specific code, creating a plugin architecture is probably better, and the plugins can be built and delivered as separate modules:

```
...
if (customerType == PAYING_CUSTOMER) {
    editor = "FullFledgedEditor";
}
...
```

If you have a lot of this type of configuration, you might make up time by generating the code from the configuration files and throwing the configuration files away. If you have too many variations, it's probably an indication that you can't handle the complexity you've created, and the solution needs simplification.

Configuration parameters that must vary in and around runtime are the parameters that actually need configuration files. When your environment forces you to use configuration files, make sure the intersection with them is as limited as possible. This will greatly simplify any immediate and future refactoring work.

7.4 Summary

In this chapter, you've seen a few patterns for avoiding cluttered graphs:

- Group common prerequisites in a grouping node
- Extract preparatory prerequisites
- Group a repeated set of prerequisites as a templated change
- Graph concurrent goals with common prerequisites together
- Split the graph
- Explore options

You've also learned a few patterns for changing code:

- Merge, reorganize, split
- Move code directly to a new package
- Move code gradually to a new package
- Create an API
- Use a temporary shelter

In addition, we showed you some code tricks and tactics that we've used for restructuring software. These are just a few patterns and tricks we've found useful, and there are certainly more to be discovered. We bet that the more you use the Mikado Method, the more recurring structures and patterns you'll find.

This is the end of the book, but it's not the end of your Mikado Method journey. One of the most important things to take away from this book is to try things and see what happens. We hope you'll try the Mikado Method and see where it takes you. There are still vast amounts to learn about it, and to learn about restructuring code. We hope to see your thoughts on the matter, and to learn from your experience. Sharing is caring. :-)

In case you don't want to put the book down and start restructuring that big ball of mud just yet, there are still three appendixes you can explore. The first is about technical debt and how to analyze where your problems come from. The second is about things you should think about before starting a Big Change. In the last appendix, we'll revisit the loan server, but this time in a dynamically typed language, to see how to get feedback when there's no compiler to lean on.

Try this

- If you've ever tried the Mikado Method, did you make any changes to the graph to suit your specific needs? What changes? Why?
- What did you think were the three most interesting patterns? Why?
- Can you think of any occasions when any of the patterns in this chapter would have been useful?
- Have you discovered any patterns of your own?

appendix A
Technical debt

This appendix covers
- Understanding technical debt
- Focusing on sustainable development and avoiding shortcuts
- Sources for redesigning and restructuring

Outside of the software world, you take out loans to finance different sorts of investments or expenses. You then have to pay back the principal (the money you borrowed) and interest (a time-based fee for borrowing the money). You take out loans both privately and in business-related situations.

The basic idea behind taking out a loan is to delay the payment for a purchase, from a time when you don't have the purchasing power to a time when you do. Sometimes this means you pay back a little at a time over a longer period, perhaps over decades for expensive things such as a house. Sometimes it means you pay back everything in one lump sum quickly, within a week or sooner. Now, what has this got to do with software development?

Imagine the following scenario: The product owner of the site you're developing comes in shouting, "We need to add social media integration to our customer support flow! And we need it by next week! We have a potential Top 100 customer we must impress!" This is the break you've been waiting for. Everybody on the team drops what they're doing and starts hacking away at adding the new feature.

No one cares that the code isn't designed for adding social media integration, and that there aren't any abstractions that support it. With grease and pure force, the new functionality is implemented using a global flag and `if` statements like `if(flag=="SocialMedia")` ... across the codebase, among other code good-practice violations. Everyone knows that this will take a lot of time to clean up later, but before that happens there are other important things that will suffer from this code frenzy.

Good practice or best practice?

Often in business you'll find people using the term "best practice" for a way of doing something—for a process or a method. In our opinion, that term is misleading in several ways:

- It implies that if you follow the best practice you're all good. But the reality is that if you do the *wrong* thing in the *right* best-practice way, it's still the wrong thing to do. For example, you could take code that isn't used and cover it with tests and refactor it, instead of just throwing it away.
- Which practice is "best" is so highly context-dependent that there's no universal solution that deserves being called "best practice."
- It implies that there's no better way to do something, no room for improvement. In a complex field such as software development, there's usually a better or equally good practice, and there's always room for improvement.

For these reasons, we use the term "good practice" to express that we find something beneficial, but likely with room for improvement or with alternative ways to get the same, or a better, result. The Mikado Method is a good practice for restructuring legacy code.

By behaving this way, you have, metaphorically speaking, put yourself in debt—*technical debt*. You now have to spend a little extra time to understand what the code does, and you have to put some extra effort into making changes. This *extra time* is equivalent to *interest*. The *principal* of the loan is the time it will take to get the codebase back into shape again. This is why these types of problems in code are often called "technical debt." The phrase *technical debt* was originally introduced by Ward Cunningham in the experience report "The WyCash Portfolio Management System" at OOPSLA '92 (http://c2.com/doc/oopsla92.html).

So far, you've learned how the Mikado Method can get you out of a big mess and, in other words, repay your technical debt. Now it's time to learn how to spot the early warning signals and see where the technical debt traps are.

But as in real life, not all debt is bad. You'll learn what type of debt you must take on, or should take on, in order to hit the market window or seize an opportunity. You'll also learn to see the big picture—that some technical debt doesn't originate from the technical team, but from the business side, or even from outside of the company.

A.1 How you get into debt

Like debt in the real world, the reason for taking on technical debt is to cut yourself some slack now, such as to get the social media integration working for the important client. The cost is having to clean up afterward, and living with the mess you've created until you've cleaned up.

> ### Definition of technical debt
>
> *Technical debt* is any existing technical structure that prevents you from effectively and efficiently making relevant and necessary changes to your software. The *interest* on the debt is the extra time you spend to deal with that structure. The *principal* is the structure itself. When repaying, the *payment* is the time it takes to refactor the structure.

As a metaphor, debt is quite easy to understand, but it has a bad connotation relating to loss of freedom, and of owing something to someone. While debt is debt, regardless of where it originates, understanding where the code problems come from can help you mitigate the root cause, or realize that the cause was a good investment, or perhaps just let you come to peace with the stressful situation of having to deal with it.

There are several ways to categorize debt builders. Table A.1 and the following sections categorize debt builders as acceptable, unavoidable, unnecessary, and bad. These are ways of looking at technical debt from a utility perspective. Note that it's the debt *builders* we're talking about, the cause of the debt, and not the resulting code. In some cases, a specific builder may produce certain types of problems, but in general the problems created can be of any kind. Table A.1 lists different categories of technical debt builders. The different builders will be explained in detail in the following sections.

Table A.1 Categories of technical debt builders

Category	Characteristics	Examples
Acceptable	Short-term loss for long-term gain	■ Making a trade-off to hit a market window ■ Waiting for the right abstraction ■ Reflection and learning about your domain or technology ■ Receiving new requirements that render the current solution insufficient

Table A.1 Categories of technical debt builders (*continued*)

Category	Characteristics	Examples
Unavoidable	Caused by uncontrollable events	▪ Working on the edge of chaos ▪ Inherited debt ▪ Staff turnover ▪ Complying with new regulations ▪ Changes in demand
Unnecessary	Good intentions produce bad outcome	▪ Working under stress ▪ Having insufficient knowledge ▪ Making premature optimizations ▪ Adhering to the not-invented-here syndrome ▪ Adhering to the proudly-found-elsewhere syndrome ▪ Creating vendor lock-in or framework leakage ▪ Writing one-way code ▪ Writing too-clever code ▪ Suffering from technical policies
Bad	Totally without benefit	▪ Lack of communication ▪ Unprofessionalism ▪ Habitual corner-cutting ▪ Creating excuses for writing bad code—the broken window syndrome ▪ Lack of respect ▪ Unresolved disagreements

A.1.1   *Acceptable debt builders*

Acceptable debt is when you take on debt as an investment to enable a gain of some sort, in the short or long term, that has a greater value than the cost of the debt. It would be better, of course, to get the gain without getting into debt at all, but in the context of debt, this is the good kind.

MAKING A TRADE-OFF TO HIT A MARKET WINDOW

This category of technical debt builder is where you have a known conflict between creating the most apt technical structure and meeting a delivery deadline. If there are considerable financial or market-position gains to be made from meeting the deadline, the cost of having to deal with a less appropriate implementation might be worth it.

Adding social media integration in the example earlier is a good example of this type of debt. Debt can be accepted to meet a deadline, but the debt is best repaid immediately after the deadline. Alternatively, you accept paying interest on that piece of code for a longer period of time before you pay back the loan by refactoring. If deadlines are constantly stacked up and there's never any time to repay accepted debt, this isn't an investment anymore—it has turned into credit-financed interest payments. This is generally a bad idea. It will keep you floating for a while, but sooner, rather than later, the debt will accumulate and you'll risk spending most of your time paying interest, and very little time creating and delivering new features. In some businesses, not being able to deliver new features means closing up shop, and for most companies it means getting a decreased return on invested capital.

Given a reasonably well-structured codebase, a rushed delivery often forces you to violate the abstractions in the code. When the new information, encoded in the mess, is to be placed in proper abstractions, substantial rearrangements are often needed, and such changes are well suited to the Mikado Method.

WAITING FOR THE RIGHT ABSTRACTION

Reducing debt often boils down to finding the right abstraction for your application. In some cases, the abstractions are obvious from the domain. At other times, you'll need to try a few variations on your implementation to see where you can abstract and generalize it. You might have to put up with some temporary debt as you look for a good abstraction.

We once worked on a system with an object data structure that was programmatically navigated for aggregation, validation, transformation, and presentation with several different traversal implementations across the codebase. After a while, we realized that the underlying structure was a composite pattern, and the traversal could be implemented with a visitor pattern. After implementing that, with a great deal of help from the Mikado Method, the logic that previously was duplicated across the codebase was implemented in a single place. There were also a lot of conditionals for the traversals that were only interested in objects of certain types, or with certain attributes, so we added a filter pattern. This allowed us to remove all those conditionals and place each type of conditional in its own reusable class. By finding those abstractions, we were able to replace pages of code with one or a few lines. As time went on, we found more and more things we could implement with those abstractions, simplifying the codebase and removing technical debt even further. Realizing what we were looking for took us a while, and we couldn't have been rushed into this epiphany.

> **COMPOSITE AND VISITOR PATTERNS** The composite and visitor patterns are described in *Design Patterns: Elements of Reusable Object-Oriented Software* by Erich Gamma et al. (Addison-Wesley Professional, 1994). The composite pattern is a way of creating an object structure, usually a tree, of related but heterogeneous objects without requiring the objects to know exactly what other objects are in the structure. The visitor pattern is an abstraction of how to traverse such a heterogeneous structure.

As in this example, you might have to incur some temporary debt while waiting for the epiphany of a good abstraction. Sometimes waiting is a conscious choice, and sometimes you wait because you have no choice. In either case, this is usually a good thing, because jumping to conclusions can cause an even worse situation with overly complex structures. This process can't be forced, but it's essential to software development, so it's most definitely acceptable.

REFLECTION AND LEARNING

Many developers have a different idea about how they should have implemented their solution after they've completed it. They did the best they could at the time, but the more they learn about the domain and the system, the more ideas they have about how their system could be even better.

Developers learn things from discussions with colleagues, from reading on the internet, and from attending sessions at conferences. With the incredible amount of knowledge available, a single person or team just can't know everything, or even know how to apply the things they already know about in the best possible way. The things you learn can be minor details, or they could suggest a major, Mikado Method–sized overhaul of the application. Learning is an integral part of software development, and when you learn something and realize that your solution wasn't up to par, this is totally acceptable.

Learning is essential. It implies that you reflect on your work and your solutions. You discuss your problems and solutions with others, and every now and then you get a pointer to something you didn't know before. With this knowledge, and sometimes using the Mikado Method, you can morph the system into a new and better shape.

NEW REQUIREMENTS FROM STAKEHOLDERS

In order to keep up with competition, extend an advantage in the market, or accommodate new sales, your company stakeholders will update their vision and goals for the product you're developing, resulting in new requirements. If you're unlucky, you could end up in a debt situation, where the previous solution worked just fine, but the new requirements invalidate the previous designs and architecture. Until that moment, the application was fit for its purpose, but from that point on, adding more features in the old way just adds to the trouble.

Ola once worked with a start-up online bank that decided to add another type of account to their offerings. What before was a codebase rather fit for its purpose immediately felt a bit more cumbersome and unwieldy. By changing the current abstractions to accommodate the new account type, he once again streamlined the application for what it was supposed to do.

This debt builder usually comes from learning at the business level, where the product you're developing gets better, so it's an acceptable debt builder.

A.1.2   *Unavoidable debt builders*

Some things in life just can't be avoided, and especially not in real-time business situations. Unavoidable debt builders are those that are just a normal part of developer life.

WORKING ON THE EDGE OF CHAOS

Software development involves constantly making decisions about which path to choose. Generally, the less chaotic the environment, and the more informed the decision-maker, the less risk there is of making bad decisions. Unfortunately, software development is a relatively chaotic field and the problems are ill-posed, at best. This makes it very hard to create the solutions that you, in hindsight, will consider the best, or even good. The debt that comes from this chaos is far from optimal, but you can't slow the world down, or simplify it, as you please.

If you've ever been working hard, but with that uneasy feeling that your solution might not be exactly right, or that it is right but you're not sure how it should work, and no one has the time to explain, that feeling might be a sign of a chaotic situation. Our best suggestion for avoiding or mitigating trouble is to be transparent about what you do and why, to expose problems early, to reflect upon them, to get feedback on them, and to take action without unnecessary delay. Symptoms often get harder to see the longer you're exposed to them. Take a step back for a moment and look at the situation—how you got where you are today—and maybe you'll see things you're currently unaware of.

INHERITED DEBT

Often, you'll get to handle troubled legacy code written by others—inherited debt. This isn't a delight, but it's something you have to deal with as a software developer. If the people involved in creating the inherited version are still around, you can talk to them to get a hint of why things are the way they are. The reasons may still be valid, and knowing what they are may help you avoid ending up in the same situation again.

On the other hand, the reasons may not be valid anymore. Once, Ola was asked to take over a system where the original developers were about to quit. The system was written using an object-relational mapping framework, and the performance degraded horrifically as the amount of data grew, partly because of the framework itself, and partly because of the objects created by it. Using this framework was the easy path functionality-wise, but only for the initial load. It took about a year and the assistance of a colleague to start getting the functionality performant, slowly removing the old structures piece by piece, making extensive use of the Mikado Method.

STAFF TURNOVER

Figure A.1 Staff turnover

Whenever you visit code for the first time, you can feel awkward. You're not 100% sure what it does, or how to implement things. It always take some time to get up to speed on a codebase. The same thing happens when you replace members on a team. The departing people take some unique knowledge with them, and the new people, especially when under deadline pressure, might add things in ways that add to your problems.

If you've ever come in as a replacement for someone on a team, you know the hopes everyone has for you, and you've probably felt like you were letting people down when your solutions haven't matched their expectations for that environment. It takes some time to get up to speed, and in the meantime debt might be created. When you're new to a codebase, take some time to experiment with the code and document your findings with the Mikado Method. If you can pair with someone who's familiar with the codebase, or just discuss your findings with others, you can get on a fast track to knowing how the application is stitched together. You can also teach others about the Mikado Method and possibly create even more mutual benefit.

Staff turnover is unavoidable, and it isn't bad *per se*. In the short term, there might be a dent in productivity when you're getting someone up to speed, but in the long term, the added knowledge and perspective often improves speed and structure in a solution. It could be viewed as *learning*, but the reason for this learning is that knowledge was lost when the previous team member left, so it's placed in the *unavoidable* category.

NEW EXTERNAL REGULATIONS

Changed regulations or laws can sometimes require significant changes to the architecture and implementation of a product. This is a sort of technical debt that's not caused mainly by the development team, but by forces outside of the team, and even outside of the company.

When the European market opened up for online gaming, such as poker, governments all over Europe required that every transaction be approved by a central national authority. The companies that wanted to compete in those markets had to adapt their implementations to those rules.

These kinds of changes are hard to predict. When you know you're working in a market that's heavily regulated, you can only prepare for it—you can't anticipate it. By automating the building, packaging, documenting, and verifying of your product as much as possible, you're best prepared for whatever changes come along.

New regulations can have a significant impact on your system, requiring large changes. With regulatory compliance as the Mikado Goal, and a clear graph, there should be little argument over any changes tied to that goal.

CHANGES IN DEMAND

The market, or the customers, do change their minds from time to time. Things come in and go out of fashion, and new technologies make existing products obsolete. There's usually little you can do about it but try to adapt. Sometimes the associated changes are just a cost, but sometimes they could harness possibilities. Change isn't always bad.

For example, Flickr, one of the largest online photo-sharing sites, started out as a photo upload tool in the massively multiplayer online Game Neverending. The tool proved to be much more popular than the game, and it was extracted to a chat room with real-time photos. The chat room was also later discontinued, in favor of the current website for uploading and storing photos. The game, like the chat room, was discontinued as the photo service was refined. During those discontinuation transitions, the amount of technical debt—code that was in the way—in their codebases should have been substantial.

A.1.3 *Unnecessary debt builders*

Some debt originates from the excessive ambition of developers or management, from lack of experience, or from systemic problems. These are unnecessary debt builders, but because there's a positive and ambitious undertone in the activities that caused the debt, we don't place them in the bad-debt category.

STRESS

Figure A.2 A situation of stress

Stress makes you less aware of the current situation, leading to tunnel vision where decisions are often based on an unusually incomplete or distorted set of data. Those decisions tend to create solutions that aren't optimal. You can be pretty sure that in the social media integration example, the extra stress will cause additional debt to be created, beyond that created by consciously cutting corners.

All people have different thresholds when it comes to stress; at low levels of stress, humans tend to produce slightly better results, but high levels invite you to take shortcuts and make unnecessarily short-sighted solutions, adding to the problems that already exist in the solution. Sometimes you're aware of the stress, but other times stress creeps up on you. Excessive stress, frequent or extended, is often a systemic problem and can only be solved by making changes to the system. Are the developers in the team pushed to meet deadlines beyond reasonable expectations? Are the teams not permitted sufficient control over their workload? The underlying systemic problems must be dealt with.

Stress comes from caring about the outcome of the situation, and caring is a good thing that should be nourished. Indifference or apathy would be much worse. Management is always responsible for creating a healthy environment, and the excellent book *Behind Closed Doors* by Johanna Rothman and Esther Derby (Pragmatic Bookshelf, 2005) gives great insight into how to become a better manager. But the problems can't be blamed exclusively on the system or the managers; all people involved have a personal responsibility to warn their managers and colleagues when working conditions are so unhealthy that they cause bad code.

INSUFFICIENT KNOWLEDGE

Figure A.3   Insufficie nt knowledge

When you lack tool or programming-language knowledge, you risk creating an implementation that's unnecessarily bulky, or that does the right thing but in an awkward way, thereby adding to the technical debt. In addition, if you have no understanding or a poor understanding of the business and the domain you're working in, you're likely to build up debt. Just as a lack of technical knowledge can contribute to bad constructs, insufficient domain knowledge can lead to similar problems because you're missing important pieces of information. This is also true if the person specifying what to do lacks knowledge of the domain.

The lack of correct information can lead to problems ranging from minor defects to using incorrect assumptions as the basis for important parts of a product. The cost of fixing this at a later stage might be high. Try to verify your assumptions with real code, real tests, and real users as early as possible. Try to get together with the business side, or the customers, to learn how they talk about and interact with the domain. If you find that things have gone horribly wrong with your implementation, the Mikado

Method may help you out of that, but it's not a replacement for communicating with the people involved.

PREMATURE OPTIMIZATION

Making optimizations before you've tested your application with real data often leads to an overly complex design that rarely targets the right bottleneck, and that needless complexity is just added technical debt. In a complex system, it's virtually impossible to foresee where the bottleneck will be, or even to predict where the next bottleneck will be if you've already identified your current bottleneck.

We've seen several incomprehensible pieces of code that were the result of premature optimizations, sometimes in parts of the code that had neither performance nor load requirements. It was optimized only because "code should be fast." Untangling that code can be a challenge, and in ugly cases you might find the Mikado Method helpful.

Structure your applications well, write the clearest code you can, and then optimize when you must, based on real usage, or preferably on crafted load and performance tests (based on expected or real usage). Good structure often leads to good performance as well. If you have extreme performance or load requirements, you'll need to consider performance at an early stage in your architecture, but even in those cases, the majority of the application won't be on the critical path of performance and your focus should be on clarity.

NOT INVENTED HERE

Figure A.4   Not invented here

The not-invented-here syndrome manifests itself as an unwillingness to use existing software components, frameworks, products, or knowledge. Time and energy is spent on writing proprietary code for components that are commonly available, instead of focusing on the core business. Because the component isn't part of the core business, its maintenance is likely to suffer, sooner or later making it a debt rather than an asset.

When you find a local implementation that can be replaced with an external library, it's often easiest to encapsulate the functionality behind local interfaces, and then replace the implementation with the external library. This is almost exactly what you saw in section 2.2, where we encapsulated the database calls. As in that example, the Mikado Method is often useful when the implications are many, or when they go deep into the codebase.

PROUDLY FOUND ELSEWHERE

The opposite of *not invented here* is *proudly found elsewhere*. This leads to a *framework frenzy*, where no piece of code can be developed; the focus is always on analyzing and choosing an existing library or component that contains the feature. Developing a system becomes a *scrapheap challenge*, where the system is built by fitting together different libraries that do what's needed and a million things more. Navigating and improving such a system is often difficult because the libraries are entangled with the system, and just penetrating such a system means wading through unnecessary complexity.

The decision to introduce an existing library must be balanced not only against the cost of developing your own code for that functionality, but also against the cost of decreased control and increased complexity. In the book *Domain-Driven Design: Tackling Complexity in the Heart of Software* (Addison Wesley Professional, 2004), Eric Evans discusses strategic domain-driven design: when is an existing library more effective, and when should you consider developing your own? It comes down to the strategic mission statement for the product or service and following the consequences of that statement; if the code is what creates your competitive edge, according to the statement, you should develop it yourself, even if there's software available that does the job. If not, you can use a standard library. The important thing is that you *must* be able to adapt and change the strategic parts of your software to keep your edge.

Replacing frameworks can also be a tough job, requiring the Mikado Method. The process is similar to when you replace a local implementation with a library, but the purpose is the opposite. Take the code that does the job and encapsulate it with interfaces, and then make your own implementation of those interfaces.

VENDOR LOCK-IN OR FRAMEWORK LEAKAGE

When you use a framework and let that framework leak into most corners of your codebase, you're suddenly in a *vendor lock-in* situation. You've let the third-party library take over your application instead of using the library to solve a problem.

If you want to use a third-party library, the abstractions should come from your domain, and then you should implement those abstractions to encapsulate the library. That way, you don't let the library dictate your implementation. The library merely becomes a tool to help solve a specific problem, and it'll be much easier to replace if necessary. If your framework has already leaked, use *not invented here* or *proudly found elsewhere* to contain the problem.

Some vendor lock-ins can be acceptable, such as choosing a platform for development. But care should be taken so that, for instance, licensing for the platform doesn't limit the development, testing, or deployment of the solution.

ONE-WAY CODE

One-way code is when a codebase is unnecessarily restrained so that you can only do things one way. Where abstractions are used, they're used to limit the freedom of an implementation rather than create options. Performing any task, however simple it may be, might involve making changes to the entire codebase. If a customer asks for a new feature, it may not be feasible to implement it within the existing architecture. This is *not* a template situation for being productive in creating good software.

> ### Ola and Daniel remember
>
> We were once in a situation where dynamic, context-dependent menus were considered for an application, but the existing framework for the menus didn't support that, so the team had to change the framework to allow for more dynamic handling. As they did that, they realized that the initialization of the menus was tangled up in the initialization of the application, so the initialization of the application had to change as well. But that could only be done if a lot of global variables and singletons were removed first. Those global variables were in turn used throughout the application, so the team had to refactor all the code where these globals were used. This, of course, took quite a while longer than the initial estimate indicated it would.

One-way code is riddled with limitations. Either the author deliberately restrains the flexibility without having a business case for that, or it happens as a result of the programming style of the author. In either case, if these restrictions aren't part of the business case, and they rarely are, this puts unnecessary limitations on future development.

The opposite of limitations is *options*. Good code has abstractions that put the fewest possible restrictions on future development, in order to preserve options. This is *not* the same thing as making something "future-safe" by implementing code for all future scenarios that can be imagined. This is putting as few constraints as possible on the code to minimize the risk of having to change it when adding more code.

To resolve such limiting code, you'll often need to deal with a lot of dependencies. This is a situation where the Mikado Method can help to get you on the right track.

TOO-CLEVER CODE

Too-clever code is code where the author has used all available tricks known, creating a solution that's way more complex than the problem solved.

> ### Ola remembers
>
> Ola was once involved in a project where he and his pair-programming partner came up with a really clever solution. They used built-in abilities in the programming language and managed to create a very flexible solution. The code parsed an XML file and objects were created from the XML structure, depending on what elements it contained. The code was compact and highly efficient, but it lacked something. Two weeks after the code was deployed, a bug appeared. Two other team members looked at the code and were blown away. Not by its cleverness, but because they had such a hard time understanding the code. They just handed the code over to its originators, saying "We don't know what to do. You guys will have to fix this yourselves!"

One would think that a clever solution would be preferable. After all, "clever" has a positive connotation. But programmers would take a clear, easy-to-read, and understandable solution over a clever one any day. As a rule of thumb, *one point of clarity is worth more than one hundred points of cleverness.* Sometimes, this rule is in conflict with keeping the code free of duplication. When that happens, clarity is more important than removing all duplication.

The computer is just as good at executing clear code as clever code, and sometimes even better. The Java Virtual Machine (JVM) is a good example of this. The JVM has built-in optimizations for about 200 common programming patterns. Clever code can throw it off and might even result in *worse* performance because it can't find an optimization for the code.

To deal with clever code, change the program piece by piece by making sure the intentions of every piece of code are clear. This is like unrolling the implementation. You might have to use the Mikado Method when doing this, but more often it involves working on a smaller scale, method by method or class by class.

TECHNICAL POLICIES

Many organizations and corporations have technical policies that state what products are allowed to be used. Often the idea behind this is to simplify the work for IT operations, in an attempt to limit the number of technologies they have to handle.

In the eyes of the operations manager, this seems a rational decision. But different tools are good for different tasks, and using the wrong tool will force developers to create technical debt in the shape of workarounds. This means that interest has to be paid throughout the lifetime of the product. If you're trying to provide the best value for the money, or to compete with the best in the market, this could be crippling, or even fatal, for the business. Sometimes it will work just fine, and the products implied by the policy might be sufficient, but in other cases this will incur a debt that will take a toll on the profitability of the product.

In any competitive market, technical decisions should be made based on the product and its usage. Any technical policy should be a preference rather than a dictate. If the technical policies are lifted, the Mikado Method can help when migrating to using more appropriate tools.

A.1.4   *Bad debt builders*

Some debt is bad in the sense that it comes from a lack of respect for customers, coworkers, managers, employees, or shared resources. When you see these types of debt builders, you can be fairly sure that the problems go deeper than just the technical parts of the application.

LACK OF COMMUNICATION

When different parts of an organization isolate themselves or excessively formalize their communication, other parts of the organization build structures or behaviors around that. Instead of people just talking to each other, you get not one, but *two* unnecessary filters between the people who are trying to communicate. This leads to distrust, disrespect, an us-versus-them mentality, and a poor flow of information. This, in turn, leads to the different parts of the organization trying to solve problems in isolation, creating multiple structures for the same purpose within the organization, often including technical solutions. That leads to technical debt situations.

UNPROFESSIONALISM

Technical debt isn't an excuse for letting your system or development environment decay into a mess. You should always do the best you can, and apply good development practices such as using just-in-time design, incorporating test-driven development or the like, writing clean code, taking care of the continuous integration environment, and so on. To dismiss this responsibility for a system is just plain unprofessional.

HABITUAL CORNER-CUTTING

It's common to be asked for estimates and then face pressure to reduce them in the hope that this will result in work being done more quickly.

> Manager: *How long do you think this task will take?*
> Programmer: *Well, I looked into it, and I'd say four days.*
> Manager: *Four days?!!*
> Programmer: *Yeah, this new editor that we're creating looks a lot like two others...*
> Manager: *So...*
> Programmer: *...so I was thinking we might pull out the similarities in a base editor...*
> Manager: *Isn't there a faster way?*
> Programmer: *I guess we could finish one, then just copy that and do some small changes...*

To be done sooner, do less instead.

When you cut corners, you start on a downward spiral that steadily adds to the needless complexity of the application. It's very easy to end up in a situation where you compensate for previously cut corners by cutting new corners, adding complexity upon complexity. This is like taking credit to pay the interest on your loans. If you don't start improving the code, but keep cutting more corners, you'll get deeper and deeper in debt with every change you make.

BREAKING WINDOWS

In criminology, there's a phenomenon often referred to as the *broken window syndrome*, first presented in 1982 in an *Atlantic* article by James Q. Wilson and George L. Kelling called "Broken Windows" (http://mng.bz/Cw7O). The title comes from studies of houses left unattended. When a well-cared-for house is abandoned, it can stay untouched for a long time, perhaps even years. But if someone breaks a window in the house, it isn't long before the house is completely vandalized. The phenomenon is manifested in our unwillingness to break or stain something nice, but when the first scratch on the surface is made, the rest will soon be ruined. This principle holds true with code: deterioration often starts with one small thing, like a broken window.

Similarly, working on code that's already messy can be demoralizing, and it's easy to just wreck some more of the code, creating more technical debt.

Creating trouble-free code in that situation is very cumbersome. The easiest way is to fix the codebase by fixing one piece at a time, and then to not break them again.

LACK OF RESPECT

Sometimes a team member knows what's expected, and is capable of complying with those expectations, but they still play by private rules. This can mean anything from checking in code that doesn't compile to refusing to share knowledge with other developers. It's a way of saying, "I'm more important that you," and that kind of behavior is bad for a software development team for several reasons.

First, it will make the current state and the expectations more unclear. This, in turn, will have an impact on the code. It increases the risk of having different rules for different parts of the codebase, adding to your problems. Developers risk becoming more keen to take ownership of certain parts of the code and to build protection against the other parts, causing technical debt to grow.

UNRESOLVED DISAGREEMENTS

When there are unresolved disagreements, such as about how to implement certain things, there's a great risk that you'll start building technical debt. If a team can't settle on an implementation, the application is likely to have two or more ways to implement a feature. It may be that all the suggested ways are perfectly valid, and that the difference is a matter of taste. But even then, having to learn and navigate several different implementation styles takes a serious toll on the development effort.

Try to resolve any disagreements early. If the situation becomes difficult to manage, bringing in an outside facilitator for that particular task is probably worth the cost. As a last resort, consider making changes to the team if important problems aren't resolved.

A.2   *More about technical debt*

We often use the metaphor of *technical debt* when we talk to non-technical people and try to explain how bad code affects progress and profitability, especially when we communicate with people who work with management, economy, and financing rather than technology. Often, they're unaware of the consequences of an ill-structured codebase, but they're very familiar with the do's and don'ts of debts. In general, they're terrified by the fact that they were put in debt without even knowing it, grateful for the new insights, and they slowly become frustrated when they realize they have to pay it back.

A.2.1   *Lactic acid*

Debt isn't inherently bad, but if it isn't handled properly, it'll eventually introduce more problems than you bargained for. To illustrate this, let's look at software development through our sports glasses for a moment.

There are situations where a short sprint can win the race. In a bike race, riders use this strategy to gain advantage over their competitors. A perfectly timed spurt at the very end of the race, or a sprint during a critical part of the race, can literally leave the competition behind.

The price of this strategy is an increased load on the system. If the racer doesn't get a breather shortly thereafter, the lactic acid produced during the sprint will trigger the opposite effect and slow the rider down. If they go for too long without clearing the acid, they might even hit the wall and collapse.

Deliberately using bad structures or cutting corners can give you a temporary advantage over the competition. It can be viewed as the equivalent of sprinting, which will result in the equivalent of lactic acid—technical debt. Used properly, this approach can truly be a performance booster, but using it as a regular strategy will bring you to your knees.

The body has a natural process for ridding the system of lactic acid, but software doesn't. If you want to keep your product in a healthy state, you need to take into account the time it will take you to rid the codebase of the accumulated debt.

A.2.2 *What is the interest?*

Different debts have different levels of interest. To illustrate this, consider Kenny, an ordinary guy with a weakness for betting. Kenny has several loans: one on his house and one for his new car, and he also borrowed some money from a relative. On top of this, he has a gambling debt to a mob-associated loan shark. Not a very nice guy. If Kenny comes across some money, where should he start to pay it back?

In this case, it might look rather easy. Paying back the loan shark is likely to be a higher priority because those kinds of loans come with very high interest, along with very persuasive methods for getting repayments.

Technical debt in software projects comes in different shapes and with different interest rates, but the interest depends on what you set out to do, not what type of debt you have. In fact, a single type of debt might have different interest rates at different times. It can be zero interest if it's in a part of the code you hardly ever touch, or "mob interest" if it stands in the way of delivering important features.

When you spend time paying back debt by randomly refactoring code, you might be prioritizing repaying the loan to mom and dad before the loan to the mob. But in software development, the difference between the types of debt is much more subtle. In order to identify your mob debts, you need a way to find them. The Mikado Method can help you sort out the critical paths in your change effort to find your mob debts.

> **ZERO-INTEREST TECHNICAL DEBT** If you don't need to touch or read a part of a system that's part of the debt, you don't need to pay any interest. It's likely unwise to repay that debt, because there are usually more urgent needs in other parts of the system. Focus on the important parts, and the parts that you change frequently.

From a debt point of view, it doesn't matter how you got into debt. You still have to pay the interest every time you come across that part of the system. If you ever want the interest payments to go away, you need to repay the principal. *Debt is debt, no matter the cause,* but to avoid getting into debt again and again, it's important to know where it came from and avoid the creation of debt altogether.

A.3   *Influence and type*

Technical debt doesn't only come from technical work. It also comes from the surrounding organization, from the integration of supplied APIs, and from the greater society we live in. Another way to look at technical debt is to assess it in terms of its *influence* and *type.*

Influence is the extent to which your organization has control or influence over the process. Was the debt externally imposed (out of your control) or internally incurred (created by your organization)?

The second dimension, *type,* indicates to what extent the debt is related to technical details or has more of a market focus. Is the debt related to technical and operational decisions, or is it the result of a change in laws and markets, visions, or business models?

Figure A.5 shows these factors in a matrix. The matrix consists of four categories. Let's look at them a bit closer, starting with the upper-left corner.

Figure A.5   Influence and type quadrant

A.3.1 Third party—technical and imposed

Technical and imposed debt is related to technical changes outside of your control. An example is when BigCorporation buys SmallCo, your database vendor, just to discontinue the product. You have no influence over that decision, but you have to deal with the consequences by either changing your implementation or by living with the fact that you no longer get any support.

Debt from this quadrant can be very expensive to pay off, depending on how your system is structured. But still, it must be done if you don't want to throw your solution away and start afresh, and starting afresh is often is a bad decision.

We were once developing a product in which a map engine was integrated. Unfortunately, there was a bug in the map engine, and the bug fix was only available in the latest major version, in which the APIs had changed significantly. Because the old API had leaked into the application in several places, we had quite a lot of work to refactor those parts of the code. We had put ourselves in a bad situation and ended up in a vendor lock-in or framework leakage situation (see section A.1.3).

If an application is built up by calls to different frameworks, as described in section A.1.3, the risk of getting into trouble increases. The risk of running into problems with discontinuations or other major changes should be balanced with the gains of introducing a framework.

A.3.2 Bigwig—market and imposed

In this quadrant, the rules or regulations have changed and there's not much you can do about it. You either comply or your product is unusable, or in the worst case, illegal.

Things keep changing, and you'd better get used to it. New laws are created, which could mean that an application that was really fit for its purpose yesterday may have to change a lot today in order to comply. The market can also change, and customers may change their behavior. You can try to change the course of events, but unless you work in a very large organization, you'll probably not be able to influence the decision.

In the northern parts of Europe, especially Scandinavia, young adults are less and less likely to get a phone number tied to a physical address (a number for their house or apartment). They grow up with a mobile phone and stick with that. This slight change in behavior isn't something a service provider can control or predict. But consider how this change is imposed on companies. A simple registration form that worked perfectly well a couple of years ago might now need attention because the phone number validation has changed or the mobile number that once was optional is now considered the most important one.

More examples of debt builders that relate to this category are new external regulations and changes in demand (section A.1.2).

A.3.3 The boardroom—market and incurred

Software developers often experience the effects of management making quick decisions and swift changes in order to keep up with competitors. The challenge is to keep up with and embrace the changes.

Some business decisions can have a bigger impact than initially expected, such as corporate policies. These decisions (or rather, the lack of options) often steer you toward early limitations in projects, sometimes even before the projects have started. For example, *"We must use BigRelationalDatabase, it's a corporate policy."* BigRelationalDatabase might be a really good relational database, but when the project needs to store big chunks of loosely structured data in a massively distributed system, it might not cut the mustard. By forcing technology onto a project, a debt is created that will diminish the returns, or even push the project over the edge.

Examples of debt builders that relate to this category are making a trade-off to hit a market window (section A.1.1), technical policies (section A.1.3), and new requirements from stakeholders (section A.1.1).

Consider a loan institution, like a bank. They're humming along nicely, and one day the owners of the bank stumble across an opportunity. They receive an offer to buy their competitor's customers at a very reasonable price. The deal is quickly closed, and soon the only thing left is to import the competitor's customer database into the existing back-office system.

Most of the new customers have contracts similar to the ones already in place, but some are different. Some have a loyalty bonus in the form of an individual, significantly lower, interest rate. There are also customers who aren't amortizing on their loans during their first six months—they're just paying interest. Neither of these two contract types can be accommodated in the existing system. Deciding to expand its business has put the bank in a situation where structural changes need to happen or a lot more manual work will be introduced. If the former is chosen, the back-office system that was working fine before just isn't any more.

Even though turning down or following through on a deal is a business decision, its impact can be more readily handled if the technical side is involved early on.

A.3.4   *Propeller hat—technical and incurred*

This quadrant is where most of the technical debt we've seen comes from. It can be the result of anything from sloppy coding, to a don't-touch-it-it-works mentality, to ambitious and well-intended over-engineering. They all create technical debt.

Early choices on architecture and design that once looked like good decisions can become the biggest hurdles when it comes to effective software development, forcing you to create workarounds that add complexity to your solution without giving anything in return. But it's a balance, and some decisions have to be made. Choosing a database too early is often a bad idea, but so is staying too long with saving your data to a flat file.

The most sensible technical changes often start with a hunch and maybe a feeling that you're missing a point. The code may feel awkward, inflexible, and stale like yesterday's bread. Sooner or later that feeling is followed by a new way of looking at things and usually an idea of how to improve the system.

When you've decided to make an improvement, make sure you implement it all-out to avoid leaving the codebase semidisrupted. We've seen our fair share of semidisruption; one case that comes to mind is where Apache Struts was almost replaced by WebWorks, which in turn was almost replaced by the Spring Framework, leaving the system with no less than three different ways of presenting and accessing data. Like growth rings on a tree, the system presents its structural shifts to its caretaker.

Although sound changes stand the best chance of leading to improvement, the change can add to the debt unless everyone is aboard and the change is fully implemented.

Watch out for these examples of debt builders and red herrings that relate to this category of debt: waiting for the right abstraction (section A.1.1), insufficient knowledge (section A.1.3), premature optimization (section A.1.3), not invented here (section A.1.3), proudly found elsewhere (section A.1.3), one-way code (section A.1.3), too-clever code (section A.1.3), and breaking windows (section A.1.4).

A.3.5   *Borderliners*

Some of the sources of technical debt can't easily be put into a single category. Rather, they span several of these quadrants, or their origin differs from time to time. This is due to the fact that technical debt is often created when internal or external borders of communication are crossed.

A.4   *Attacking the technical debt source*

Poor internal structures constitute a multitude of problems that might all need to be handled sooner or later. If you look closer, you'll find that there are no less than four different ways to deal with a problem:

- *Absolve*—Do nothing; just forgive the people or the process.
- *Resolve*—Take knowledge acquired in the past from a similar situation, and apply it to the current situation. This is the preferred way to deal with problems, and it's what we're taught and tested for in school.
- *Solve*—Sit down and analyze the problem, and try to find a solution that's better that the current one.
- *Dissolve*—Eliminate the cause of the problem.

In order to show how a problem can be approached in several different ways, we'll illustrate it with a story, once told by Russell L. Ackoff in *Idealized Design* (Prentice Hall, 2006). Throughout the story, you'll see examples of absolving, resolving, solving, and finally dissolving the problem.

In London, double-decker buses have a driver and a conductor. The conductor collects fares and issues receipts from the back, as passengers board the bus. When all have boarded, the conductor signals to the driver through the front mirror that everyone is on board and they're ready to go.

To make things a bit more complicated, there are incentive programs in place—one for the driver and one for the conductor. The driver is paid more if they stay closer to schedule; the conductor is paid more the fewer fares he misses collecting, which is controlled by undercover inspectors. The driver is highly dependent on the efficiency of the conductor.

To prevent delays during peak hours, the conductor lets everyone board the bus and collects fares and issues receipts between stops. Sometimes the conductor isn't fast enough, or fails to signal the driver when everyone has boarded. This results in a growing hostility between the drivers and conductors.

When this problem surfaced, management chose to ignore it, hoping that the problem would disappear on its own. This is the problem-*absolving* approach. In an ever-changing environment, problems can disappear by themselves, but they didn't in this case. The problem actually got worse, so they had to do something.

They decided to change the incentive system, which they thought was causing the problem. Ackoff calls this reversion to a previously working situation *resolving*. But the conductors and drivers had gotten used to their extra money and rejected the idea.

Next, management decided to *solve* the problem and find the best solution. After thinking about the problem for quite some time, they came up with the idea that the drivers and conductors should share the incentive payments. This wouldn't affect their paychecks. The company wouldn't have to pay more, and it would encourage the conductors and drivers to work together. If they had started out with an incentive system that looked like that, the problem might not have surfaced or would have taken longer to discover. But at this time, conductors and drivers were reluctant to work together, and even more so when it came to sharing money.

Management was on the verge of giving up, and as a last resort they consulted an expert, who happened to be familiar with problem *dissolving*. He dove into the problem—actually, he stepped back and took a broader view of the system, which is really important when you want to get to the bottom of a problem.

The consultant found something really interesting, which made him propose a redesign of the system. During rush hour, there were more buses on the streets than there were bus stops. Conductors should get off the bus and stay at the bus stops! If they got off the bus and collected fares from people at the bus stops during rush hour, they could still signal to the driver that everyone was on board and ready to go. But more importantly, the passengers could get on the bus a lot faster. When the peaks were over, the conductors could work on-board again. The problem had been dissolved.

His proposition had another advantage. During peak hours, fewer conductors were needed because there were fewer stops than buses, which meant a huge savings in salaries for the company!

A.4.1 Get to the bottom of the problem

In general, you want to solve the *essential and novel* problems that are at the core of your mission statement and domain, because that's what your customers are paying you for. You usually do that by applying a series of resolutions—previously applied and known solutions—to parts of the problem you're solving. In addition, you want to dissolve any unnecessary or accidental problems.

For the parts of the system with technical debt where you don't have to pay any interest, you can do nothing and absolve the problem. To pay back debt, you can apply technical solutions or resolutions to the problems. The Mikado Method is a tool for helping you solve your novel debt problems, while utilizing any resolutions you have. The solutions are typically a graph or a subgraph, whereas a resolution is often what you write in a single node, like breaking a circular dependency by using the Dependency Inversion Principle.

In contrast, the *creation* of technical debt is usually the kind of problem you'll want to dissolve. To do that, you'll likely have to change the system you're working in, how work is arranged, how change requests enter the organization, how decisions are made, and so on. A shift in attitude is required, and you'll need to step back and take a good hard look at the situation and the work system.

This can be difficult when you're deeply involved in the details of the implementation. This is true not only because of the level of your involvement, but also because going to the root of the problem and dissolving technical debt requires a slightly different approach for each of the previously discussed quadrants. Figure A.6 identifies some phrases that suggest where the origin of the debt might be.

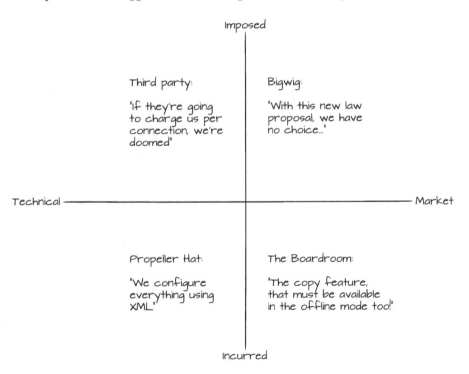

Figure A.6 Phrases that hint where technical debt originates from

A.4.2   *Third party—create defensible space*

The disadvantage of being tangled up in API calls or tied to a specific solution to a problem becomes real when you're forced into change after change due to changes in the underlying API. The trick when you work with third-party software is to minimize the collateral damage of any changes you can't control, and identify situations that could lead to problems that might spread.

If you're not careful in your use of third-party libraries, for example, the external dependencies can leak into your codebase, much like a wildfire spreads over a prairie or savanna. And much like a wildfire, third-party libraries can be hard to contain once they've started spreading. This wildfire is also fueled by the broken window principle. ORMs, 3D engines, or report tools can easily be become the wildfires of a codebase.

Firefighters know that stopping a fire is a lot easier if the correct prevention techniques are implemented, such as education, careful handling of open fires, and defensible space. Defensible space acknowledges that a fire needs fuel. Cutting down corridors of trees in a forest, or requiring enough space between buildings in a suburb are examples of defensible space across which a fire can't easily spread.

Abstractions or *layers* are the defensible space of a computer program. Eric Evans calls them *anti-corruption layers* in his book *Domain-Driven Design* (Pearson 2004). When you're able to see the fire early on and use abstractions and layering properly, many of these problems will be dissolved, thus minimizing the effects of third-party API changes later on.

A.4.3   *Bigwig—probe and prepare*

The problems that come from when the bigwigs, or the markets, change their minds are very hard to dissolve, and instead you need to *probe and prepare* for this type of change. You need to do your market research, keep in touch with customers, listen to the news, and keep up to date with current political decisions to anticipate what will happen.

In general, regulatory and legal changes can be hard to anticipate. What you can do is make sure your organization is able to respond quickly to *any* change. This means letting the people doing the job make the decisions about how to do it, have spare work capacity (slack) in the organization, have automated validation and verification processes in place, and have as little work in process as possible at any given time. When you're working with code, using the Mikado Method with frequent check-ins is a good way of keeping work in progress low.

When your decisions are heavily influenced or regulated by external or governmental instances, we recommend making those variation points easily configurable. Keep your options open by separating the logic that varies depending on external decisions from the logic that stems from internal decisions.

A.4.4   *The boardroom—talk and learn*

Changes to business models and great new ideas are probably the most natural and sane causes for change in a codebase. But when the program manager repeatedly makes decisions that cause large changes to your program, you have a problem.

If technical and non-technical people don't have an understanding of each other's work, friction will appear and the nimble solution will continue to be unidentified, or unimplemented. The non-techies need to get an understanding of how their decisions affect implementation details, and techies need to understand the relevant parts of the business domain to make good technical decisions.

To achieve this, non-techies and techies need to teach each other and learn from each other, to build the knowledge and the respect needed to create awesome products. This communication can't be expected to be built on an occasional argument.

The easiest way to get started is for one group to invite the other to talk about both business and technical details, such as technical debt, with the goal of learning and understanding each other's work and challenges. Once you're speaking the same language, both sides are more likely to make the right decisions. This also helps mitigate the problem of creating technical policies that damage development.

A.4.5 *Propeller hat—form an opinion and align*

Awkward technical solutions, sloppy coding, absent or inadequate coding standards, and different opinions on what code should look like, or even what paradigms should be used, are also drivers of technical debt.

The road to better code starts with forming an opinion about what great solutions look like. This opinion shouldn't be static, even though some people tend to believe so. It's actually a work in progress; it's always subject to improvement. By continuously and actively working on a team's opinion, and aligning development and design ideas with that opinion, it's easier to come to agreement on where to take the existing code, what parts to improve, and how to implement new things. Forming a team opinion takes some time and a lot of effort, but unless you talk about it, you'll be running without direction, which is an even worse use of your time.

Looking at other people's code or other paradigms for inspiration and ideas is an excellent way to broaden your perspective. You should look for the qualities you want in your own work, and then figure out what parts of your current opinion to replace.

A.5 *The way out of technical debt*

Sustainable change can't be forced; it requires a *willingness to change*, and this goes beyond the software development team—it includes the whole organization. If you want different output from the system that created what you have today, you need to change it, which essentially means a change in behavior. You can't expect different results from a system without a change.

Apart from different behavior, you also need *discipline* and *integrity* from the people who develop the software. Real improvements to a messy codebase can only be made by moving away from the current situation and then continuing in that direction for a long time. For this, the developers need *support* and *commitment* from management.

You also need to be *patient*. You can't expect an organization to change over the course of a week. Rewiring a human brain for new habits and ways to do things normally takes around a year with plenty of practice, and it's easy to see that discussing and changing old habits should be pretty high on the agenda, continuously.

Making use of an effective *process* for the change helps a lot. This is where the Mikado Method can help in repaying the current debt and getting the product in shape at a competitive price.

Technical debt *is* a tricky thing. You can't just put up a lot of money to pay the debt and hope that the problems are gone the next day. You do need financing for your activities, but primarily you must pay with sweat and hard work.

Technical debt isn't limited to the code; it can manifest itself in anything from code to build scripts, folder structures, version control systems, tests, environments, operating systems, configuration files, and more. When we're using the Mikado Method, we don't limit the nodes to code. The nodes can be *anything* in the system that we need to take care of.

A.6   *Summary*

Just fixing problems as you run into them isn't enough; that should be pretty clear by now. If you just fix problems, you'll end up feeling like you're Sisyphus, the ancient Greek king who, according to the mythology, was condemned to perpetually roll a immensely heavy boulder up a hill, only to have it roll down again before reaching the top, and having to roll it up again. Unless you change the system, addressing the way the work works, you're doomed to the same fate as Sisyphus.

Changing the process of how software is developed will look different depending on a lot of things, such as the type of application you're developing, the size of the team, and a lot of other parameters. It's also important to remember that reworking, redesigning, and restructuring your system can never be avoided entirely, but examining where your changes are coming from can help you create strategies for minimizing the disruption. Try to mitigate your debt builders as early as possible, and pay back your loans with the highest interest first.

Try this

- What alarm bells are ringing for you in your current environment, and which are sounding most frequently?
- What alarms have you experienced in previous projects? What did you do? What should you have done differently?
- Can you think of times when you introduced technical debt into a system?
- What types of technical debt can you see in your current, or a previous, system? Can you find some that resulted from hitting a market window, unprofessionalism, ignorance, external events, or learning?
- What types of events caused your debt?
- What parts of your code are troublesome to read or change? Do you read that code often? Do you change it often?
- For a piece of code that has some debt, can you estimate how much less time you'd spend there if you could improve the code? What would that improvement constitute? What stops you from changing it?

appendix B
Setting the stage
for improvements

This chapter covers

- Technical preparations for a restructuring effort
- Personal preparations
- What to think of before, during and after a restructuring effort

At this point in the book, you should be pretty confident with the technical aspects of restructuring code the Mikado way. Now we'll show you a few things that can give you advantages and boost your work right from the start. You want to make sure that you spend your time wisely and direct your energy on the essential parts of the problems.

In this appendix, we've gathered some tips, tricks, and good practices that can really make a difference when you restructure code using the Mikado Method. We'll present a mix of technical and organizational advice that we've found very useful in solving and mitigating common problems. This appendix is organized to give you a rough hint about when the advice is most applicable—before, during, or after your restructuring. We hope you'll find a few gems in here.

B.1 Before your restructuring

This section presents things you should think about before heading out on your restructuring. It's a rather long list, and you probably don't need to have them all in place before you start. Look at your context and see what needs to be done, if anything.

B.1.1 Shorten your feedback cycles

Every developer has at some point implemented a feature and had a user report a bug in a seemingly unrelated part of the application. Every developer has at some point wondered, "How could this thing possibly affect that?" And every developer has also thought, "If I only knew then what I know now..."

When you deal with code improvements, you're much better off if you can verify that your changes don't break some other functionality, and this is why programming benefits a lot from closing feedback loops and shortening feedback cycles. You get to know as soon as possible what your changes have affected and minimize users having to report bugs.

The faster you get the feedback, the faster you can dare to go. You'll also want a development environment where you can try things and get feedback from failure safely, in order to learn how the system behaves at its boundaries. The more things you can try without disturbing or depending on others, the better.

AUTOMATION

One way to simplify the Mikado Method dance is to have an easy way to verify that a change didn't break anything. Quickly running compilers and tests is one thing, but for a complex product you need an automated build process. Automation will give you consistency and repeatability, which is very important for reliable feedback. In fact, try to automate as much as possible, as soon as possible. If you need the results of the automation, it's time well spent.

> **DON'T AUTOMATE WHAT YOU DON'T NEED** Spending time on automating things you don't need is an utter waste and should be avoided. Only produce results that are asked for and that produce *mutual benefit* for all parties involved, including you.

A typical build process setup involves the following steps:

1. Pull all code from a versioning system
2. Compile
3. Run micro tests
4. Put together artifacts
5. Deploy

6 Run macro tests

7 Create documentation

8 Create the distributable artifact

It's best to pick out parts of that process depending on the type of change you're making to get the fastest relevant feedback. For instance, if you rename a local variable in a method, you only need to compile to check that you didn't miss anything. On the other hand, if you change the internal structures of an algorithm, you'll probably want to run the micro tests to check that it still works as expected. If you're pulling apart your system into new packages, you'll probably want to run the entire build. The book *Continuous Delivery* by Jez Humble and David Farley (Addison-Wesley Professional, 2010) offers detailed advice on how to automate building, testing, and deployment.

COMPILER SUPPORT

For statically typed languages, a compiler gives even faster feedback than tests if something breaks, because compilation precedes running tests. There are also so-called *eager compilers* in many development environments that check code as it's typed, and that feedback is almost instantaneous.

Early signs that something broke after a change, such as compiler errors, are important input when you create a Mikado Graph. If you don't have a statically typed language, micro tests are the first level of feedback.

In this book, we talk a lot about using the IDE's refactoring automation for many atomic and composed refactorings. But for an automated refactoring to work properly, it's essential that the code compiles. Before we discovered the Mikado Method, we often tried to refactor code in a noncompiling codebase, usually with very poor results. Then, when we couldn't compile our code, we had to revert to refactoring using search and replace, which is *much* slower and more error-prone than the automated refactorings of an IDE.

AUTOMATED TESTS

Our best friend when we're up against a bigger refactoring or restructuring is *automated tests*. When we refer to automated tests, we mean pieces of code that run a part of the system and assert that the expected functionality is there, *without human intervention*. Tests like that can be written both on a macro level and on a micro level.

Languages without static typing require you to execute tests to verify changes because there's no option to get feedback from a compiler. Automated tests can be viewed as the compilers of nonstatically typed languages, in that they actually invoke the code and force the runtime interpreter to check it. If no tests are in place before making a change in a dynamically typed language, it's a good idea to make "Cover area X with tests" a prerequisite to the change in the Mikado Graph, or even to make adding tests a separate graph before you start on the actual goal. These types of tests are often referred to as *characterization tests* (as described in Michael Feathers' *Working Effectively with Legacy Code* (Prentice Hall, 2004)), which are tests written to define the actual functionality of the code. IDEs for dynamically typed languages usually provide some refactoring support, but when dynamic language features are used, refactorings might occasionally fail.

Macro-level tests

Automated tests that work the entire system, or parts of it, from the outside like a user would are particularly valuable when a system needs to change. The Naive Approach partly relies on this safety net and it also tells you what prerequisites you should consider. Those tests are sometimes called *macro, system, functional,* or *acceptance* tests. They typically launch a GUI, click buttons, enter text, select check boxes, and more, just like a user would. By doing so, they exercise the system in an end-to-end fashion, and it's also very common for these actions, in turn, to store state in a persistent manner, generally by using some sort of database. As the suite of tests is run, it verifies the *business value* of the system, as well as its wiring and plumbing. It's this end-to-end aspect that makes these tests so useful when you make structural changes, because you don't want the functionality to change as internal changes are made.

The downside of such tests is also their end-to-end characteristic—they often take a long time to execute. In return, they're able to provide loads of high-quality feedback, but that feedback arrives more slowly than the feedback from micro-level tests. Improving the execution speed and tightening the feedback cycle is possible to a certain degree, but dramatic improvements come at the price of the amount and quality of feedback they provide. Making major improvements in execution time often means bypassing important parts of an end-to-end test, like keeping data in memory instead of using the actual database. In order to get faster feedback, you need a complement, namely, micro-level tests.

Micro-level tests

Micro-level tests provide the fastest feedback you can get, only bested by the speed of generating compiler errors in statically typed environments. If you don't have either tests or a compiler, you'll be severely crippled in your ability to use the Mikado Method; you'll have to rely on manual tests and analysis, both which are relatively slow.

The micro-level tests we're talking about don't trigger the use of any external resources, such as files, sockets, or screens, and this is what makes them so fast. They only test small chunks of logic and should execute entirely in memory. This means that hundreds, thousands, or even tens of thousands of tests can run within seconds. When they execute that quickly, it becomes possible to verify a lot of the logic in the code in a very short time. The downside is that they normally don't verify that a user can actually perform a business-value function in the end product.

Tests on a micro level can cause problems if they're written a certain way. If the tests use knowledge about the structure and implementation details of the code they test, they're on the same level of detail as that code. Hence, for every piece of code that needs to change, several tests have to change as well. For instance, when using refactorings, you often change a lot of structure at the same time, which can break a substantial number of micro tests. Fixing them can be a daunting task, and in that way, poorly constructed micro tests can hold the code hostage.

You can usually solve that problem by removing those tests, but before you remove the tests, you should usually add a replacement for the tests you're removing—a higher-level test. The job of the higher-level test is to verify the module's behavior in a way that's less dependent on the way the application is structured. This often implies testing a small cluster of classes that perform some cohesive service for the application. Sometimes this becomes a macro-level test, and sometimes it's a micro-level test on that cluster of classes. Such tests are usually more stable in the face of change. When that higher-level test, or maybe several tests, are in place, the old tests can safely be removed.

ADD TESTS "ON THE WAY OUT" If the codebase doesn't have a sufficient number of tests, such that they don't verify the behavior you think they should, a test is clearly missing. This is normal, especially when you work on legacy code, but too often you'll find this out too late. To mitigate nasty surprises, we've found that it's best to cover the code with tests as we explore the graph, rather than when we make all the changes. We add high-level tests when we're still exploring the graph. This is the classic "cover (with tests) then modify" approach.

Load and performance tests

In addition to the macro- and micro-level tests that verify the functionality and logic of the application, load and performance tests are used to verify that a change doesn't introduce severe bottlenecks.

Load tests usually simulate having multiple clients accessing an application to see, for example, how many simultaneous users or requests the application can handle. This normally requires the system to be set up in a somewhat realistic fashion, which usually results in rather long feedback cycle times.

Performance tests measure how fast certain requests or algorithms are performed in the system. Performance tests may or may not need the system to be set up in a realistic fashion, and can sometimes give fast feedback.

From the Mikado Method perspective, we prefer faster feedback while exploring a system and growing a graph, so load and performance tests can be a bit too slow. But if you have those types of tests, run them as often as you can, such as over lunch, or during the night, so that you're alerted if any of your changes have degraded performance significantly. Keep in mind that sometimes you need to first make structural changes and then optimize the new structure, meaning that performance will be degraded for awhile. During this time, the system isn't releasable, and extra care must be taken to avoid getting stuck in this situation for too long.

Tests of other system properties

In many applications and domains there are other properties, such as security and regulatory rules, that limit what can be done in an application, or specify what must be done. Because the changes from the Mikado Method could break such properties, just like any changes you make to your system, it's equally important to get feedback on such properties and use that information to build your Mikado Graph.

Try to automate those verifications as well. Be creative. A colleague of ours implemented a plugin for his automated tests that tested the rules of the system and generated regulatory documentation at the same time. This might not be directly applicable to your context, but it shows the creativity that might be needed to avoid long feedback loops.

MANUAL FEEDBACK

Automation can provide fast feedback on things that are measurable by a computer. By putting a person in the loop, you can get another dimension of more complex feedback.

Manual testing

In some settings, teams of testers manually click through (or use other means to stimulate) the system under test to verify that it acts as expected. We recommend automating the repetitive tasks of testing as much as possible via micro- or macro-level tests. If this is done properly, the automated tests enable faster feedback cycles, and they also contribute to the confidence in the system by acting as *executable specifications.* In a Mikado Method setting, where maintaining momentum is usually important, waiting for system-wide manual testing kills the flow and focus.

Manual testing is still needed, but the time invested should be used to explore the system and go beyond the scripted tests rather than finding errors on a daily basis. Repetitive tasks are perfect for machines. Thinking outside of the box is something humans do a lot better.

Deploying and then letting the users report problems is also a way of getting feedback. We don't recommend this as a strategy for finding errors, especially not in a Mikado Method setting, but releasing and getting user feedback is essential in order to build the best product possible.

Pair programming and mob programming

One of our favorite ways to get fast feedback is to use pair programming or, if you have the opportunity, mob programming. When done properly, the co-driver(s) will give you immediate feedback on the code you're writing. You can also get feedback on your ideas in a design discussion, before you write any code. The feedback can be at many levels, from details about the programming language or shortcuts in the development environment to paradigm philosophies and principles of software development.

> **CODE REVIEWS** Programming with other people—in pairs or in a mob—isn't the same as a traditional code review, where a developer's code is scrutinized by another developer. Pair or mob programming gives instant feedback, in context, whereas a code review is usually performed after the fact, with the potential for plenty of time wasted on a bad solution or a bad Mikado Method path. Although a code review can provide valuable feedback, we value the fast feedback when programming together more.

When we pair or mob program, we let the co-driver focus on strategic decisions so the driver can focus on tactical decisions. We also give the co-driver the responsibility of updating the graph.

BALANCING SPEED AND CONFIDENCE In the ideal Mikado Method situation, you'd have full test coverage of the whole system, and it would run in the blink of an eye, so you'd know immediately what problems a change caused. In reality, though, you must strike a balance between how long you spend verifying a system, and how sure you are that you've found all the problems your change introduces. You can adjust the balance by adding good tests and making the tests faster, but there will always be a trade-off between speed and confidence when using the Mikado Method. The more critical the system is, the more you should shift the balance toward confidence, adding and improving tests, and spending time verifying the system after the changes you make. On the other hand, if time to market is more important, the balance should shift toward speed and away from confidence. The latter choice involves some hoping for the best, but it's a valid option when a significant deadline must be met.

B.1.2 Use a version control system

We've seen businesses that don't use a proper version control system (VCS), and we can't stress this enough: the VCS is one of the most important tools in a software project.

A VCS is an application that keeps track of all the changes made to files in a filesystem. The beauty of using a VCS is that you can revert, or roll back, all the changes to a specific date, or to a specific tag or label created to identify a version. The more often code is checked in, the more fine-grained the history is. Other names for a VCS are *revision control system* or *source control module*.

The Mikado Method uses the revert functionality of the VCS systematically and extensively. Without it, you can't expect any real progress at all.

PET PROJECTS ARE ALSO PROJECTS Even when we're working alone on our pet projects, we use a VCS to save us from any wasted time and agony. There are good VCSs available for free that are easy to set up, so there's really no excuse for not using one. If you think your VCS at your day job could be better, evaluate another one when you work on your pet project.

B.1.3 Use automated refactorings

Another thing we've covered to some extent in this book is the automated refactoring support of your IDE. Most modern IDEs have automation support for an abundance of atomic and composed refactorings from Martin Fowler's *Refactoring* (Addison-Wesley Professional, 1999) and other literature.

When we're working with a codebase, we make constant use of these tools to improve, change, delete, restructure, and implement code. With these automated tools, you can make changes that span the entire codebase, changing and moving thousands of files with a single command.

Because modern IDEs, or changes using regular expressions, can affect literally thousands of files, we don't rely on the undo or redo function of these tools too much. If one change creates one or two errors, you can use the undo function of the IDE, but if there are more than three or four errors, it's probably better to undo using the VCS.

B.1.4   Use one workspace

Before you start changing code, it's good to have all the editable code in a single workspace in the IDE, so you can make as much use of the refactoring tools as possible. If the code is spread out over several different workspaces, changing the code using automated refactoring becomes very cumbersome, because some code is changed properly and some isn't changed at all. This can hide compilation and runtime errors, or delay the discovery of such problems until the right workspace is opened.

B.1.5   Use one repository

When making extended changes to a codebase, it's simpler, more robust, and development performant to move all related code into a single repository root. This is something we strongly recommend. If you have reason not to do so, the benefits from having different repository roots must be carefully weighed against the increased overall complexity of the development environment.

We've seen cases where a single codebase is spread out over several VCS repository roots. This makes configuration and version management more complex and increases the risk for anyone involved to make mistakes. When you make changes across repository boundaries, it's more difficult to maintain consistency and integrity across the different repositories. Taking care of the release-reuse versioning of the different repositories can also be cumbersome.

B.1.6   Merge frequently with the main branch

If you use a VCS, you always work in branches. The checked-out code at your local workstation is an *implicit branch* of the central main branch. Each developer has one such branch and possibly more locally defined branches in addition to any explicit branches created centrally in the versioning system. The longer you wait before checking in your local implicit branch, the harder the merge becomes, because the trunk and your code will diverge from the point when you checked it out.

When we use the Mikado Method, we try to merge our local branch with the main branch frequently, sometimes as often as 10 times a day. This may sound like a lot, but it allows everyone on the project to have the very latest code to build their changes on; likewise, it allows us to build our changes on the latest code our colleagues provide. One of the main characteristics of the Mikado Method is the small safe steps that continuously take the code in a new direction. When you work like that, the only sane approach is to work with one branch or very short-lived local ones.

What you really want to avoid is branches that *diverge* for a long time. The more they diverge, the harder they become to merge. The divergence will increase with the rate of change and the time between merges. With a large codebase and with the use of modern refactoring tools, you can sometimes change and move hundreds or thousands of files with a single command. This makes the rate of change very high, and the only variable you can affect is the time between merges.

Refactoring branches

A common, but *bad*, idea is to make a separate branch for the improvement efforts, and to keep on implementing new functionality in the main branch, with the intention of merging these two branches when the improvements are done. The rationale is usually that implementing new features shouldn't be disturbed by improvements.

This is far from optimal and not the Mikado Method style of merging, mainly because the branches have different goals and will diverge very quickly. The better you become at using the Mikado Method, the faster they'll diverge. A common, but equally suboptimal, solution to that problem is to merge the refactoring branch with the development branch continuously, but only from the main branch to the improvement branch.

As the improvements move in one direction and the new features in another, the merges will become more and more difficult, eventually choking the improvement efforts. The preferred solution to that problem is to merge both ways, but that's like having only one branch to begin with.

Our recommendation is that the number of "central" branches be kept to an absolute minimum, with preferably only one main branch and possibly a branch that's created when problems in the production environment arise and need immediate attention.

There are VCSs that can help you with complex merges, provided that there's a fine-grained check-in history in each of the branches. But even then, there will always be cases where that fails. Use this VCS ability as an extra safety net instead of letting your improvement effort stand or fall with it.

Moving to "trunk development"

Learning how to work in a single branch is one of the things that makes companies such as Google, Amazon, and Yahoo successful at developing profitable software quickly. The most common pattern for enabling working in a single branch is the *latent code pattern*, where you can turn features on and off. This means that you can deploy half-finished features that are disconnected from the execution flows. This is also called a *dark release*.

B.1.7 Scripting languages to the rescue

Some improvements are difficult to make with the basic refactoring and regular expression tools of an IDE, such as when you need more complex search-and-replace operations or to access different sources of data to produce the result. Tasks like that, however, are easy to perform with most scripting languages. Sometimes when you're using the Mikado Method, the number of edits required to fix a single prerequisite can be in the hundreds. If there is a pattern, using a scripting language can help immensely in making such edits.

B.1.8   Use the best tools

Get the best tools for the job and learn how to use them. In a for-profit context, the time spent discussing whether or not to buy a tool is usually worth more than the cost of the tool. On top of that, tools are usually so cheap that using them once pays for the whole investment. If work is carried out in a pro bono environment, there are many free tools that are sufficiently good and sometimes better than their commercial counterparts.

> **BE A TOOLSMITH**   The best tools are not necessarily the most expensive ones. Sometimes it can even be more cost-effective to take a simple free tool and extend or modify it than to buy an expensive tool that doesn't do exactly what's needed. Occasionally, building your own tool might even be warranted. As for any application, start out small with a clear business case and add functionality incrementally as long as you can warrant it.

B.1.9   Buy the books

Investing in knowledge pays good interest, and books are a cheap way of extending your knowledge. If the advice from a book is applied only once, the book has probably paid for itself. Managers should keep that in mind, and always give approval when their employees ask to buy a work-related book. You could say that we, as authors, are a bit biased about this, but we also run a company where our employees are encouraged to buy the books they think they need, at our company's expense.

B.1.10   Know the dynamic code

Fast feedback and fast graph exploration is a lot harder if there are dynamic, or reflective, parts in the code. It's important to know what parts of a codebase are dynamic, and to specifically verify those parts using automated tests, or to use the *frozen partition* trick from section 7.3.2 of this book.

Sometimes, these dynamic parts are needless complexity that can, for example, be replaced easily with proper abstractions. We always try to minimize the use of dynamic parts, and we're often surprised how well that works.

B.1.11   Consistency first, then improvements

There are two things in a codebase that are good to keep consistent: the formatting of the code and the programming style. When you keep the formatting consistent, your brain can make more sense of a complex situation and doesn't get distracted by irrelevant formatting differences. By keeping your programming style consistent, you can also reduce the cognitive load of having to understand different solutions to similar problems.

When formatting the code, there are several tools you can use to get a consistent result. In terms of programming style, it's important to keep adding code in the same style as already exists in the system, until a change to a new style is performed.

If the code is formatted the same way everywhere, with regard to line endings, blank lines, and curly braces, it's easier to modify the code with scripting languages and regular expressions.

B.1.12 *Learn to use regular expressions*

Most development environments have tools to perform search and replace using *regular expressions*. A regular expression is a powerful text-matching pattern that's processed to find and replace text in files in very intricate ways.

There are a few different regular expression dialects for different platforms, but they usually contain approximately the same functionality. To avoid overly complex regular expressions, start by making the code consistent, as described in section B.1.11.

B.1.13 *Remove unused code*

One of our favorite code improvements is removing unused code. After removing the code, the system reads better, compiles faster, and takes up less disk space and working memory. Of course, the code removed must not perform any work that's relevant to the system. When removing unused code, go for the low-hanging fruit and don't try to clean-sweep the codebase.

There are a few categories of unused code, and we've taken some inspiration from the horror genre to describe them.

GHOST CODE

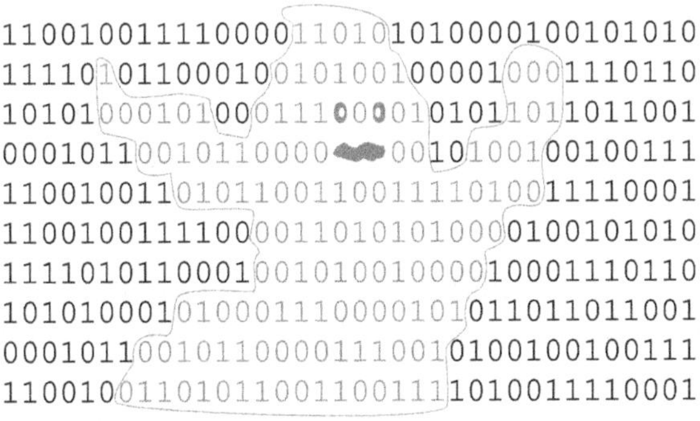

```
11001001111000011010101000010010101 0
1111011011000100101001000010001110110
10101000101000111000010101101 1011001
0001011001011000001010010010 0100111
11001001101011001100111101001 1110001
11001001111000011010101000010010101 0
11110101100010010100100001000 1110110
10101000101000111000010101101 1011001
0001011001011000011100101001001 00111
11001001101011001100111101001 1110001
```

Figure B.1 Ghost code

Sometimes you stare at code that's commented out, thinking, "Why is this still here? What is it saying? It's probably very important, or it wouldn't be here. Let's keep it."

Programmers sometimes feel the urge to comment out a particular piece of code, perhaps to short-circuit the execution, or just to save it for later possible use. But there's no reason for that commented-out code to stay in that state for more than a couple of minutes. Code that's commented out is *ghost code*, and like any ghost, it should move on to the other side as quickly as possible. In this case, it should be deleted. If it's not, it will haunt you as long as it remains in this world. On the upside, ghost code is easy to locate with a normal text search.

You should use the VCS instead of keeping old code in commented-out blocks all over the codebase.

ZOMBIE CODE

Figure B.2   Zombie code

Zombie code is the living dead code. It's not part of any business value flow; it's only called from automated tests, like unit tests or other unused code. It's just walking around, feeding off the living code by taking up maintenance resources without giving anything back.

This kind of code is very hard to distinguish from real code. It looks like real code, but it isn't really used. It's also hard to locate, because it's covered by tests and may not be marked by static analysis.

To kill it, cut off its head, which is usually the unit tests. This will make the zombie code plain old dead code.

DEAD CODE
Nothing invokes dead code. There are no user calls from a UI, no calls from tests, nor any other usage from anyplace else. If a compiling language is used, it's somewhat easier to find these dead parts, because static code analysis can help you. Dead code is of no use at all and should be given a proper burial by deletion.

FINDING REMOVABLE CODE

When you look for dead or zombie code, try to run the system using the acceptance test suite with code coverage turned on. This way you can exercise the parts of the code that an actual user will use. Better yet, if the system allows for some overhead, monitor it in production. Then look through the coverage reports to find uncovered code. The covered code is clearly used and can be ignored. The uncovered parts are candidates for more detailed analysis.

Ghost code can usually be found using a regular expression in a text search. The trick is to look for the start of a comment, and then any characters that are common in code, but uncommon in normal text. Parentheses and semicolons are good candidates, depending on your programming language.

B.1.14 *Prepare yourself mentally*

Improving code takes time as well as determination and a vision, but mostly it requires courage. Fear of changing code is not an option, although respect for its complexity is. Errors will be made, and the important thing is to deal with them as soon as possible. Leading, and especially leading change, can be lonely at times. Find strength by including the people around you instead of pushing them away.

B.1.15 *Prepare others*

You also need to communicate with the people around you, telling them what is about to happen and explaining why the codebase needs to be changed, in terms they can relate to. A good way to kick off the dialogue is to review the main goal of the Mikado Graph, and to explain in a broad sense how the goal will be achieved, perhaps showing a draft Mikado Graph. Take the time to explain the consequences if this isn't done, as well as the upside of it being implemented. You might also need to explain that this is the job of every single person in the company, especially the developers. The Mikado Graph provides a visual tool through which the goal, scope, opportunity, and consequences can be discussed without going into technical detail.

B.1.16 *Measure code problems*

There are many tools out there that provide help when analyzing a codebase, as well as plenty of relevant metrics, or code quality parameters, that can give a hint regarding the state of your code:

- When you get confused by how many ways the execution flows due to conditionals, the *cyclomatic complexity index* will give you a number to quantify that confusion.
- When your mind is spinning from dependencies going back and forth between your packages, you can draw a dependency diagram, or take a look at efferent and afferent couplings in Robert C. Martin's book *Agile Software Development* (Prentice Hall, 2002).

- When you need to know how much you can trust your tests, first look at the quality of the tests, and then check the code coverage of the tests. If the tests look good in that they assert the right things, and most of the code is executed by the tests, all is well. Otherwise, you'll have to find the parts that aren't tested, and determine what the impact of that is.

These are just a few of the available metrics, and all metrics are good in that they provide numbers you can learn from, and you can see how they change as you make changes to the codebase. They can give you some idea of where you might have problems, but there's more to developing software, and especially legacy code, than just improving metrics.

The Mikado Method starts with what needs to be done, and even though a piece of code scores well on metrics such as complexity, package coupling, and coverage, you might have to change it. At the same time, you might never have to read or change the parts of the code with really bad numbers.

In addition, your *gut feeling* often tells you where the real problems are. It might take some initial working with the codebase to get that gut feeling, but you usually bump into the worst problems every other day. Code metrics are a good way of getting some backing for that gut feeling, but you shouldn't base a restructuring effort on metrics alone.

B.1.17 *Hire a critical mass of change agents*

If bad development habits led to your problems, and that isn't changed, the problems will never go away. You need to change the way the system is developed, and that requires a lot of effort and determination. Our experience is that on a software development team, 25–50% of its members have to support a new way of working to make a sustainable change.

The fifth principle of the Agile Manifesto states, "Build projects around motivated individuals. Give them the environment and support they need, and trust them to get the job done."[1] It's the same for an improvement effort: find the people who want to make the improvements. If the goal is to gradually restructure the code, you want to pick the people who want to work that way. If they can't be found inside the company, search outside of the company for consultants or new employees. To improve your chance of finding the right people, let the people inside the company who want to work that way select the people they want to work with.

For more detailed advice on change, we recommend reading *Fearless Change* by Mary Lynn Manns and Linda Rising (Addison-Wesley Professional, 2004).

B.1.18 *Encourage collective code ownership*

In Extreme Programming, collective code ownership is mentioned as a good practice, and it's one of the cornerstones of software development teamwork. It basically

---

[1] See www.pmp-projects.org/Agile-Manifesto.pdf.

means that any person on the team in a software project is allowed to change any part of the code. (See *Extreme Programming Explained*, second edition, by Kent Beck, Addison-Wesley Professional, 2004.)

The opposite approach is giving some people the exclusive right to change certain parts of the code, by conventions in a team, or by rules and procedures in a company. Denying developers access to some parts of the code might seem like a good idea at first glance—what they can't change they can't ruin. The problem is that when you restrain access to code, this increases the resistance to change it. Necessary restructurings become very tedious to perform, to the point where building large workarounds is easier than fixing the real problem.

When doing larger restructurings with the Mikado Method, you can end up in any part of the codebase and the system, and you need to be able to perform the necessary changes. At the same time, you must, of course, make sure the users of the system aren't affected.

B.2   *During the restructuring*

There are a lot of ways to initiate and maintain an effort to improve a codebase. This section discusses some things to keep in mind when you're in the middle of a restructuring.

B.2.1   *All things are relative*

Try to always be sensitive to what other team members think is problematic in the code. Just because your last project was even worse doesn't mean their concerns aren't relevant.

The shared purpose of always changing the code for the better is a great way to boost morale and feel good about what you're doing. If you stop improving because the code is in fairly good shape, you'll end up in triple trouble: first by losing the ability to improve, second by losing the good morale, and third by ending up with bad code. Our best advice is to *never stop improving the code*, no matter how good it may seem.

B.2.2   *Be aware of the code*

To effectively reflect on the code you create, you need regular input from other programmers. One of the best ways to see code through fresh eyes is to practice pair programming or mob programming. Then you get the eyes of the other people in the room, and an additional perspective, namely, the one where you reflect on how you think others perceive your work. Pairing or mob programming also enables informal discussions about newly produced code in a fitting context with one or more people who most certainly have knowledge that complements your own.

Another opportunity for reflection can be achieved by using the Pomodoro Technique (see *Pomodoro Technique Illustrated* by Staffan Nöteberg, Pragmatic Bookshelf, 2009. This technique suggests 25 minutes of work followed by 5 minutes of some other activity. By focusing on something else for 5 minutes, your brain gets a chance to restructure new information and knowledge. Compare this to all the bright ideas that come to mind when standing in the shower, or when folding laundry. Pausing regularly makes it possible to use new information sooner, and it also gives your brain a chance to refocus. Pair programming, or pair work in general, often fits nicely with the Pomodoro Technique. When mob programming, switching programmers at 15-minute intervals works well.

B.2.3 Create an opinion about what good code looks like

In order to improve, you need to have an opinion about what constitutes good code. You need to set a current standard for your team. After that, the hard work begins: the job of keeping the code up to, or above, the standard you've set. Discuss the standard with others, and raise it when a better way of doing things appears. The standard will never be perfect, but rather something that is always being perfected.

B.2.4 The road to better often runs through worse

When you're working with small-scale improvements, the code improves incrementally and is in a little bit better shape after each change. But when a larger refactoring or restructuring is started, you'll sometimes feel as if the code is heading off in the wrong direction. The stepping stones leading to better code actually make the situation look worse!

Imagine a situation where a lot of related functionality is spread out in several places throughout the codebase, and you use the *temporary shelter* pattern to move it all into one big and ugly class, just to get an overview. At this stage, the code wouldn't get through any decent code review.

This is only a transient state though, and the code will eventually be moved into more appropriate places. When you start finding the connections and abstractions in the code, you can create better homes for the pieces of code, making it all look better.

This also applies to when you implement new functionality. You want the code to tell you the abstractions needed in order to avoid overdesign. This often means that you create a small mess to get to know exactly what's needed and to get an idea of what the right abstractions are, and then you refactor to those abstractions.

If you're afraid to make the system look a bit worse initially, you might never find the ways to make it look good eventually.

B.2.5 Code of conduct

Dealing frequently with legacy code can be frustrating, and it's easy to revert to *code bashing* or *code baisse*, such as, "This code sucks!!" or "What kind of idiot wrote this crap?!" Phrases like that are often formulated in a programmer's mind, uttered between gritting teeth, or even shouted out loud in team rooms and over cubicles.

If you bash each other's code, eventually you might stop speaking with each other, not daring to ask for help, and actually becoming afraid of each other. Name-calling only leads to negativity and a downward spiral.

For those situations when you need to blow off some steam, find a *safe space* for it, like an agreement with a colleague that it's OK to be very open and direct.

Often the real problem isn't the code, but something else, and the code just gets the blame. Finding what you're really upset about often helps relieve some of the agony. Remembering that the code you're bashing might be that of a future friend, or the result of your own actions, might help too.

When working with spaghetti code, big balls of mud, or just a plain mess, keep your focus on developing good code. And after all, it's just code.

IT'S JUST CODE Yup, it's just code. Relax!

B.2.6 *Find the ubiquitous language*

You should always strive to bring technical and business people as close to each other as possible. Invite everyone to discussions and create, or rather discover, the common or *ubiquitous* language and understanding for your domain. Try to incorporate this language in the code, represented as names of classes, packages, methods, and functions.

This often requires a closer collaboration between developers and the business side than most organizations are used to. For more details, tricks, and tips, check out Eric Evans' *Domain-Driven Design* (Addison-Wesley Professional, 2003) and Gojko Adzic's *Specification by Example* (Manning, 2011).

B.2.7 *Pay attention to your gut feelings*

Nicely formatted code, well-balanced comments, and documentation could at first glance make the code look good. But it might also be a way to just "pimp the code" and trick its readers into thinking it's better than it actually is.

Many developers have a good gut feeling for code, but without experience, that gut feeling is hard to trust. After a couple of years of experience, some developers start to understand that they're actually right when they feel something is overly complex, whereas others just seem to get numb to the pain.

Try to listen to what you feel about the code, questioning how things are done and looking for better ways. You don't want to get numb.

> **Ola remembers**
>
> When I started out programming, I was doing a lot of web development. At that time there weren't a lot of fancy web frameworks, so there was a fair amount of text parsing, database handling, and even some low-level HTTP stuff to be done. The only frameworks available were the ones that we developed ourselves.
>
> I was working on a rather big web project. This time we had developed some sort of action classes, a dispatcher, and support for views. Very basic stuff. But it still made the development go faster.

(continued)

One day I was struggling a bit more than usual with some difficult code in a view, and I turned to a more seasoned colleague for some help. I explained the logic and the flow of the code, how this affected that, and how the state of this parameter made the program enter this code. It was a huge mess with nested conditionals, state scattered all over the code, and way too many responsibilities in a single class.

After 10 minutes of explaining, I looked at my colleague and sort of waited for him to point out what I had missed. I didn't get the response I was looking for though.

"Ola, this is too complex, I don't get this," my colleague started. "It doesn't have to be this way…"

What did he mean by that?

It took at least 5 minutes for that to sink in. Maybe even a week for it to *really* sink in. What did he mean? I don't need to have 20 `if` statements? How am I supposed to do it any other way?

Looking back at this incident, with years of experience, it's easy to laugh. But for me to see this back then, when I was digging an ever deeper hole, creating a more complex mess every day by adding one `if` statement at a time, it was a totally different story. I had a blindness to flaws that kept me from seeing that I was creating a complex mess. In addition to that, I had insufficient knowledge about what good code is supposed to look like. I also lacked that hard-to-describe skill that experienced programmers have—the ability to distinguish good code from bad code, which can be harder than one first thinks.

B.3   *When the crisis is over*

Once you've gotten your head above the surface, you want to keep it there and start swimming, and eventually get dry land under your feet. The following sections describe what you need to do to get out of the water and stay there. This behavior takes a little bit of effort to keep up, but the joy of working in such a way will give you much more energy back when things start to look good, feel good, and work well.

B.3.1   *Refactor relentlessly*

For every change that's made to the system, try to take a step back and see if there are more parts that can be simplified, split up, or removed completely.

There are some great books out there describing how to make the code better, such as

- *Refactoring* by Martin Fowler et. al (Addison-Wesley Professional, 1999)
- *Refactoring to Patterns* by Joshua Kerievsky (Pearson, 2005)
- *Clean Code* by Robert C. Martin (Prentice Hall, 2008)
- *Implementation Patterns* by Kent Beck (Pearson, 2008)
- *Test-Driven Development* by Kent Beck (Addison-Wesley Professional, 2002)

There are also great tools in most development environments that make it easier to carry out a lot of those smaller refactoring and restructurings.

All this knowledge and all these tools are of no use unless they're put into practice. Play with your tools and your new knowledge to see how they work. Playing around is without a doubt one of the best ways to learn how to perform refactorings and restructurings.

B.3.2   Design never stops

A software system is a model (or several models) of the real world, usually modeling the business you're developing for. Like any model, it represents a few concepts of the real world in order to be able to perform some tasks. But the real world will change, and so will your understanding of it. The model should then change too, based on your knowledge, to favor your business.

For that reason, design is something that never stops. You constantly need to rework the model, introduce new concepts, and think about how you can make the model serve its purpose most effectively.

Also, the natural habitat for a software system is in production. If the software isn't making money, saving money, protecting property, or avoiding costs, no benefit or value will come out of it. This means that you need to be able to stay out of trouble and at the same time keep deploying new increments of value into production. This requires you to design as you go.

B.3.3   You ain't gonna need it—YAGNI

Never develop a feature because *you might need it later on*. You most likely won't, and if you do, you can implement the change then and there, later on.

This is one of the most important rules of software development. Few things add complexity as much as speculative development, and it only makes changing the code harder in the future. The cheapest software to write and maintain is the software that's never developed.

B.3.4   Red-green-refactor

The test-driven development mantra is *red-green-refactor*, and it describes the three parts of test-driven development:

1 Write a test for the functionality you want to implement. Then run the test, expecting it to fail. When you run the test in an IDE, there's often an indicator or a progress bar that turns red to signal failing tests; hence, *red*.

2 Implement just enough code for the test to pass, and nothing more. This results in the indicator turning green as the test passes; hence, *green*.

3 If all tests pass, you can safely *refactor* to remove duplications, reorganize the code, and clean up.

If any test fails after such a refactoring, revert the code to the last green state and continue from there. This approach makes sure a lot of problems are discovered before the code reaches other developers or the users.

The tests are good to have, but the refactoring step is immensely important. If you omit it, the code will be tested, but complexity will build up in the codebase. Eventually, you can't refactor the built-up complexity within a single task. This might force you to take on even more complexity in a workaround, and then you'd need to ask your stakeholders for permission to plan time for a major cleanup. It's better to continuously refactor.

B.3.5 *Continue using the Mikado Method*

Even though the crisis is over, there are usually more things to take care of in a codebase that just emerged from a crisis. The Mikado Method can, of course, be used for day-to-day work on nontrivial tasks. In addition, it's good to keep your tools sharp, just in case you need them. When you use the Mikado Method continuously, you're up to speed with it when you *really* need it.

B.4 *Summary*

In this appendix, you've seen a plethora of things to think about before, during, and after using the Mikado Method in a change effort.

A very important aspect is getting sufficient and timely feedback, preferably from automated tests, but also from compilers and other tools, as well as from your colleagues using pair or mob programming. In addition, by setting up your technical environment in a helpful way (such as for main branch development), you can move more quickly toward your goal.

Any change effort must also include the people involved, starting with you and your team, extending to the team's surroundings and possibly to the entire company.

When the crisis is over, you should continue improving the codebase bit by bit to avoid falling back into that hole again.

Try this
- Of all the preparations described in this appendix, what do you have in place in your organization or team?
- What preparations would you need to make before making a bigger change in your codebase?
- What preparations would you omit? Why?
- Which of the preparations are you unable to do? Why?
- Is there any preparation that feels more difficult than others? Why? What would make it easier?
- How do you verify that your application works after a change?
- What metrics do you generate from your codebase? Do you know what they mean?

(continued)
- Find the automated refactoring tools in your IDE (you might need a plugin). Try each of them. Think of an occasion when they would have been useful.
- Find the regular expression option in the search dialog of your IDE. Write different regular expressions to locate things in your codebase. Can you find what you expect? Does formatting the code consistently improve your success?
- Try to write regular expressions to replace code in your system, using parentheses to pick parts of the found string to use in the replacement. In particular, find the negating match and use it.

appendix C
Dealing with
dynamically typed languages

This appendix covers

- Getting fast feedback from dynamically typed languages
- Driving change with tests

How you use the Mikado Method differs a bit from how you get fast feedback when it comes to different kinds of languages. The biggest difference is probably between statically typed and dynamically typed languages. This appendix will show you how to work with a dynamically typed language.

Even if you work mostly with statically typed languages, there's value in reading this appendix because there are dynamic aspects in statically typed languages too, such as the reflection capabilities in Java. But if you work with dynamically typed languages like JavaScript or Python, this appendix was created with you in mind.

In this appendix, we'll work with a variant of the code in chapter 5, and we'll assume you've read chapters 1–3, and the first part of chapter 5. Because of this, we'll skip the description of the problem and solution and go straight for the code.

First, though, we'll look very quickly at why dynamic languages require a slightly different approach.

C.1 How to get feedback in a dynamic environment

Statically typed languages offer rapid feedback from the compiler in the form of compiler errors, but these aren't available in a dynamically typed language. You need another way to generate fast and repetitive feedback. One way to do this is to run the actual program when you make a change, but we think that approach is much too slow. We generally choose another approach: automated tests.

We don't think that there's much to debate about whether tests are good or not; we believe they're absolutely crucial when you're dealing with dynamically typed languages. In fact, we believe they're equally crucial when you're dealing with statically typed languages. As a consequence, we're not going to argue about their value, nor will we debate whether we should "test first" or "test last." We'll use a test-first approach, and the tests will drive the change here.

> **Feedback from debugging**
>
> Another way to get feedback from your code is running it in a debugger. A useful debugging environment provides means to inspect the state of your code and data and also allows you to analyze it at a pace that suits you. There are pros and cons with debugging, but it's definitely something we do from time to time.
>
> The biggest challenge with debugging is getting the application in a certain state—exposing the problem we're trying to fix. That's why we combine debugging with tests. This gives us the best of both worlds: repeatability and quick setup from the tests, and analysis and code inspection at a very detailed level from the debugging environment.

C.2 The loan server (again)

Imagine the loan server from chapter 5 again and how that's used. It consists of three basic services:

- Apply
- Fetch
- Approve

These are web services, and the API is described in chapter 5.

Our mission here is to separate the approve functionality from the rest of the application's functionality so that they can run in separate environments. The difference in this appendix is that we'll look at an example that uses JavaScript and Node.js. Before we change the code, we'll go through it so you can get an overview, and then we'll look at how we can approach a change without breaking the code.

> ## Node.js
>
> Node.js is a software platform written in JavaScript that's mainly used to build server-side applications. It contains a built-in HTTP server library that makes it easy to run a web server without using external software, like the Apache web server. This gives the user (the developer) more control over how the web server works.

C.2.1   A run-through of the Node.js code

The code we have today is a small mess, and all the code resides in just two files: loan_-server.js and repository.js. Let's look at the contents of loan_server.js first.

Listing C.1   The initial loan_server.js code

```javascript
'use strict';

var url = require('url');
var http = require('http');
var fs = require('fs');
var repository = require('./loan/repository.js');

var APPLICATION = "apply";
var FETCH = "fetch";
var TICKET_ID = "ticketId";
var APPROVE = "approve";

var srv = http.createServer(function (req, res) {

    var nextId = function(application, callback) {
        fs.readdir('loans/', function determineNextId(err, data) {
            if (err) {
                throw err;
            } else {
                var id = data.length + 1;
                repository.toDisk(application, callback, id);
                callback(JSON.stringify({
                    ticketId: id
                }));
            }
        });
    }

    res.writeHead(200, {
        'Content-Type': 'application/json'
    });
    var url_parts = url.parse(req.url, true);          ◁─┐  nextId() and
    var query = url_parts.query;                          │  repository are used to
                                                          │  save an application
    if (query.action === 'apply') {                    ◁─┘
        var application = {
            amount: query['amount'],
            contact: query['contact'],
        };
```

```
            nextId(application, function printTicket(ticket) {
                res.end(ticket + '\n');
            });
            return;

        } else if (query.action === 'fetch') {
            var ticketId = query[TICKET_ID];
            repository.fetch(
                ticketId,
                function printFetched(application) {
                    res.end(application + '\n');
                });
            return;
        } else if (query.action === 'approve') {
            repository.approveLoan(
                query[TICKET_ID],
                function printTicketAfterApprove(ticket) {
                    res.end(ticket + '\n');
                });
            return;
        }
        res.end('Incorrect parameters provided\n');
}).listen(8080);
```

> fetch method uses repository to get a result and then return it

> approve method is same as fetch, except an application is approved and stored first

The following listing shows the repository code, which handles most of the writing and fetching of data from disk. We won't use that in our example; it's just here to give you a complete picture of the whole loan server codebase.

Listing C.2   The initial repository.js code

```
var fs = require('fs');

var LOAN_DIR = 'loans/';

var repo = {
    toDisk : function(application, id) {
        application.approved = false;
        application.applicationNo = id;
        fs.writeFile(LOAN_DIR + id + '.data',
            JSON.stringify(application),
            function(err) {
                if (err) {
                    throw err;
                } else {
                    console.log('Stored');
                }
            });
    },

    approveLoan : function(ticketId, callback) {
        fs.readFile(
            LOAN_DIR + ticketId + '.data',
            function(err, data) {
                if (err) {
```

> Stores a loan to disk

> Puts a loan in an approved state

```
                throw err;
            } else {
                var application = JSON.parse(data);
                application.approved = true;
                fs.writeFile(
                    LOAN_DIR + application.applicationNo + '.data',
                    JSON.stringify(application),
                    this.doneWriting);
                callback(JSON.stringify(
                    {ticketId: application.applicationNo}
                ));
            }
        });
    },

    fetch : function(ticketId, callback) {                  Fetches a stored
        fs.readFile(LOAN_DIR + ticketId + '.data',          loan from disk
            function(err, data) {
                if (err) {
                    throw err;
                } else {
                    callback(data);
                }
            });
    },
};

module.exports = repo;
```

Before we change any code, we need to make sure we haven't broken anything. The authors of loan_server.js didn't write any tests, so we need write them now. We'll start with the assumption that we want to test fetch, apply, and approve in that order, so that goes into our Mikado Graph, which produces a picture like the one in figure C.1.

Now that we have a graph, it's time to create the first test and drive the change from there. When we start with a test, we create an expectation on the code, which we create an implementation for. When that expectation is later met, we not only have a

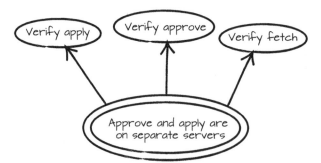

Figure C.1   The goal and the test prerequisites

working program, we also have a regression test in place. We won't initially drive much change, because we want to cover the code with tests before we change it. But that will change slightly over the course of our restructuring.

As you can see in the following test (listing C.3), we're creating a seam in the code. We do that so the code can be tested more easily. We could test the code on a different level, with cURL for instance, but that requires more setup and would make the test depend on a filesystem and an active network connection. We don't want to rely on those for regression tests.

---

cURL

cURL is a command-line tool for transferring data with URL syntax, supporting HTTP, HTTPS, and IMAP, among other protocols. That makes it a great tool for when you want to fake or test sending data to a web server.

Listing C.3   Our first test

```
exports['Loan Server'] = {
    setUp: function(done) {
        done();
    },
    'fetch': function(test) {
        var launcher = loan_server.launch();
        test.equal(launcher(), 'Test', 'Should return something');
        test.done();
    },
};
```

> Introduce launch method to get a handle to server code

When we run the test it produces the following results:

```
Testing loan-server_test.jsF
>> Loan Server - fetch
>> TypeError: Cannot call method 'writeHead' of undefined
>> at server.start (lib/loan-server.js:29:10)
>> at Object.exports.Loan Server.apply (test/loan-server_test.js:11:13)
>> at Object.exports.Loan Server.setUp (test/loan-server_test.js:7:2)
```

This tells us that we forgot something when we called `launcher()`. Upon closer inspection, it looks like we need to pass an `http-response` to our test when we call the launcher. We actually need to pass a request as well, so let's do that and see what happens. The updated graph is shown in figure C.2.

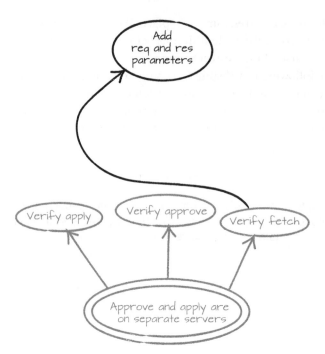

Figure C.2   Response (res) and request (req) are needed as parameters

C.2.2   *Extending the test*

Once we add the request and the response to the test, it looks like this:

```
'fetch': function(test) {
    var launcher = loan_server.launch();
    var req = {};
    var res = {
        writeHead : function() {}
    };
    test.equal(launcher(req, res), 'Test', 'Should return something');
    test.done();
}
```

With this addition, the test results tell us this:

```
>> Loan Server - fetch
>> TypeError: Parameter 'url' must be a string, not undefined
>> at Object.urlParse [as parse] (url.js:96:11)
>> at server.launch (lib/loan-server.js:30:26)
>> at Object.exports.Loan Server.apply (test/loan-server_test.js:16:13)
>> at Object.exports.Loan Server.setUp (test/loan-server_test.js:7:2)
```

OK, now we need to provide the server launcher with something else, and from the look of the output it seems we need a URL on our request. Let's see if we can add `fetch` to that URL and maybe get a more sensible response. See figure C.3.

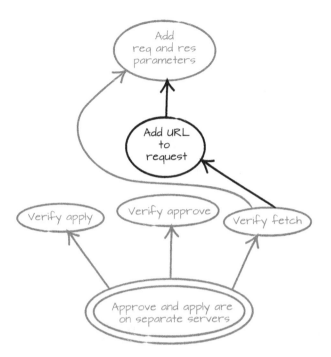

Figure C.3   Request needs a URL

We now add some more to the test, as follows:

```
'fetch': function(test) {
    var launcher = loan_server.launch();
    var req = {
        url : 'action=?fetch&ticketId=1'
    };
    var res = {
        writeHead : function() {}
    };
    test.equal(launcher(req, res), 'Test', 'Should return something');
    test.done();
}
```

After running the modified test we get the following result:

```
>> Loan Server - fetch
>> TypeError: Object #<Object> has no method 'end'
>> at server.launch (lib/loan-server.js:59:10)
>> at Object.exports.Loan Server.apply (test/loan-server_test.js:18:13)
>> at Object.exports.Loan Server.setUp (test/loan-server_test.js:7:2)
```

This is what it looks like to drive changes with tests. You modify the test, and then the code. In between you add nodes to the graph. Our updated graph now looks like figure C.4.

The error message we got from the test tells us that the end method on the response is called, which makes sense because after we've fetched data, we want that

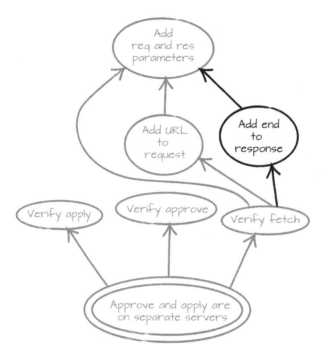

Figure C.4   end needs to be faked too

to be returned from our server. We add the method to the response stub that we use for testing purposes, like the next listing shows.

Listing C.4   The test is growing.

```
'fetch': function(test) {
    var launcher = loan_server.launch();
    var result;
    var req = {
        url : 'action=?fetch&ticketId=1'
    };

    var res = {
        writeHead : function() {},
        end : function(data) {
            result = data;
        }
    };

    launcher(req, res);
    test.equal(result, 'Test');
    test.done();
}
```

> data is stored in result variable so we can use it to assert its content later in test

Notice that we pick up the data from the end function and use that in our assertion. But we're not there quite yet. The result from the server tells us this:

```
Testing loan-server_test.jsFatal error: ENOENT, open 'loans/1.data'
F
>> Incomplete tests/setups/teardowns:
>> Loan Server - fetch 0 [ 'Loan Server - fetch' ]
Fatal error: A test was missing test.done(),
so nodeunit exploded. Sorry!
```

It looks like we're getting everything right, but we're not getting the response we were hoping for. After a brief investigation, we realize that's not very strange, because we're trying to read applications from a loans directory that doesn't exist at this location. The applications reside in a directory relative to the server path, not the tests path.

This leads us to the conclusion that if we want full control over the tests, we need to control the repository as well. We add that to the graph and then extend the test. The updated graph can be seen in figure C.5.

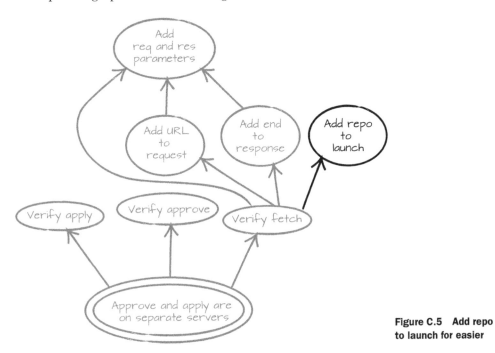

Figure C.5   **Add repo to launch for easier**

Listing C.5   An ever-growing test

```javascript
'fetch': function(test) {
    var repo = {};
    var launcher = loan_server.launch(repo);
    var result;
    var req = {
        url : '?action=fetch&ticketId=1'
    };

    var res = {
        writeHead : function() {},
        end : function(data) {
```

```
                result = data;
            }
        };

        launcher(req, res);
        test.equal(result,
            '{applicationNo : 1,
                amount : 10000,
                approved : false,
                contact : "donald@ducks.burg"}');
        test.done();
    }
```

To be able to test the loan server fully, we added a repository to the launch() method. This means that now we need to modify some production code as well.

In the following code, we've added an argument to the launch function **❶**, and the repository is passed in as we launch the server **❷**. For this to be of any use, we've also made sure that the repo argument is used in the fetch() method **❸**.

Listing C.6   Modified loan_server.js

```
var server = {
    launch : function(repo) {                                    ◄───┐
        return function (req, res) {
            var nextId = function(application, callback) {
                fs.readdir('loans/', function determineNextId(err, data) {
                    if (err) {
                        throw err;                    repo is sent in as a parameter
                    } else {                             to launch() method  ❶
                        var id = data.length + 1;
                        repository.toDisk(application, callback, id);
                        callback(JSON.stringify({
                            ticketId: id
                        }));
                    }
                });
            }

            res.writeHead(200, {
                'Content-Type': 'application/json'
            });
            var url_parts = url.parse(req.url, true);
            var query = url_parts.query;

            if (query.action === 'apply') {
                var application = {
                    amount: query['amount'],
                    contact: query['contact'],
                };
                nextId(application, function printTicket(ticket) {
                    res.end(ticket + '\n');
                });
                return;
            } else if (query.action === 'fetch') {
            var ticketId = query[TICKET_ID];
```

```
            repo.fetch(
                ticketId,
                function printFetched(application) {
                    res.end(application + '\n');
                });
            return;
        } else if (query.action === 'approve') {
            repository.approveLoan(
                query[TICKET_ID],
                function printTicketAfterApprove(ticket) {
                    res.end(ticket + '\n');
                });
            return;
        }
        res.end('Incorrect parameters provided\n');
    }
  }
}

var srv = http.createServer(server.launch(repository)).listen(8080);
```

② repo parameter is used here rather than the global "repository"

③ Repository is passed to server as we launch it

When we run the test now, something interesting happens. We no longer get an error that tells us that it can't locate the file loans/1.data. We get another missing method:

```
>> Loan Server - fetch
>> TypeError: Object #<Object> has no method 'fetch'
>> at server.launch (lib/loan-server.js:44:8)
>> at Object.exports.Loan Server.apply (test/loan-server_test.js:24:2)
>> at Object.exports.Loan Server.setUp (test/loan-server_test.js:7:2)
```

By now we know that this means. We need to add a method to our stubbed repo.

Listing C.7 The test grows.

```
'fetch': function(test) {
    var res = {
        writeHead : function() {},
        end : function(data) {
            test.equals('Called\n', data);
        }
    };

    var repo = {
        fetch : function(ticketId, callback) {
            test.equals(1, ticketId);
            callback('Called');
        }
    };

    var launcher = loan_server.launch(repo);
    var result;
    var req = {
        url : '?action=fetch&ticketId=1'
    };
    launcher(req, res);
    test.done();
}
```

tickedId is expected to be 1

callback is expected to be called

If you look carefully, you'll see that we've shifted our testing tactics slightly. We no longer expect to get a result from the launcher; we merely expect that the correct methods will be called. Instead of testing a state at the end, we verify that the behavior we expect is there, and we expect that the repo method fetch() is called with 1 as the ticketId. We also expect that the callback will be called.

Something is wrong here, though. The test doesn't test everything correctly. The fetch() method is replicating the behavior in the repository and is short-circuiting the real code. In order to test this correctly, we need to modify the test slightly and the production code as well. We need to be able to control what gets called back. Let's add that to the graph (see figure C.6) and then change our test code so it looks like the following listing.

Listing C.8   The test shifts in its approach.

```
'fetch': function(test) {
    var wasCalled = false;

    var response = {
        writeHead : function() {},
        end : function(data) {
            wasCalled = true;
        }
    };

    var repo = {
        fetch : function(ticketId, callback) {
            test.equals(1, ticketId);
        }
    };

    var request = {
        url : '?action=fetch&ticketId=1'
    };

    var launcher = server.launch(repo, server.serveResult(response));

    launcher(request, response);
    test.equals(true, wasCalled);
    test.done();
}
```

This change in our test forces us to change the production code, and the biggest change is that we've added a serveResult() method to our server that uses the response. To make this work, we add a function to the production code:

```
...
    serveResult : function(response) {
        return function printFetched(application) {
            response.end(application + '\n');
        }
    }
...
```

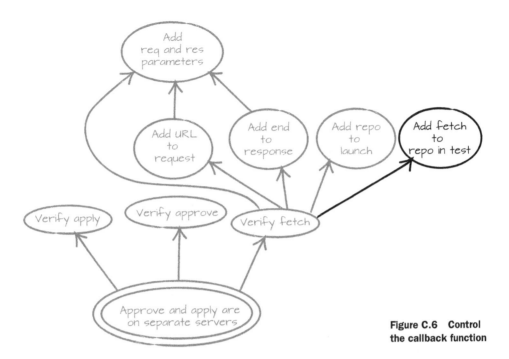

Figure C.6 Control the callback function

We also changed how it's launched. The actual fetch code now looks like this:

```
...
    } else if (query.action === 'fetch') {
        var ticketId = query[TICKET_ID];
        repo.fetch(
        ticketId,
            returnResult(res)
        );
        return;
    }
...
```

And this is how the server is now launched:

```
var srv = http.createServer(server.launch(
    repository, server.serveResult)
    ).listen(8080);
```

And with that, we've completed our test and also that part of the graph that deals with the changes to the fetch functionality. If you look at the form of the Mikado Graph, you'll see that it fans out, and a lot of prerequisites were created because we were experimenting with tests. This is often the case when you cover code with tests before you change it. The same thing will happen with the "Verify apply" and "Verify approve" prerequisites.

We won't do a detailed run-through of the approve and apply prerequisites—you should have the idea by now. If you want to see what a graph and the restructuring of approve and apply look like, we suggest you download the code from the Mikado Method GitHub repository and try it yourself. We will, however, show you what the apply graph ended up looking like when we tried to restructure loan_server.js some more. It's very small (see figure C.7) because most of the work was done in the fetch verification.

If you combine both the apply and fetch graphs, and also add the approve part, the graph gets pretty big. There's a lot of work involved in covering code with tests afterward, and most of this work could have been avoided if we had tests from the beginning. The work of adding tests overshadows our real task, which was to separate the servers, but without the tests, we didn't have the courage to do so.

By now you should understand the general idea of letting tests, instead of the compiler, speak to you.

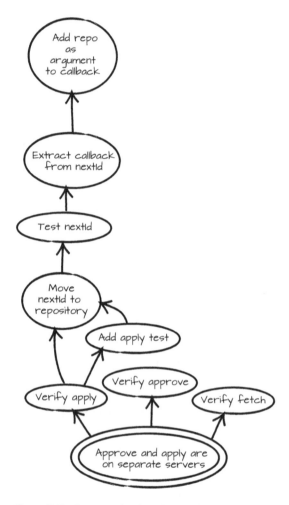

Figure C.7   An example of testing apply

Tests on a different level

Sometimes when you move methods and functions between units, such as classes and files, you can't be 100% sure that you haven't made a mistake. And sometimes moving things and other small changes are absolutely necessary in order to introduce a seam. In those cases, we suggest you test your program on a different level, maybe using an integration test or by running the program. We mentioned cURL earlier, and that we didn't want to rely on it for regression testing. But as an intermediate solution in the transition between two states in a refactoring, it can be a quick way to make sure nothing gets broken.

C.3 *Summary*

In this appendix, you've seen how you can drive small changes to code with tests. This is useful in cases where you need to loosen a system enough to get it under test, and then modify it even more. This is particularly important in situations where you can't rely on a compiler. The Mikado Method is about taking risky changes and transforming them into boring ones by breaking them down into safe steps. Getting to a safe step in JavaScript, as an example, differs slightly from similar changes in statically typed languages.

There are more differences between dynamically and statically typed languages than just the type system, but our main point is that when you use JavaScript or Python or any other dynamically typed language, the level of certainty that static typing offers isn't there, so it needs to be replaced with something else. We prefer that something else to be a solid base of tests. If you don't have that now, start creating it.

Table C.1 Static versus dynamic typing and the Mikado Method

Static	Dynamic
<ul><li>Try a change—see if you get a compiler error.</li><li>Change a method signature with an IDE, which does the job for you safely.</li></ul>	<ul><li>Try a change—run the tests—see if there's an error.</li><li>Change a method signature, find all the references by searching the codebase for a potential match, and then change all those places manually or maybe with a regex.</li></ul>

Try this

- Change a piece of dynamically typed code. What's the most common error you make?
- Write a unit test for your code. What was hard about it?
- Imagine a restructuring and then draw a graph without actually changing code. Now make the change as the graph suggests. How did that feel?

index